A Eucharistic Ontology

A Eucharistic Ontology

Maximus the Confessor's Eschatological Ontology of Being as Dialogical Reciprocity

Nikolaos Loudovikos

Translated by Elizabeth Theokritoff

HOLY CROSS ORTHODOX PRESS
Brookline, Massachusetts

© 2010 Nicholas Loudovikos

Published by Holy Cross Orthodox Press
50 Goddard Avenue
Brookline, Massachusetts 02445

ISBN-13 978-1-935317-08-1
ISBN-10 1-935317-08-3

On the cover: Icon of St. Maximos the Confessor by Vassiliki Loudovikos.
Cover design: Steven Klund

Comment from Yannis Spiteris, O.F.M. Cap., Catholic Archbishop of Corfu, from his article "Attuali tendenze della teologia greca," *Orientalia Christiana Periodica* 71 (2005), 299–314.

Library of Congress Cataloging-in-Publication Data

Loudovikos, Nikolaos.
  [Eucharistiake ontologia. English]
  A Eucharistic ontology : Maximus the Confessor's eschatological ontology of being as dialogical reciprocity / Nicholas Loudovikos ; translated by Elizabeth Theokritoff.
    p. cm.
  Includes bibliographical references.
  ISBN-13: 978-1-935317-08-1 (alk. paper)
  ISBN-10: 1-935317-08-3 (alk. paper)
  1. Maximus, Confessor, Saint, ca. 580–662. 2. Lord's Supper—History of doctrines—Middle Ages, 600–1500. 3. Ontology. I. Title.
  BR65.M416L6413 2010
  234'.163—dc22
                                                        2010015341

CONTENTS

Chapter 2
THE BEING OF THINGS AND ITS *LOGOI*

Chapter 3
THE COMMUNION OF ENTITIES THROUGH
THEIR *LOGOI*

Chapter 4
THE BECOMING OF ENTITIES THROUGH THEIR *LOGOI*

Foreword

Eucharistic Ontology was first published in Greek in 1992. Parts of it have been translated into various languages and much debated, something that caused considerable academic trouble and no less profit to its author. This English edition is not completely identical to the Greek, but rather should be seen as a second revised edition of the work. Thus, I have prepared a new introduction and a sixth chapter specifically for the English edition in an effort to engage some of the recent discussion. The text has also undergone some significant corrections and additions. However, only little discussion of very recent Maximian bibliography has been attempted, as the scope of this book still remains, I believe, unique in the midst of Maximian scholarship. For exactly that reason the book is still worth translating.

My subsequent books have explored the consequences of the sort of understanding of Patristic theology portrayed here. Two of them, *Closed Spirituality and the Meaning of the Self* (1999) and *Apophatic Ecclesiology of Consubstantiality* (2002), will soon appear in English, thus forming a kind of trilogy, respectively comprising eschatological ontology, anthropology, and ecclesiology as parts of a developing line of thought. I frequently refer to these books in this work.

I must express special thanks to this volume's translator, Dr. Elizabeth Theokritoff, for her long and laborious patience with my writing. I believe that her final achievement is excellent. For the pages I wrote in English I am of course fully responsible. I also express my special gratitude to the President of Hellenic College–Holy Cross Greek Orthodox

School of Theology, Rev. Nicholas Triantafilou, to Dr. Anton Vrame, Director of Holy Cross Orthodox Press, and to Aimee Ehrs, a member of his staff. My students Fr. Demetrios Harper, Philip Navarro, and Alan Brown discussed with me some difficult linguistic points of the work. I am especially grateful for the friendship of Rev. Dr. Philip Zymaris, who showed a great deal of care and encouragement for the publication of this book in English.

Finally, the work of translating the book into the English language was made possible by the sponsorship of the Holy Monastery of Vatopedi of the Holy Mountain. So I must express my deep gratitude to the Abbot for his generosity, goodwill, and faith in the value of this project.

Fr. Nicholas Loudovikos
Thessaloniki, July 2008

Introduction

Toward a New Understanding of Eschatology?

I.

Can we talk about eschatology in an ontological and not merely historical or existential way?

If this is a deep yet hidden desire of the twentieth century's eschatological thought, as I shall try to show later on, then we still need to read authors such as St. Maximus the Confessor. But our first surprise would then be that the catalyst of this illuminative link between eschatology and ontology is the Eucharist. Western scholars have failed so far to give us an adequate account either of this Father's eucharistic theology or, still more, any suspicion that this is connected with his ontology and his eschatology. No doubt that the Eucharist has been an original element of Church's self-awareness (everyone knows that today!) but no one could probably articulate this in purely ontological language—being as an event of "enkoinonetic" becoming, of becoming-in-communion in Christ and life as gift-sharing—before Maximus. And furthermore, being as a dialogical existence which brings to the fore precisely the mode of being which was able to undergo change, forming and deifying created nature without escaping it: the "enousion" person, person-in-essence.

An ontological explanation of Eucharist, eucharistic understanding of ontology: eschatology now emerges exactly as the ontological realization of Eucharist, of the eucharistic consummation of ontology. The eschatology of St. Maximus, then, is a eucharistic ontology, an ontological factor that causes beings truly to be, experiencing even now the certitude of becoming-in-communion of the eschatological Sabbath

1

rest. The uncreated breaks the bounds of the created, entering into history through every eucharistic incarnation of Christ. Maximus, therefore, can also help us to rethink and to essentially correct what we call eucharistic theology and ecclesiology today.

II.

BUT MANY CLARIFICATIONS AND EXPLANATIONS of terms and concepts must follow even briefly. What do we mean by a historical or existential understanding of eschatology? And what do we mean by the term ontology in this book? In the end, how do we understand the Eucharist in an ontological context? And what is ontological eschatology?

This long discussion must of course start from eschatology. I call a *"historical understanding of eschatology"* the eschatological claims of different authors converging upon the need to shape a strict historical context for our understanding of Christian eschatology. Daniélou, von Balthasar, Cullmann, Moltmann, and Pannenberg are some of these authors. What expresses the opposite tendency is of course the *"existential understanding of eschatology "* as an a-historical or very slightly historical understanding of the end-times doctrine, as either an existential authenticity or personal fulfillment, etc.—such as can be found in Bultmann, Barth, and others.

The existentialist core of Bultmann's theology is commonly acknowledged. For him the paradox of Christian eschatology as he understands it (attributing his understanding to John and Paul) consists, we suppose, not in a historical event of eschatological consummation of the world, but in an existential event of individual authenticity expressed as the repeated appearance of God in the Christ-event and the here-and-now personal acquaintance with it.[1] Eschatology does not concern history but human existential authenticity, as individual "historicity" of a personal awakening in my internal truthfulness—and here of course Heidegger sheds his philosophical light upon the possible content of this truthfulness. These views certainly correspond with Barth's first theological period where he seems to agree with Bultmann on the sheer anthropologico-existentialist conception of revelation—later on (in his *Kirchliche Dogmatik*) he will criticize this one-dimensional approach[2] trying to reach the depths of Christian Trinitarian theology.

Against Bultmann's demythologized eschatology, Moltmann proceeds to a remythologizing of theology, admitting belief in the resurrection of the dead and accusing Bultmann of having drastically reduced the New Testament vision of a new world to a [subjectivist] individual eschatology.[3] History now becomes an essential element of Christian eschatology as the Church is conceived as a historical messianic community in the sense of God's Kingdom in the world.[4] History thus becomes eschatological exactly because eschatology entered history in the form of the crucified and risen Christ. Moltmann calls his claim "a future eschatology" while Barth's and Bultmann's positions are called by him "an eschatology of the present."

We must not forget, of course, that the first reaction against Bultmann was by Cullmann. He was the one who stressed so powerfully the meaning of time and history for Christian revelation.[5] Cullmann's view is that there is a sacred history which co-extends with general history, having Jesus Christ as its midpoint, and claiming a final judgment upon the facts of the latter. Thus the drama of human history can be read and faced through this sacred history that will finally consummate it. Pannenberg converges with Cullmann in the affirmation of the meaning of history for Christian revelation.[6] Furthermore Pannenberg accuses Hegel (and of course Bultmann) of abolishing the meaning of the future in history, a meaning that can be grasped only in the light of the final consummation of history in the resurrection of Christ. In his *Systematic Theology* he develops a "theology of history" in the sense that he tries to reach an understanding of history in its wholeness—not only the facts but also their meaning. Christ's resurrection thus belongs to history and can be historically investigated, yet it also has a meaning beyond history. But here the question lies open: In what way can we understand Christ's resurrection as a *meaning* and not only as a fact? How can we incarnate this meaning in the midst of history without abolishing the latter? How can we in other words, maintain both meaning and "happenedness" in history the latter consummated in the former? How, furthermore, can we reconcile historical fact with the existential approach to eschatology? If I understand them properly, Moltmann, Cullmann, and Pannenberg (as well as von Balthasar and Daniélou) do not attack meaning or existential authenticity in their dispute with Bultmann and the theology of the Word, but they rather seek a more solid ground in time and space for it. Thus "eschatology of the future" does not really completely contradict the "eschatology of the present" although it is very difficult for the authors mentioned above to achieve a convincing connection between them.

It is only after the above findings that we can come to what I called an "ontological eschatology" in the beginning of this text. This ontological interpretation of eschatology which maintains real history while it constantly opens it to its last uncreated meaning, is impossible without making Maximus's decisive step as this is described in this book: the association of eschatology with the doctrine of the uncreated *logoi* of beings that forms the Maximian ontology.[7] The doctrine of the *logoi* is an eschatological ontology, as they form not immovable archetypes but divine wills, destinations and existential vocations for the creatures, waiting for the human *logos*/response. An eschatological dialogue is thus inaugurated, that is a dialogue of ontological character as it forms the very essence of beings that will be fulfilled in the end times but starting from now, as beings are not just given, but also talked about, concerning their mode of existence. Thus the essence of beings for Maximus can be found, in a way, not in the "origins" but fundamentally in the "end" of beings: beings *shall be* as they really are, the kingdom to come is the kingdom of the ontological/eschatological consummation of things.

But how does the Eucharist enter this problematic? As we shall see step by step in this book, it is only in the Eucharist where the eschatological meaning of Maximus's ontology can be deciphered. The Eucharist explains eschatology and is itself explained eschatologically at the same time, by and in the doctrine of *logoi*, thus forming the only way of understanding this sort of deep connection of ontology with eschatology that marks not only Maximian thought, but finally the Greek patristic tradition as a whole.

This is why we still need Maximus the Confessor's thought today. We can find there what is sought consciously or unconsciously by Moltmann or Pannenberg: an ontological way of bridging the gap between meaning and history here and now, a way of safeguarding both existential authenticity and socio-historical course, an ontological way of bringing the *eschata* within history without losing either of the two, a way of mutual verification of both.

III.

But let us now make a small philosophical parenthesis demonstrating the philosophical parameters of our discussion of eschatology. As we have already noted, the meaning of historical beings to which we refer is *uncreated*—it consists, more precisely, in a *dialogue* between created human *logos* and the divine uncreated *logoi* of things, which, according to Maximus, are all becoming apparent by the Incarnation of the

Logos. This *dialogue* with the *Logos* via his *logoi* forms human historical openness to the uncreated, bringing divine meaning and wisdom[8]—to beings and history. The fact is that without this opening, and without this kind of eschatological wisdom, not only theology but also philosophy remains within the limits of an intra-worldliness, binding always being with thought, even if it wants to break the limits of our understanding of the philosophical subject. In Heidegger's philosophy, for instance (to touch on the pinnacle of the philosophical obelisk established by Descartes), there is exactly this identification of "thinking" with "being" which pervades his thought just below the surface, from *Being and Time (Sein und Zeit)* to *Introduction to Metaphysics (Einführung in die Metaphysik)*, despite all the changes over the course of his development. This identification is expressed in the last analysis as an essential affinity between "thinking" and "being" (however much the emphasis falls on the "being" not the "thinking"), as if "being" were bounded by the potentialities of "thinking," as if "being" and "thinking" belonged equally to this created natural world as it offers itself to philosophical experience. Thus Heidegger in his testament entitled *The end of philosophy and the task of thought (Das Ende der Philosophie und die Aufgabe des Denkens)* talks directly about the end of philosophy, understood as the end of metaphysics or ontology in our times (these having anyway been swallowed up by the sciences), and locates the only future for thought in the free mythopoetic quest for truth through thinking; and he does not seem bothered by the fact that the linkage of thinking and truth is a survival of the same essential identification of thinking with being. That identification once again yokes philosophy to a rationalistic subjectivism (which in fact is always central to Western metaphysics, even when, as with Heidegger, it appears to be allergic to the metaphysical subject), thus leading it to the same creation-centeredness, the same confinement within the thought of creaturehood. The end of ontology of which Heidegger speaks is, in our eyes, the definitive confinement within the thought of creaturehood with its essential linkage between thinking and being or, later, between thought and truth, in the context of the individual created being. Buber has been able to show us how strong and decisive is the centrality of this kind of subjectivity in Heidegger's work and how it affects his understanding of intersubjectivity.[10] Thus even if Heidegger aspires to authenticity and meaning he is himself the one who finally provides this meaning, bound with his own limits of experiencing the truth: thus Heideggerian authenticity, which so much inspired Bultmann's eschatology, tends to become the absolute narcissism of understanding the others as "selfobject" in Heinz Kohut's psychoanalytic terminology, for example.

But we cannot close our parenthesis without mentioning Levinas, who used eschatology in his philosophical ontology, as well as very briefly, the contemporary phenomenological trends, which tried to follow the same way. Thus for Levinas eschatology puts us in relation with being as an exteriority beyond totality and history.[9] This escape from the impersonal totality of the objective historical and political being, relates us with the infinity of being as this is revealed in the relationship with the other.[11] Thus subjectivity is not despised but is now conceived as established upon the idea of the infinity of the moral openness to the other.[12] But how is this eschatological openness/relationship to be understood? Here we come to the core of Levinas's thought and its problems. Levinas speaks of a "Liturgy of the Neighbor" that can be understood as "a movement of the Same toward the Other which never returns to the Same"; the radical heteronomy thus established forms the very nature of subjectivity beyond any autonomous conception of the self.[13] As Michael Purcell puts it, for Levinas, "subjectivity is always and already in a situation of intersubjectivity, and only ever, realizes itself as the *other-in-me*, a situation which realizes the self as *for-the-other*."[14] But then if we connect all these claims with a theology of the Liturgy, such an economic logic in which giving also implies giving back destroys the gift as gift: "these conditions of possibility define or produce the annulment, the annihilation, the destruction of the gift," for within such a cycle, the logic of the gift is also the logic of the debt that the one to whom the gift is given owes the giver.[15] Thus "responsibility, as a liturgical self-giving for the other person, is out with the economic cycle of exchange. Expressed eucharistically, liturgy is absolute kenosis."[16] Here Levinas meets Derrida and Caputo. But Levinas finally understands eschatology also as a self-sacrifice for a future time where the self has no place: " thus the liturgical sense of the work as *for: for* a time without me, *for* a time after my time, *for* the time of the other, *for* the other."[17]

Radical heteronomy, gift without return, dialogue without reciprocity, future without me, absolute kenosis: do we have here a dialogical eschatology like that described above? Certainly not. As divine Incarnation here is missing, Levinas fails to understand the genuine reciprocity of love. Reciprocity now does not mean repayment, but inspiration, learning of wisdom. What is horrible is that without that reciprocity this supposedly kenotic, perfect, and self-sufficient love-for-the-other easily changes once again into a narcissistic ego-centrism, another mechanism of unconscious defense in Freudian terms. Love is dialogical: what makes it true is first that it always waits for the other to witness that he is loved and, second, that it loves to be loved, it desires the final nuptial meeting, the cross-fertilization. True love does not perfectly know what to do with the other, unless the other reveals himself by his own love for the lover. The true love *takes into account* the other and safeguards his freedom—that means that it knows when to retreat, to pause, to vanish, to come back again. Love is the dialogical, eschatological wisdom of reciprocity—as proposal, learning, attendance, and burning desire.

Marion's phenomenology of gift has also to be carefully considered. We could possibly accept, I think, some basic thoughts of his only after the critique made in the sixth chapter of this book. The problem is that phenomenology tends to replace ontology—usually in an unconsciously idealistic way—and forgets the explosive, undiagnosed, untold, unconscious sides of gift-exchanging. Phenomenology tends sometimes to ignore *that being really exists*—and not only in favor of our numerous reductions. The undiagnosed side of the uncreated ontological intervention into createdness belongs to the essential core of eschatological ontology: it inaugurates a real free reciprocal dialogue of unexpected finality where beings finally take their real being, as we shall see in the course of this book. Here theology is, once again, wiser than philosophy.

IV.

BUT LET US RETURN (as we cannot avoid this question of historical clarification) to the Greek patristic tradition and modern Orthodox theology in order to see how the kind of eschatology we are dealing with was able to emerge. We shall make a sharp distinction between two types of eschatology that can clearly be discerned in the patristic words: first, a type of eschatology which we shall call an *ecstatic or transcendental eschatology*, traced mainly in Origenist and Evagrian tradition; second, an *eschatology of being as gift* traced in the more "Chalcedonian" part of patristic thought and culminating in Maximus the Confessor. Let us make some remarks here. Concerning the first type of ontology, I have two specific points to make. First, in both Evagrius and Origen ascension to God is *ecstatic*, that is, an outlet from nature[18] in the form of an intellectual contemplation of the divine. In both the body does not participate forever in the final glory of divine participation as it vanishes in a final dissolution. This position is quite clear in Evagrius, while in

Origen, Crouzel insists that we can also find evidence for the position that the state of the glorious body is final.[19] On the other hand, Daniélou correctly insists that for Origen the acquisition of bodies results from the Fall, all spirits being originally disembodied. Embodiment being a result of the Fall, the *apocatastasis* is a kind of return to pure spirituality of an ethereal body.[20] We thus see that here nature is identified with fall and eschatology is an ecstatic outlet from it. Second, *Apocatastasis,* as a return to a pure spirituality is the final goal of this ecstatic eschatology. For Origen (as for Evagrius) the end is identical to the beginning. No other *telos* will emerge for creation except the return to the initial sameness. Even Christ for Origen is a mediator between the human and divine realms and that means between the realm of the God-contemplating Demiurge (*Logos*), and the created images of the highest divinity's mind.[21] That means that Christ, by his unfallen *nous*, comes to his creation for the final transcendence/return to pure divine intellectuality.

Origenist eschatology is not *creative* at all. The historical process will yield nothing new or unexpected; although Origen defends freedom of choice, freedom as dialogue is completely unknown to him. *Apocatastasis* implies no real dialogue as it is the reign of sameness. Both history and existential authenticity are practically abolished in this Platonizing eschatology, where intellectual contemplation replaces any real transformation of beings, as this has been conceived by the balanced incarnational theology of Chalcedon and expressed in the sacramental theology of its adherents.

We thus have already come to the second type of eschatology, following our initial distinction. The *eschatology of being as gift*, realized as a dialogical reciprocity, is the consequence of a balanced Christology, which of course follows a balanced Trinitarian theology such as that of the Cappadocians. We shall leave the important discussion for the book, confining ourselves for the moment to emphasizing that this theological balance refers primarily to the question of the relationship between person and nature. This eschatology of being as gift of dialogical reciprocity, the ontological expression of which is the Eucharist, where the circulation of gifts takes place, presupposes the *non-ecstatic conception of person* as we saw it in the Origenist/Platonizing theology. Briefly *person here is not an ecstasis out of nature, but refers to a personal ecstasis of nature itself.* Maximus will show us that nature exists as an ecstatic personal vocation, rather than as an immutable "given." Nature is something that is planned, given and discussed in the perspective of this eschatological formation, and finally emerges in the *eschata*. Person refers exactly to this eschatological/dialogical mode of existence of nature. It is the very formation and not the escape from nature that makes the person really exist.

Modern Orthodox theology seems to have confused the above issues. I have critiqued the personalism of Berdyaev, Yannaras, and Zizioulas in various books (some of which will soon be available in English), and this Introduction is not the place to repeat my criticism. Here I shall only say a few words concerning the subject of this book—the eucharistic ontology of being as dialogical reciprocity and its misconceptions. One can find much evidence for this in John Zizioulas's most recent book, *Communion and Otherness*.[22] Following unconsciously a long Kantian tradition, brought into Orthodox theology by Berdyaev, along with a Hegelian affirmation of relationship as constitutive of being and a Heideggerian identification of being with its ecstatic mode of existence, Zizioulas identifies nature with blind necessity and person with freedom as an ecstatic outlet from nature—and falsely attributes his position to the very quintessence of Greek patristic tradition. Thus for Zizioulas nature is practically—though not explicitly—identified with fall as we saw in Origen. Therefore:

> it follows from this that though *man's nature is ontologically prior to his personhood* as we have already noted, man is called to an effort *to free himself from the necessity of his nature and behave in all respects as if the person were free from the laws of nature.*[23]

For some reason nature here seems to be something passively given to person before he exists—but a "given" nature for Maximus, as we shall see, is already a personal nature, given personally and received personally, and thus not bound with necessity but open to a dialogue of love. It is clear that here Zizioulas identifies nature with necessity, and person (not grace!) with the liberation from this nature/necessity. It is essential to note that, as the last part of his final phrase shows, Zizioulas clearly means that he wants to liberate us not from a nature that has for some reason (that is, sin!) *become necessity,* but, as he says, from the *very laws of nature,* that is, from *nature as it is.* Even Incarnation itself does not transform anything, but only supports the great escape from created nature to the *how* of the divine person that vouchsafes freedom, exactly because he has himself reached a full dominion over his own nature—hence Zizioulas's polemic against the patristic Christology of the *communicatio idiomatum.*[24] What he seems to need is rather a *Christology of an escape* from the *what* of nature to the obvious freedom of the *how* of the person. But do we need Christology at all in order to achieve such an escape?

I don't of course intend to fully criticize Zizioulas's book in this introduction. In his Trinitarian theology as well as in his ecclesiology and his theory of intersubjectivity, Zizioulas seems to copy Levinasian heteronomy (that is, Levinas's concept of asymmetrical relationship where the Other prevails and dominates the I) with an essential alteration: Zizioulas changes Levinas's *ethical* priority to a completely *ontological* one. Thus God the Father, the Bishop, the Other, are *ontologically prior* to the rest of the persons, thus tending to create a kind of dictated otherness where reciprocity and dialogue become unrealistic indeed. But how then can we have real communion? Thus the so-called eucharistic theology of nowadays must be profoundly corrected.

V.

It is thus clear that, given the above presuppositions, it is very difficult to speak of nature as a dialogical/ecstatic personal event of dialogical reciprocity, or this ontological and eucharistic eschatology we find in Maximus. Nature is already a gift, it is already in the order of grace, Maximus seems to assert. And furthermore, nature as gift is already and always personal, already and always reciprocity; nature is an eschatological, dialogical becoming and not just a frozen "given." Out of the above context nature (along with person) can turn out to be death, but within it, *nature can be freedom,* claims Maximus, establishing a precious understanding of eschatology as eucharistic ontology, as we shall see, page by page, in this book.

Notes

1. See his *Geschichte und Eschatologie*, (Tübingen 1979³⁾, p. 172 ff.
2. *Kirchliche Dogmatik*, I/1 (1932), p. VIII.
3. J. Moltmann, *Theologie der Hoffnug. Untersuchungen zur Bengnündung und zu der konzequenzen einer christlicher eschatologie* (München, 1985), pp. 20, 35.
4. See J. Moltmann, *Kirche in der Kraft des Geistes*, München, 1975, p. 315 ff.

5. See his classical work *Christus und die Zeit. Die urchristliche Zeit und Geschichtauffassung* (1946).

6. See W. Pannenberg, *Offenbarung als Geschichte* (Göttingen, 1982[5]).

7. It is somehow misleading that ontology is usually identified with metaphysics in general (see for example, *The Cambridge Dictionary of Philosophy*, [R. Audi ed., Cambridge University Press, 1999, p. 564]). Here we take the term ontology in the simplest of its meanings as talking of being of things, that is, of what makes them to be as full entities. In this sense the uncreated logos of a being causes its very essence/existence. But this does not mean that these *logoi* are necessarily "metaphysical" in the sense that they are not empirically real, i.e., that they merely are high products of our own intellectual speculation. For Maximus, as we shall soon see, *logoi* are divine wills—that means absolutely real acts of a personal divine Being.

8. This could be a first positive reaction to David Ford's insightful book *Christian Wisdom. Desiring God and Learning in Love* (Cambridge: Cambridge University Press, 2007). We could perhaps say that for Maximus wisdom is exactly this creative encounter of human *logos*, considered as human desire as well as existential reasoning, with the divine *logoi*/wills of Christ.

9. E. Levinas, *Totalité et Infini. Essai sur l' exteriorité* (Martinus Nijhoff / La Haye, 1974[4]), p. XI: «L' eschatologie met en relation avec l' être, par delà la totalité pour l' histoire, et non pas avec l' être par delà le passé et le present.»

10. Martin Buber, *Das Problem des Menschen*, (Verlag Lambert Schneider, 1948), 2.

11. Levinas, p. XIII: «une telle situation est l' éclat de l' exteriorité ou de la transcendance dans le visage de l' autrui. Le concept de cette transcendance, rigouresement developpé, s'exprime par le terme d' infini.»

12. Levinas, p. XIV.

13. E. Levinas, *En decouvrant l' existence avec Husserl et Heidegger*, (Paris, Vrin, 1988), pp. 190–191.

14. See M. Purcell, *Levinas and Theology* (Cambridge: Cambridge University Press, 2006), p. 142.

15. Purcell, p. 145.

16. Purcell. p. 147.

17. Purcell, p. 152.

18. Com. Joh. (I,30); Keph. Gnost. 18.

19. See H. Crouzel, *Origen*, trans. A. S. Worrall, (Edinburgh : T&T Clark, 1989), p. 259 ff.

20. See Jean Danièlou, *Pères de l' Eglise au IIIe siècle: Origène* (Paris : ICP, 1986), pp. 299–301.

21. See Ed. Moore, "Christ as Demiurge: The Platonic Sources of Origen's Logos Theology in the Commentary on John," in *Philotheos*, 8 (2008), pp. 200–207, where the absolutely Platonic presuppositions of such a claim are joyfully stressed.

22. John Zizioulas, *Communion and Otherness* (Edinburgh: T&T Clark, 2006). For a thorough criticism of this book, see my "Person instead of

Grace, and Dictated Otherness; John Zizioulas' Final Theological Position",
Heythrop Journal, forthcoming, currently available at www.3.interscience.
wiley.com/journal/120120515/issue.

   23. Zizioulas, *Communion and Otherness*, p. 166.

   24. Ibid., pp. 238, 277

Chapter 1

Maximus's Eucharistic Theology and Its Ontological Dimensions

1. Maximus's Eucharistic Theology and the Scholars Who Have Studied It

THE STUDENT OF ST. MAXIMUS's eucharistic theology will be under pressure from the outset to join in the pessimism of scholars regarding the difficulty of describing the texture of this theology and articulating it with any accuracy. Thunberg expresses the assessment of scholars as a whole when he attributes this difficulty primarily to the scarcity of source texts in Maximus's work itself.[1] The meticulous Sherwood, affirming the difficulty of interpreting this aspect of the Confessor's thought, finds the reason in the fact that Maximus "has nowhere left us a complete exposition of the Eucharist," as well as in the "luxuriousness of allegorical interpretation which passes with the utmost ease through the various modes by which the soul is nourished."[2] Because the word of God is the natural nourishment of the soul, so, in Sherwood's view, the paramount concern for Maximus is that the soul should be nourished, whether this takes place through Scripture, through theological contemplation, through the Mysteries, or through inclusion in the Body of Christ; "it matters only that the soul is fed."[3] Thus, according to Sherwood, even in the *Mystagogy* Maximus deliberately passes over certain problems out of fear lest "his inadequacy" should reflect on the work of Dionysius.[4]

So because Maximus "has never expressed his thinking on the Eucharist with clarity" (W. Völker),[5] there are only two known studies specializing in his eucharistic theology, those of G. E. Steitz[6] and W.

13

Lampen[7] (and of course that of Thunberg, to which we have already referred). These two studies disagree in general, as the second is a refutation of the first, but they express the same impasse, because Steitz's article is "quite superficial"[8] and Lampen's cannot be considered complete,
even though he adduces a greater number of texts.[9] Nevertheless, Sherwood himself presents a collection of fourteen passages from Maximus
with a eucharistic reference (and it is obvious that he has adopted the
order of these passages as first presented by Steitz), of which six refer to
the priesthood and two to the sacrifice of Christ, while the remaining
six deal with the "obscure" subject of communion.[10] He describes these
texts as "difficult for us of another mentality to savor and understand";
but even so, his examination of them enables him to affirm that for Maximus, the Eucharist is at the heart of the Christian life.[11] A. Riou, too, is
impressed by the "total silence" to which Maximus is inclined, attributing it to his reverence for the nature of the mystery on the one hand, and
also to the fact that he himself was a simple monk and not a member
of the clergy.[12] Von Balthasar has considerable hesitation about adopting such an explanation,[13] whereas Bornert looks for specific historical
factors bearing on the approach Maximus takes.[14] Lastly, Thunberg believes that Maximus's behavior in this case, though it may not satisfy the
analytical scruples of the scholars studying him, does reflect the saint's
profound reverence for this crowning moment of the Divine Liturgy, to
which Maximus gives especial emphasis by his silence.[15]

Concealed in these short studies and brief references by scholars
are fleeting traces of Maximus's outstanding spiritual style and his ek-
static movement toward the unifying, living center of universality in
Christ, a movement that is holy and indeed "foreign to our mentality."
For in reality, there is in the written work of Maximus the Confessor a
eucharistic teaching of deep significance, the theological ramifications
and consequences of which may ultimately prove profoundly fruitful
and exceptionally crucial for contemporary theological thought. His vision is great indeed: it is the mystery of the recapitulation of the created
order in Christ through communion and by providence, according to the
loving good pleasure of the Father.

This chapter will attempt to observe the semantic aspects of Maximus's references to eucharistic theology (and we should repeat here that
we have added several new eucharistic texts to those already cited by
other scholars). It will do so with a focus on the overtly or covertly repeated appearance of key concepts similar and comparable in meaning,
which would permit further generalizations in interpreting Maximus's

thought. This way of proceeding will lead us, by a roundabout route, to the very heart of Maximus's universe. The saint's fruitful wisdom produces extraordinary assemblages of spiritual theorems and exhibits a rare poetic unity. Our endeavor is always to keep listening to the word of the holy Father himself.

2. "Eucharistic Communion" and the "Eucharistic Becoming" of Things

IN THE SEQUENCE OF THOUGHT in Chapter 24 of the *Mystagogy*,[16] the "invisibly present grace of the Holy Spirit" acts "during the holy synaxis" of the eucharistic rite, in an altogether special way, "changing and transforming and truly *reshaping* [each of those present] into a more divine state, conformably to his own self, and leading him toward that which is symbolized by the Mysteries being performed." Grace reshapes "each of those present" "truly," that is, existentially and ontologically, not in an imaginary way or according to the aesthetic fancies of some supposed "religious feeling." This is further evident from the truly amazing phrase that follows, which impressively disconnects the ontology of the mystery from the gnosiological approaches to it, ". . . even if he is not aware of it—if perhaps he is among those who are infants in Christian faith—even if he is unable to see the depths of what is taking place, or to perceive that the grace which is indicated by every one of the divine symbols of salvation is working within him, leading him in an order and sequence from things imminent to the final goal of all things."

Here Maximus goes beyond the usual philosophical principle that any ontology is implicitly linked to a gnosiology;[17] through the Grace that loves mankind, God works ineffable mysteries of marvelous changes in Christian believers as they are deified, and this activity of His which makes them human is not determined by the degree to which their cognition is involved—their infantile state does not prevent "the grace of salvation" from leading them in "order and sequence" from "things imminent" to the eschatological fullness of the symbols of the synaxis.[18] In what follows, Maximus sums up the liturgical process up to its culmination and fulfillment in the Eucharist, and at the same time describes the existential becoming of the rational beings who find themselves within the theurgic orbit of the Divine Liturgy. Let us see how: the first Entrance indicates the laying aside of unbelief and the increase in faith, the lessening of malice and progress in virtue, a (relative) removal of ignorance and an increase in knowledge among those who are existentially moving with the flow of the liturgical process. With the hearing of the divine words, all of the above (faith, virtue, and knowledge) are consolidated into unshakable habits and attitudes. The divine hymns that follow indicate the soul's voluntary assent to the virtues and the spiritual pleasure and delight they produce. The reading of the Holy Gospel indicates the end of the earthly mind as an end of the sensible world. After this, when the doors are closed, we have the transition and transposition of those who have made themselves of part of this liturgical becoming from this corruptible world to the spiritual world of the soul, at which transition the soul closes its senses like doors, purifying them from the idols of sin. The more perfect and mystical and novel doctrine and knowledge, that which has to do with God's economy for our sake, is signified by the Entrance of the Holy Mysteries. Next comes the moment of the kiss of peace. What has until now been a liturgical progression, which has already led to the most profound spiritual knowledge about the divine Economy, will now extend to "the *identity* of all with all, and first of each with himself and with God, an identity in concord, oneness of mind and love." Here we have a first but extremely eloquent reference to the profound communion which indeed, as will become apparent later, forms the essence of eucharistic becoming,[19] a communion of full identity first of each person with himself, then with all the others and finally with God, grounded in concord, oneness of mind and love. This communion makes possible the recitation of the Creed, which Maximus calls a "confession," as fitting thanks for the wonderful ways whereby we are saved. With the Thrice-holy Hymn that follows, the unity and communion among believers is extended also to the angels as "union and equality in honor," so as to achieve praise of God as "tuneful harmony." There follows the prayer "through which we are accounted worthy to call God Father," by which is indicated a still higher degree of communion with God, our "adoption in very truth by the grace of the Holy Spirit." The result of this is the experience, in the hymn "One is holy" that follows, of the "unifying grace and *familiarity* with God Himself." And as the process of liturgical becoming unveils ever-deeper realities of communion, the moment of Holy Communion or "divine partaking" arrives. (It is significant that Maximus speaks of "partaking," *metalepsis*, a term that already reveals a profound communion.) We read: "By the holy partaking of the pure and life-giving mysteries [is signified] the communion and identity with Him which can be achieved by participation through likeness. It is through this that man is accounted worthy to become no longer human, but god." An obvious parallel to the above is the following passage from *To Thalassius*, which, however, has no direct eucharistic reference:[20]

> Participation in supranatural divine [things] is the assimilation of those who participate to that in which they participate. The assimilation of those who participate to that in which they participate is their identity with it, actively achieved through assimilation. The identity of those who participate with that in which they participate, which can be actively achieved through assimilation, is the deification of those accounted worthy to be deified. And deification is the encompassing and ultimate end of everything that exists in time and in eternity, according to the general description of all times and ages. The inclusion and ultimate end of the times and ages and everything that exists within them is the inseparable unity within those who are being saved between the absolute very beginning of things and their absolute and literal end.

Following on from this, "those accounted worthy" are energized by "the energy of God, direct and infinite and stretching to infinity, all powerful and exceeding in strength," which is "the ineffable and more than ineffable delight and joy of those in whom God's energy works, flowing from the union beyond speech and understanding; no concept or word or thought can be found in all the nature of things to describe this delight." If we make a comparative study of these two passages, we observe that participation in God is grounded and set in motion "through likeness" and leads to communion and identity with God "by participation" and also to the experience in God of the "inseparable unity" of the literal beginning with the literal end; an eschatological experience, the experience ultimately of the "deification of those accounted worthy to be deified." We shall see throughout this book how this profound eschatological experience forms the very essence of Maximus's thought, and especially his ontology. Beyond the initial connection of Divine Eucharist and deification (cf. *Mystagogy*, Epilogue, 708C: "And the partaking of the holy and life-giving mysteries [. . .] indicates adoption by our God, and union and familiarity and divine likeness and deification"), what emerges as the "essence" of deification is the fact of communion and identity with God through participation.

The precise meaning of this communion and unity and identity of the saints with the Holy Trinity is described for us by Maximus in his text *Another contemplation of how the saints transcend material duality, and what is the unity perceived by the mind in the Holy Trinity*.[21] There we have a description of how the saints first pass beyond "material duality," that is, the matter and form of which bodies are made, or flesh and matter, and are then granted "to hold converse with God and be mingled with the most pure fire"; they

> have completely thrown off sense perception and the things perceived by it through a disposition marked by firm action; by means of the intellect alone, they behold [the soul] ineffably assimilated to God, wholly united in a way surpassing knowledge with Him in His totality in intellect and reason and spirit, as the image to its archetype, possessing the likeness as far as is attainable by assimilation; and so they learn in a hidden manner what is the unity perceived by the mind in the Holy Trinity.

In other words, the saints are guided to the knowledge of the unity-in-communion of the Holy Trinity.[22] Further on, Maximus speculates that "the material dyad" may refer to the incensive power and the desire; for if someone keeps these in subjection by the mastery of the reason, or even abandons them altogether; if he comes alone to the immovable enchantment, knowable in love through reason and contemplation; he has restricted himself to only one of the many movements, the pure and simple and undivided movement of the most noble power of desire, and according to that movement has wisely established for himself a state of permanence, moving around God without end in identity of eternal movement according to his desire—then such a one is truly blessed. He has achieved not only true and blessed union with the Holy Trinity, but even *that unity which is perceived by the mind within the Holy Trinity*, because he has become as far as possible simple and indivisible and single in form, in conformity with the Holy Trinity who is simple and indivisible in essence.[23]

The unity of the Trinity brings about the unity of the natural powers of the participant. Furthermore, the communion and identity of the saints with the Holy Trinity by participation means that the saints are "united in essence" in accordance with the essential unity perceived by the mind in the Holy Trinity: this belongs to the ultimate texture of the eucharistic event, which is thus not simply an experience of communion, but an ontological fact of communion. As we read in the *Mystagogy*, Chapter 1:

> The holy Church is an image of God, as has been said in that it brings about the same unity among the faithful as does God, despite the fact that those who are united in the Church through faith differ in language and come from different places with different customs. *This same union among the essences of things, without confusion between them, is effected by God Himself.* As has been shown, He smooths out the difference between them and converts it into identity by reference to and union with Himself, as the cause and beginning and end.[24]

The union-communion of the essences of things is a union of which God is the author. In consequence, the ecclesial-eucharistic communion between beings and God makes the Church an image of God, an ontological fact of relational unity.[25] Eucharistic communion, as an ontological fact, is a consequence and image of the only true ontology, that constituted by "the unity perceived by the mind in the Holy Trinity."

We should add that the relational texture of this eucharistic ontology is undergirded by the actual becoming of beings, precisely the eucharistic becoming, which is nothing other than becoming-in-communion especially for the created world, by a participatory assimilation to the unity of the Holy Trinity.

3. *The Areopagitic Legacy in Maximus and How He Develops It*

IF WE WANT TO DISCOVER THE AREOPAGITIC ANTECEDENTS of Maximus's thought and also the changes he introduces, we shall need to look at Dionysius's work *On the Ecclesiastical Hierarchy*. Evident in that work is the saint's insight that every "operation of sacred ritual," and especially the eucharistic assembly, "brings together our divided lives into a united deification; by the divine uniting of what is divided, it bestows union and *communion with the one.*"[25] This is precisely why "it is scarcely possible to celebrate any of the hierarchic services unless the Divine Eucharist, which recapitulates all the various rites, gathers the initiate into oneness through liturgical action."[26] This gathering and unification takes place inasmuch as "the most divine shared and peaceable distribution of one and the same bread and cup dictates *the same godly mode of behavior* among them, inasmuch as they are *nourished with the same food*, and sacredly reminds them of the most divine Supper, the original symbol of the rites being celebrated."[27] The synaxis "extends itself to include all the imagery of the divine, but then in unitary manner returns from them to its own inherent oneness, and unifies those who are sacredly uplifted in it."[28] It is easy to see that the saint repeatedly tries to highlight the significance of the divine Monad as author of the one-like union of the members of the synaxis: "For it is not possible for those who are divided among themselves to be gathered into one and *participate in the peaceable union of the one.* For if we have been illumined by contemplation and knowledge of the one and unified into the one-like and divine gathering, we could not endure to fall back into desires that divide us . . ."[29] The synaxis or gathering into one, and participation in the peaceable union of the one, stand as a reproach to those who are divided and fragmented because of their passions.

This communion is symbolically grounded in the distribution of the eucharistic gifts: "When [the celebrant] uncovers the concealed and undivided bread and divides it into many pieces, and apportions among all the oneness of the cup, he is symbolically multiplying the unity and distributing it, thereby performing the most holy rite."[30] Furthermore, it becomes very clear in the passage immediately following that Christ Himself becomes active in the Eucharist. There is therefore no basis for Thunberg's remark in his discussion of the latter part of *Mystagogy* 24, a passage where it is quite apparent that Christ is personally operative in the Eucharist ("He, that is to say, our God and Savior Jesus Christ, changes us into Himself . . ."); Thunberg comments that it is only in Maximus that Christ appears active in the mystery, whereas any such idea is altogether absent from Dionysius' commentary.[31] Here is the passage from Dionysius:

> By His becoming human like us, in His goodness and love for mankind, the unity and simplicity and hiddenness of the most divine Word Jesus proceeded without change to become something composite and visible. In His beneficence, he has brought about our unifying communion with Him, uniting our lowliness as humans to His utter divinity; provided that we become part of Him, as members of a body, in identity of unblemished and godly life, and do not let ourselves be

> deadened by corrupting passions and thus become unfit to
> join ourselves and share a life with members that are godly
> and full of health. For if we desire communion with Him, we
> must aspire to His most divine life in the flesh; by assimilating
> ourselves to Him in His sacred sinlessness, we must attain to
> a godlike and unblemished habit of life. In this way we will
> be granted communion with what is similar to us, in a way
> consonant with our own selves.[32]

Communion with the Oneness of God is obviously communion with
Christ. Christ is the sole author of the unifying communion between
God and man. Based on the content of this passage, we should also view
with some reservation the comment endorsed by Thunberg (which he
attributes to R. Rocques) that in the Areopagite's view of the Eucharist
"nothing reminds us of the Body and Blood of Christ, and so the eucharistic communion for Denis relates more to God in His unity (though
Trinitarian of course) than to participation in Christ's humanity."[33] The
same applies to Thunberg's conclusion that "the [Areopagite's] optic
is certainly that of the Incarnation, but the Incarnation seen as an act
through which the one and single divine nature of the Logos enters
the complex and manifold sphere of the world."[34] The Areopagite's references, in the passage quoted above, to members becoming part of a
body, to joining and sharing life with godly members and to taking on
"His most divine life in the flesh," give the Incarnation dimensions that
are truly and realistically Orthodox and not "monophysite." Also significant (though not entirely acceptable) is Thunberg's view that for the Areopagite, it is not the content of the eucharistic gifts that is of primary
importance but "the demonstrative quality of their distribution."[35] First
of all, we consider that the text does not provide evidence to support the
first part of this observation. On the contrary, the admittedly brief but
emphatic reference to incorporation, sharing in life and being joined
to the divine Flesh of Christ, makes us think that the Areopagite was
not concerned with setting priorities in his teaching on the Eucharist.
The content of the eucharistic gifts is just as important as the communal symbolism of their distribution. It is precisely because the Gifts are
so significant that their distribution has such significance in terms of
communion. Because it is exactly as a circulation of gifts that being is
constituted for Maximus.

Let us continue, however, with our quest to delineate the similari-
ties and differences between the Areopagitic *Ecclesiastical Hierarchy*

and the aforementioned works of Maximus, to which we hasten to add the text of "Questions 41" from his *Questions and Answers*,[36] studying it together with Thunberg.[37] The question is: "When the holy Body and Blood of the Lord are set out in the Prothesis, why is it the practice of the Church not to put out the same number of loaves and of cups?" And the answer is:

> Everything that is performed in the Church has a supranatural significance. Now, these symbols [i.e. the matter of the Holy Prothesis] above all are representations of and testimonies concerning the divine essence. But the divine essence is simple and not composite, whereas every created thing is composite and, as has been said, only the Holy Trinity is simple and non-composite. So it is precisely for this reason that the Church sets out a different number of loaves and cups at the Holy Prothesis, in this way characterizing the divine.

According to Thunberg, Maximus is here going further than the Areopagitic writings, where the distribution of the Gifts (as the multiplication of the absolutely unified into multiplicity) is the symbolic point of Holy Communion. Here the inequality between the bread and the cup characterizes the Godhead Itself, as simple and non-composite Trinity. And Thunberg goes on:

> Thus, to Maximus, the symbolic quality of the distribution of the gifts of the Eucharist is not only "incarnational" as in Ps.-Denis [. . .] but illuminative of God Himself, in that it points to the mystery of the Trinity (being one and three at the same time). This indicates that to Maximus the Eucharist, and the Holy Communion in particular, is linked to the communion with the God-Three-in-One and not only, as in Ps.-Denis, to the Divine One-ness, dividing itself communicatively to multiply creation thanks to the Incarnation. If to Denis the Communion refers to the *katavasis* of Divinity only, to Maximus, then, it also refers to the *anabasis,* in that it points to the Trinitarian mystery itself of One-ness in-Multiplicity (ontologically united). That is, it points to the fact that a certain multiplicity is of divine essence.

We have seen above that Maximus has in fact gone very much further than Thunberg has discovered in his perceptive remarks quoted above. In his eucharistic theology, Maximus has formulated not only the mystery of the Trinitarian unity but also the manner is which it is realized "through participation" by those who partake. At the same time, however, one cannot be absolutely certain of the accuracy of Thunberg's observation. Already in the Areopagitic passages quoted above, we have heard Dionysius talking about the synaxis even "including all the imagery of the divine," and about the members of the eucharistic assembly participating "in the peaceable union of the one." This last phrase may perhaps assume Trinitarian existence as well—how else could he speak of a "union" of Him who is already one? And then, what exactly is this "imagery of the divine" encompassed by the synaxis? Could it be the Father and the Son and the Holy Spirit in their liturgical-eucharistic manifestation during worship? However, there is a whole series of questions from the same perspective concerning the place of eschatology in the Dionysian writings, and the possible relation of the Eucharist to it. There are some modern scholars who argue that it is impossible to find an eschatological dimension in Areopagitic sacramental theology, at least explicitly. It is also true that no one has made an adequate case to the contrary (one could cite here both Orthodox scholars such as Pelikan, Meyendorff, and Golitzin, and non-Orthodox such as Roques and Farrow). "Mystical ascent" seems to predominate, while the Eucharist is taken as a kind of a symbol of this! I think that what can be considered as the Areopagite's eschatological inclination is his "ecclesialization" of the *anagogi* of Origen and Evagrius. Ultimately, Dionysius finds Christ in the Church and especially in the Eucharist, and not merely by ekstasis. That means that it is the Eucharist that makes Christ present, not mystical contemplation alone. Of course, in Dionysius we do not have Maximus's profound eschatological sense, of which we will speak in the following chapters.

These reservations apart, we consider that the main way in which Maximus goes beyond the Areopagite has to do with the discovery and ontological grounding of the notion and fact of becoming. And we speak of a "discovery" because it is not simply a matter of abandoning the pessimistic quality of movement in Origen. Maximus has actually drawn his inspiration up to a point from the positive sense given to movement in Aristotle, and has learned much from Gregory of Nyssa and the Areopagite on this subject. It is chiefly a matter of discovering the eucharistic foundation for movement-becoming, and of becoming as an ontological "fullness" of eucharistic communion. We consider that these investigations into the semantics of certain terms will provide new dimensions both to eucharistic theology and to the terms themselves. We shall later see that this notion of becoming is of paramount importance, both existentially and ontologically, if we are to understand the place of nature and history, for example, in this eucharistic ontology. We shall continue with our analysis of those writings of the Confessor relating to eucharistic theology, devoting the chapters that follow to detailed and extensive discussion of his views on the subject.

4. *The Providence and Economy of God Summed Up in the Eucharist*

IN LIGHT OF THE SEMANTIC EVIDENCE gleaned up to this point, let us examine the text of *Mystagogy* 21:[38]

> The confession made by the whole people toward the end of the mystical worship with the "One is holy" and what follows, reveals the hidden *gathering and union* of those mystically and in wisdom made perfect in God *with the One of divine simplicity—[a union] transcending all thought and understanding*, which will take place in the *incorruptible age of things intelligible*. When in that age they behold the light of the inscrutable and supremely ineffable glory, they too receive the purity of blessedness along with the heavenly powers. After this, *as the ultimate goal of everything*, the distribution of the mystery takes place, changing into itself *those who partake worthily* and showing them similar by grace and participation to that which is good of itself, in no way falling short of that good insofar as is attainable and possible for human beings. So that they too can be and be called gods, not by nature but by grace, through *God who in His totality has wholly filled them and left nothing in them empty of His presence.*

All events and entities, "things performed" by God, are going to be gathered together into an absolute, unitive, "hidden" communion with the One of divine simplicity, inasmuch as they reveal the mystic depths of the unfathomable wisdom of their Author. This mystical rite of the communion of beings crowns their long journey toward "the incorruptible age of things intelligible." The notion of time which is introduced here, and which, as von Balthasar correctly remarks,[39] is a clear reflection of the thought of St. Gregory of Nyssa, does not stop Maximus diverging from Gregory: as we have already seen, Maximus promotes movement as the fundamental element in the structure of created being, not simply as an intermediate term between God and the world.[40]

The purity resulting from "beholding the light of the inscrutable and supremely ineffable glory" then makes those who participate in it worthy of the distribution of the Gifts, which leads them to be transformed in conformity with the mystery itself, making them into gods not by nature but by grace, "insofar as is attainable and possible for human beings." This takes place, however, only with those who "partake worthily" and "as the ultimate goal of everything." Here we have the crowning moment of the spiritual life, its fulfillment.[41] Worthy members of the eucharistic synaxis experience the charismatic fullness of universalization ("catholisization") in God as they are universally interpenetrated by God,[42] the entirety of whose economy has been accomplished. For this passage is, inter alia, a small but conspicuous and clear reminder of the fact that the divine economy is summed up in the Divine Eucharist (see 696D). In other words, the fact that the Eucharist has its essence and grounding in the divine economy and providence is directly reflected in all its ontological dimensions. In their eucharistic fulfillment, the being, communion, and becoming of all existent things have as their foundation the loving Providence of God and His wise Economy in Christ.

The link between God's Providence and Economy in Christ and the divine Eucharist is manifestly present in Maximus's thought. In his *Commentary on the Letters of St. Dionysius*, we read:

> God's Providence is said to be "without beginning," but not in the sense that He exercised providence over entities which were similarly without beginning, as some foolishly maintain, saying that eveything comes into being simultaneously with God. Rather, it means that before things were made, God's Providence existed without beginning prior to any created thing in God's ideas or examplars, that is, in His eternal thoughts (which St. Paul calls predestinations, as we said in our commentary *On the Divine Names*); and it is in these ideas or thoughts of God that things yet to be made were preformed.[43]

The providence of God which is "without beginning or end" consists precisely in this providential "pre-loving" of existent things in their *logoi* or inner principles, which has the goal of bringing into being the creation which will enjoy the providential loving goodness of God. His Economy is already outlined in the assurance that this providential goodness will take the form of all the particular goods that will be required for the fulfillment of this good "pre-conception."

We will not of course concern ourselves in this work with the indisputable historical fact that the divine Eucharist was identified even from apostolic times with the totality of the divine Economy.[44] A penetrating exegesis of the prime eucharistic passage in the first eucharistic theologian, John the Evangelist (John 6:51–58), would suffice to remind us of the breadth of this subject.[45] This passage is tacitly assumed by the Confessor in those texts of his eucharistic theology which present Christ as "the living bread which came down from heaven" (John 6:51) and essentially identify the Eucharist with the totality of the God's given activity in history, the working out of the divine economy. What is of interest here is the immediately evident agency of Christ in the fulfillment of His Father's providential will, through His eucharistic incarnation which extends down the centuries. Eucharistic incorporation into Christ is the way of ascent to the Father through charismatic participation in the Spirit; it lays even now, within the bounds of creaturehood, the foundation for the eternal ontology of the "unity perceived in the Trinity," as we shall see in more detail further on. Here is that truly important text:

> [Christ] insatiably stirs our appetite for Himself, *who is the bread of life* and of wisdom and knowledge and righteousness. And by fulfilling His Father's will, He makes us worshippers on a par with the Angels, in imitation of whom we show ourselves well-pleasing [to God] by our way of life, just as they are in heaven. And from there again He raises us up in the ultimate divine exaltation to the Father of lights, making us partakers of the divine nature through participation in the Spirit by grace, whereby we shall become children of God, immaculately bearing within us *the very author of this grace, Him who is the Son of the Father by nature, who is present entire and uncircumscribed within us in our entirety;* from whom and through whom and in whom we have and shall have our being and movement and life.[46]

In this very lucid passage, there is a very clear link between being and movement and the (communal) event of living, and the final fulfillment of all these ("we shall have . . .") in our eucharistic incorporation into Christ, thus revealing the eucharistic-ontological grounding of all this. The implicit reference in the phrase "bread of life" to the well-known eucharistic passage of John's Gospel, where the Eucharist is precisely identified with the heart of the divine Economy and its recapitulation, makes clear both the Confessor's traditionalism on this point and also the adventurous depths of his personal theological explorations. J. M. Garrigues looks at this passage somewhat differently, and goes so far as to speak of "the unction of our adoption [*onction adoptive*] in Christ which was preordained for us by the Father, [which] was lost by Adam and regained by the redeeming Incarnation of Christ."[47] The union with Christ as "firstborn brother" (Rom 8:29) through likeness in the Spirit leads the human being, who has recapitulated the world in himself, "to rest for ever with the Son in the bosom of the Father, the first source of uncreated unity and ultimate end of the unification of creation in Him."[48] If we add these remarks of Garrigues's, we can already speak of the eucharistic realization of our adoption in Christ in Maximus's thought, or of the eucharistic realization of the providential good love of the divine Economy, in our adoption as sons by grace through the Eucharist. But in commenting on this same text, we must also not fail to notice the Trinitarian reference of the Eucharist. Here, too, the Eucharist relates to the unique ontology of personal communion established by the "Father of lights," into which man, too, enters when he is adopted. A communion of the Father, with the "Son of the Father" and the Spirit; a communion of the divine hypostases which bear, as we have seen, an essence that is "simple and undivided," i.e., characterized by communion.

5. *Eucharistic Enlightenment*

THE WORD—NOURISHER AND NOURISHMENT—accomplishes a series of varied and manifold "embodiments" which go to make up the sacramental process of "making the world word" in accordance with providence, because "the Word of God and God desires always and in all to work the mystery of His embodiment."[49] The sacramental-eucharistic character of these soteriological embodiments is clearly demonstrated by Maximus when he writes:

> If we thus live in accordance with our prayers, we will receive the Word as supersubstantial and life-giving bread, to nourish our souls and preserve in good condition the good things given to us. [For this is] the Word who said, I am the bread that came down from heaven and gives life to the world; in proportion to our capacity, He becomes all things for us who

> are nourished by virtue and wisdom, and *is embodied in each
> of those who are being saved in various ways, as he knows
> best.* [And all this] while we yet live in this world . . .[50]

This final statement by Maximus, which implicitly looks forward to the interpretation of "Give us this day our daily bread" that is to follow and seems mysterious to one uninitiated in Maximus's theological thought, highlights his strong eschatological sense. The bread of life is an event of "this day," yet one that reveals God's original and ultimate good pleasure for man to be made immortal:

> By "this day," I think it means this age. To make this part of
> the prayer clearer, one might say: Give us this day, while we
> are in the present life of mortality, our bread that You have
> prepared from the beginning for the immortality of our na-
> ture, in order that this nourishment with the bread of life and
> knowledge may overcome the death of sin. The first human
> being was prevented from becoming a partaker of this [life
> and knowledge] by his transgression of the divine command-
> ment. For if he had had his fill of this divine nourishment,
> he would not have been taken captive by the death of sin.[51]

The most significant conclusion from study of this passage, however, is that Maximus here identifies the Divine Eucharist with the life and wisdom or knowledge that conquers death ("the bread of life and knowl-edge," "for the immortality of our nature"; at 904A, he speaks of the "bread of knowledge," and at 905C, looked at above, he speaks of the "bread of life and wisdom and knowledge and righteousness"). What is this eucharistic wisdom or knowledge, which in vindication of Maxi-mus's insistence upon it we could call the "eucharistic enlightenment" of Christians? In accordance with the earlier conclusions of our study, what we have here is an initiation-by-participation into the "unity per-ceived in the Trinity"; it is initiation into the communal life of the Trin-ity and the realization-through-participation of that life in the life of the ecclesial community formed by mutual love and gift-sharing. We are talking about the eucharistic knowledge, by grace, of the manner of God's personal Trinitarian existence, the experience of Trinitarian unity as the charismatic life of Christian believers. Or, the eucharistic enlight-enment of Christians has to do with their understanding and experi-ence, in their own life, of truth as communion of life in the image of the Trinitarian unity.

In this same passage of eucharistic theology, where Maximus speaks of the "bread that [God] has prepared from the beginning for the immortality of our nature," he very clearly distinguishes our nature from the immortal life bestowed upon it by God; our nature may be in a state of mortality (ibid.). If our nature were filled with the divine eucharistic nourishment, it would not be "taken captive" by the death of sin. Hence death is the captivity of our nature, while immortal life is precisely the only way for it to exist in its wholeness. Living, then, is the fullness of being, its authentic realization; for Maximus, *to be* ultimately means *to live* in an absolute sense, i.e., to live immortally. And this immortal life is possible only as communion with the Trinitarian God within the eucharistic experience of the perpetual circulation of gifts (being as gift from above, life as a gift to the others, the world as a human gift to God) in the Church.[52] In consequence, the ontological dimensions of the Eucharist are dimensions of this limitless and incorruptible eternal life, consisting in mutual self-giving which is identified with eternal awareness and experience of the deifying truth of our adoption in Christ—of the recapitulation of creaturehood in accordance with providence, which is activated in the context of the Church's eucharistic communion. Maximus's thought is governed first and foremost by experiential knowledge of this truth, leading him to place the Eucharist at the apex of the mysteries of the Church, in which he is also following the patristic tradition;[53] this is made crystal clear when he writes so eloquently: "The cup is placed before the baptism, because virtue exists for the sake of truth, not truth for the sake of virtue."[54] And he goes on to explain: "Truth means divine knowledge, while virtue means the struggles which those who desire the truth undertake for its sake."[55] What stands out prominently here is the primacy of ontology in relation to ethics (askesis), and above all the eucharistic ontological foundation of the latter. This eucharistic grounding is the way Christian asceticism is rooted in truth, which thus becomes a longing to be given personal eucharistic universality, because it is divine knowledge that is truth, i.e., experiential awareness of "God who in His totality has wholly filled [us] and left nothing in [us] empty of His presence" (*Mystagogy* 24).[56] Further on, Maximus expounds in great detail the relationship between Baptism and the Eucharist, fleshing out the thought that will lead him to describe the ontological primacy of the Eucharist, as we have seen: The baptism of the Lord is the utter mortification of our propensity for the sensible world; and the cup [i.e. of the Eucharist] is the disavowal of even this present life for the sake of truth.

The baptism of the Lord typifies the sufferings we willingly embrace for the sake of virtue. Through these sufferings, we wash off the stains in our conscience and willingly accept the death of our propensity for visible things. *The cup typifies the involuntary trials which attack us in the form of adverse circumstances because of our pursuit of the truth. If throughout these trials we value our desire for God more than nature, we willingly submit to the death of nature forced on us by these circumstances.*

The baptism and the cup differ in this way: baptism for the sake of virtue mortifies our propensity for the pleasures of this life; the cup makes the devout value truth above even nature itself.[57]

The preference accorded to truth, meaning longing for God, over nature and this temporary life—a preference that forms the ultimate martyric heart of ascetic practice—is manifested and typified in the Eucharist. The ascetic leaves the immediacy of the appearance of things[58] in order to fulfill God's good pleasure concerning the world, which is to "make the world true": to give it life within the eucharistic catholicity of gift-sharing of the ecclesial body.

He produces a transmission of divine life, making Himself edible in a way known to Himself and to those who have received [from Him] such a spiritual awareness of Him. So at the taste of this food, they know with true knowledge that the Lord is good, and that He changes those who eat of it in the direction of deification through the divine quality [of this food]—because it is clearly the bread of life and power both in name and in fact.[59]

The "power" of the Bread-Christ lies precisely in the possibility for His goodness to be poured out, as divine gift communicated through the Eucharist, in order to deify those who eat it.

6. The Existential Degrees of Eucharistic Incorporation

THERE IS A CORRELATION, ACCORDING TO MAXIMUS, between the soul, the Church and the Eucharist—which is not of course to say that they are identified with each other. Through the Eucharist, the soul becomes a Church, so that the actual man-made church building, with the various services celebrated in it and the Eucharist, which sums up and unites them all, forms an image of the eucharistic restoration of the soul and its deification through grace, upon which it becomes "truly a church of God."

> It is clearly in accord with all this that the holy Church of God is likened in contemplation to the soul. By means of the sanctuary, it signifies everything that we have shown to belong to the mind and proceed from it in progression. By the nave, it reveals what we have shown to belong to the reason and the distinct properties proceeding from it; and *it brings everything together through the mystery [of the Eucharist] performed on the holy altar.* One who has been able through the rites performed in the Church, with prudence and wisdom, to attain initiation into this mystery, has made his soul truly divine and a Church of God. It is perhaps for the sake of this true Church that the man-made church, which represents it symbolically by virtue of the various divine things within it, has wisely been given to us for our guidance toward what is more excellent.[60]

In this passage, he preserves the familiar semantic motifs of communion ("everything is clearly in accord," "bringing everything together," where the contemplative and active powers of the soul are brought into unity, i.e., "the whole of the ascetic and spiritual life are [sic] unified in their one object, though they may tend toward it under different aspects,"[61] and of becoming ("guiding toward what is more excellent," which contains an implication of movement). But in addition to these motifs, there is in this passage an obvious awareness on the part of the author of the connection, through the "prudent and wise movement," between the eucharistic mystery and the existential consummation of the soul's gradual ascent to the state of perfection in which it becomes a "Church of God."

A detailed list of the stages of this ascent, with a clear eucharistic reference regarding the ways in which we partake of God the Word in the Spirit, may be found in a passage of the *Ambigua.*[62]

> Jesus who has passed through the heavens and is now higher than all the heavens, the Word of God, is forever conveying and transferring those who follow Him in action and contemplation from what is lesser to what is more excellent, and from there to what is yet higher—to put it simply, time

would fail me to tell of the divine exaltations and revelations experienced by the saints as they are changed from glory to glory, until each receives the deification fitting to his own rank. Knowing that we have the natural longing for God already mentioned, this great Teacher encourages everyone and calls us through His teaching to the spiritual eating of the Lamb slaughtered for us, and admonishes us to preserve in an orderly and serviceable form the harmony of the members of this Lamb, keeping it unbroken and unmingled, lest we be condemned for breaking apart and tearing to pieces the well-disposed harmony of the divine body, or for eating the flesh of the Lamb and Word either impudently, meaning beyond our strength, or irreverently, meaning despite our strength. Rather, let each partake of the divine Word in accordance with the meaning of each member, according to his own strength and status and the grace of the Holy Spirit apportioned to him.

First and foremost, we see in this text of Maximus the inseparable unity of the Eucharist with all degrees of spiritual ascent "from the lesser to the more excellent" and with the "change from glory to glory" up to the ultimate point of receiving deification. The receiving of the Lord's Body and Blood through the Spirit preserves the harmony of the divine members "unbroken and unmingled" in the communicant; this harmony can be damaged by the impudence or weakness of the person concerned. By the grace of the Spirit, the Christian progresses along an upward spiritual path, a process of becoming which leads to deification and is eucharistic in character, in accordance with his gradual participation in the various members of the Lord's body.

This passage is the answer to Thunberg's query as to where the Eucharist fits in: is it at the first or the final stage of the spiritual life, or indeed at every stage?[63] Thunberg regards the Eucharist as the culmination of a synergy of man and Christ, in such a way that the Eucharist is ultimately the door to man's deification.[64] I consider that we express the author's thought far more faithfully if we stress that, as is apparent from the text we are looking at and its continuation, he gives our partaking, in the Spirit, of the "Lamb and Word" an organic place in a very concrete process of existential becoming. The result is that all the degrees and achievements of our spiritual evolution have been eucharistically (meaning ontologically) grounded, and in consequence have been oriented from the beginning toward deification, "being changed according to the spiritual principle denoted by each of the members [of Christ]." And also conversely, that the Eucharist has entered into all the possible manifestations of the spiritual life, giving them their foundation and their orientation.

Let us quote the passage in its entirety:

> Thus someone will partake of the head [of the Lamb-Word], if through principles that are not demonstrable he has gained a faith that is wholly detached from reasonings about theology; for from such a faith the entire body of virtues and of knowledge is fitted together and experiences spiritual growth. Someone partakes of the ears when he receives the divine words spiritually and with understanding, and as a result becomes obedient and subject to God in his actions until death. Someone partakes of the eyes if he has a spiritual understanding of the created world, and without hindrance brings together all its principles accessible to the senses or to the mind into one single fulfillment of God's glory. Someone partakes of the breast, when he fills his heart with subjects for theological contemplation, as did John the great Evangelist, and like an ever-flowing spring pours forth in godly manner, for those who wish to learn, words and behavior expressing the providence which governs all things. Someone partakes of the hands in a fitting manner if he performs none of the works appointed by the commandment carelessly or with indifference, but keeps the practical energy of his soul in readiness and in peak condition for the fulfillment of the divine laws. Someone partakes of the stomach if he keeps the fecundity of his soul ever-flowing, and abounds in spiritual contemplation, and keeps unquenched that most ardent love which comes from dispassionate desire for intercourse with the divine. Someone will properly partake of the entrails if his intellect in its deepest searching and knowledge explores the depths of God, and is filled with ineffable mysteries. We will say something yet more daring: someone partakes in sobriety of the lower parts of the Word if he is rational is his attitude to material things, preserving his flesh altogether undefiled together with his soul, through the virtues incessantly shaping in his soul the Word made flesh in His entirety. Someone

partakes of the thighs if he puts the Word/rationality (*logos*)
in charge of the passable part of his soul and completely cuts
off the soul's impulse toward material things. Someone partakes of the knees if he compassionately inclines himself,
in accordance with providence, to those who are weak and
sickly in their faith, imitating the Word's condescension toward us. Someone partakes of the legs and feet, in addition,
if he keeps the foundations of his soul firm and unshaken,
resting on faith, virtue and knowledge, purposefully pressing
on toward the prize of his upward calling, leaping across the
mountains of ignorance and the hills of evil together with the
Word (or: through rationality) and jumping over them.

But who can enumerate everything our God and Savior
has devised for us, all the ways in which He has made Himself edible and participable in proportion to the capacity of
each person? In addition to all this, the Lord also has locks
of hair, a nose and lips, a neck and shoulders and fingers,
and all the parts of our own bodies which are applied to Him
in an allegorical sense. People partake of all these parts in a
way appropriate and useful to them when they are changed
into each of the spiritual principles signified by each part
of the Lord's body. Thus the Lamb of God is eaten, as this
great and holy teacher says, and given over to spiritual di-
gestion, changing those who partake of Him into Himself by
the agency of the Spirit, bringing them into [His body] and
transferring each person to the place belonging to the member he has spiritually eaten, in accordance with its position in
the harmony of the body; so that in His love for mankind the
Word who is in all, who alone is beyond nature and speech,
becomes the essence of all things.

In the eucharistic mystery, "He who alone is beyond nature and
speech" becomes precisely the essence of all things, the ontological
foundation of all existential movements which can be assumed into
the body of the Word. In consequence, the spiritual life of the Christian is his or her personal history of gradual participation in the members of the Lord's body. The body of Christ's eucharistic incarnation
encompasses the "innumerable ways He has devised," whereby "He has
made Himself edible and participable in proportion to the capacity of
each person." For "the flesh of the Lord is life-giving Spirit, because He

was conceived of the life-giving Spirit. For what is born of the Spirit is Spirit."[65] So the entire process of becoming that is spiritual growth is eucharistically grounded in the slain Lamb and Word, on condition that the relational truth of the "well-disposed harmony of the divine body" is protected from the abuse of impudence or unacknowledged unworthiness, which would amount to "breaking apart and tearing to pieces" the "unbroken and unmingled" unity of His members. The Eucharist is thus shown to be the quintessence, the heart and the very structure of the ecclesial body,[66] because all spiritually valid activity within that body has such validity to the extent that it has been assumed by Christ and "transferred" by Him "into the place of the member spiritually eaten by [the person acting] in accordance with its position in the harmony of the body." And indeed, this happens in such a way that the communion of members in the Lord's body is kept in undisturbed harmony. This is why Christian asceticism is profoundly communal, because there cannot be any orthopraxy in the ecclesial body that is not assumed, taken up in the Eucharist. Ultimately, all things conform to truth and are recognized and existentially authenticated to the extent that they can be incorporated through the Eucharist. Thus we see that in the Confessor's thought, Eucharist and Church are not confused; and yet Christ, i.e., the Church, is known and participated in and has substantive existence from the point of view of existent beings only in its eucharistic expression. The Eucharist thus contains the full knowledge of God's world, meaning full knowledge of the world as God wants it to be[67]—in the state to which He Himself restores it by becoming, in Maximus's bold phrase, its "essence."

In another passage of the same work,[68] Maximus extends this idea of the redeeming incarnation of the Savior distributed to each through the Eucharist, and boldly takes it to its logical conclusion. He starts by summing up what he has said already:

> As I have said, each person, according to his strength and the grace of the Holy Spirit worthily bestowed upon him, has Christ within him in a way proportionate to his own state, Christ who causes him to ascend on high through becoming dead to all things. Thus each of us sacrifices the divine Lamb as it were "in a house"—in his own order, i.e., at the level appropriate to him according to his degree of virtue. Each one sacrifices the Lamb and partakes of its flesh and is filled with Jesus.

The clarity of what this Father is saying here is quite sensational: Christ Himself brings about "lofty ascents" in the athlete of faith. Christ is at every moment the "essence" of all spiritual ascents, their foundation and author, while this upward movement is linked to the degree to which the believer becomes part of the Church body through the Eucharist:

> Jesus Christ Himself becomes each person's own Lamb *as each is capable of accommodating Him and eating Him*; He becomes the personal Lamb of Paul the great preacher of truth, and in the same way the personal Lamb of every one of the saints according to the measure of the faith of each and *the grace given to each by the Spirit.* In different ways in different people, He is wholly present in the whole person and becomes all things for all.

The innumerable distributions of Christ and His saving purposes are His multiple eucharistic incarnations, which give substance to the movement that brings individual believers into one universal whole, i.e., incorporates the many in the One—the movement that follows the eucharistic distribution of the One to the many.[69] It is evident at this point that pneumatologically, this eucharistic incarnation is formed primarily within each believer.[70] Christ thus seems to assume every human act/ energy in a synergy where human act forms a gift to God, while God gives back the divinization of this act. These multiple incarnations of Christ for the sake of those who participate in Him, His multiple acts of kenotic interpenetration and self-offering, constitute the many different ways in which he assumes all the "houses" and "ranks" and "states" through which human longing for God passes, and transforms them into divine gifts through the Eucharist, i.e., through a synergetic dialogue of love between man and God.

7. The Eucharistic Doctrine of the Circulation of Being as Gift and the Person

THE PASSAGE WE HAVE JUST LOOKED AT brings us to a new and altogether essential dimension of Maximus's teaching on the Eucharist: precisely this loving self-multiplication of the Lamb, who becomes, as a gift, "all things to all men" corresponding to the unique personal char-

acter and otherness of each of the participants, is one of the most valuable indications of the eucharistic basis for the *person* in Maximus. The
eucharistic communion of Christ with His faithful friends is profoundly
personal; it highlights the actual person in an incomparably clear and
graphic manner.

Grounding the person in the crucial distinction without separation between nature and hypostasis,[71] Maximus identifies hypostasis
with person: "hypostasis and person is the same thing."[72] We shall return
to this point many times in this book;[73] but we might spend some time
here on the indications in his thought that suggest a definition of the
person in the context of eucharistic theology. And the first thing we see
as we observe the way he confronts these questions is that through the
Eucharist, he establishes a fundamental *reciprocity* between creation,
man, and God: an open and continuous process of relationality in communion that possesses the characteristic essential to the creation and
maintenance of truly personal relationships: the *exchange of gifts*.

The notion of exchange, which is the conscious expression of an
unconscious need to place communion on a firm foundation, has been
well-described in the field of anthropology by the ethnologist Marcel
Mauss and the structuralist anthropologist C. Lévi-Strauss. According to
Lévi-Strauss, Mauss in his classic work *Essai sur le don* (1924) attempted

> to show that exchange in primitive societies consists not so
> much in economic transactions as in reciprocal gifts, that
> these reciprocal gifts have a far more important function in
> these societies than in our own, and that this primitive form
> of exchange is not merely nor essentially of an economic
> nature but what he aptly calls "a total social fact," that is,
> an event which has a significance that is at once social and
> religious, magic and economic, utilitarian and sentimental,
> jural and moral.[74]

Taking this further, Lévi-Strauss writes that "social relations consist
of the raw materials out of which the models making up the social
structure are built."[75] Thus relationships of exchange shape sociability
in modern human sciences, a fact that finds an important corollary in
modern philosophy. Gabriel Marcel, for example, can write, not conceal-
ing his Christian roots: "for me, there is nothing that cannot or should
not be regarded as a gift."[76] In Marcel, the gift establishes knowledge as a
communion of consciousnesses; the person itself is a gift. The gift thus
expresses an act of love toward God and one's fellow-man, in other words

an act of communion.[77] The way intersubjectivity thus functions among humans will be given prominence by Lévi-Strauss, and above all by Lacan (on the basis of the linguistic theories of Saussure and Jacobson) to become ultimately the foundation for the symbolic function of the unconscious,[78] in other words, the functioning of the covert communication among conscious beings that constitutes sociability.[79] In Lacan, the subjective being-through-desire exists intersubjectively by embodying the desire of the Other as his own; it exists, we could boldly say, interpenetrating or indwelling the Other as an indefinite cause for the desire and its infinite goal, although the real Other is finally lost. Thus Lacan can be placed at the pinnacle of the Western quest for an ontological foundation of the subject and for its communion simultaneously–a quest indeed most Biblical in its roots. In our age, after Levinas, Derrida, and Caputo, Marion seems to have inaugurated a significant discussion on the phenomenology of gifts, trying to overcome Husserl's egological reduction toward an opening to a communion of gifts and gifted, while Kearney focuses on the exchange of gifts as the essential core of phenomenology, as we shall see in the last chapter of this book. In our present case, the great contribution of Maximus is the eucharistic grounding for the communion of gifts, that points to an eschatological ontology of dialogical reciprocity, which will allow us to go beyond individualistic or unconscious systems of communication to attain personal communion in Christ.

Indeed, in Maximus's thought the reciprocity-in-communion between man and God is effected by "gifts offered," the inner principles (*logoi*) of creation as man's gift to God. The reciprocity-in-communion between God and man is made up of "gifts bestowed," the spiritual kernel of creation as it is given to humans though spiritual contemplation. Thus man,

> in his capacity for knowledge, takes the spiritual inner principles of existent things as offerings to God through creation. And in his capacity for action, he takes the natural laws of existent things as gifts given to him, imitating them in the way he lives and revealing in himself through his life all the majesty of the divine wisdom which is invisibly present in existent things.[80]

Elsewhere, he says clearly that

> As we bring to the Lord the spiritual *logoi* of things that have come into being, we are offering gifts, because by His nature

He has no need of any of these things. For we do not bring
the spiritual *logoi* of things as if He were in need of them in
addition to other things, but in order that we ourselves may
in some way give Him the praise due to Him, as far as we are
able, by means of His own creations. On the other hand, one
receives gifts if one eagerly devotes oneself to divine philosophy, because we by nature stand in need of ways leading to
virtue and words conducive to knowledge.[81]

And in another place:

Through the intellect, [creation] brings [*proskomizei*] the
spiritual *logoi* of knowledge contained in it to God as offerings; and on the other hand it bestows gifts on [the intellect]
in the form of the ways leading to virtue that are inherent
within [creation] according to the law of nature.[82]

And what is the aim of this reciprocal process of giving and receiving? As
Maximus writes on this point:

Someone might even say this, that the Word ordained that
gifts should be offered to God, in order to display the infinitude of the divine goodness: the fact that, as He it had not
Himself previously contributed anything, He accepts His
own gifts as offerings from us, reckoning the whole contribution as ours. In saying that this would not be inappropriate,
[Scripture] shows how great and ineffable is God's goodness
toward us. For when we offer Him His own gifts as if they
were ours to give, He receives them as if they were indeed
ours, and considers Himself indebted to us for them, just as
if they had not been His originally. (Various Texts 3.7)

The fundamental spiritual structure of communion of beings as
gifts of dialogical reciprocity becomes apparent here. God's gifts to us,
i.e., the inner spiritual principles of creation and the laws of virtue derived from them, are given back by the mind that loves God; it "brings
them as an oblation" (*proskomizei*) to God, as Maximus insists on putting it ("His own gifts as if they were ours"). Both Maximus's insistence
here on the notion of *proskomidi* ("oblation") and his liturgical expression "receiving as if they were ours His own, offered to Him as if they
were ours" (cf. "Thine own of Thine own we offer Thee, in all things
and for all things") we would regard as clear references to the Eucha-

rist and worship. The true reciprocity-in-communion is ultimately the
eucharistic reciprocity of the circulation of being as gift between God
and man, a fact that highlights the profound communion of dialogical reciprocity between them, and similarly underlines the personal
dimension as the prime characteristic of this communion. God's "ac-
knowledgement of indebtedness" for whatever gifts He receives back
from man as offerings sets man free from any sort of compulsory, imposed and un-free communion. There is a brief hymn to human free
will—in addition to everything else—in the phrase "accepting His
own gifts as offerings from us, reckoning the whole contribution as
ours": man's free offering has such value for God that He rewards it as
if what was offered belongs exclusively to man ("as if the divine goodness had itself previously contributed anything"). He does not compel
an offering from humans: He simply accepts it as a gift "because by
His nature He has no need of any of these things." This reality of an
absolutely free communion of love, which is actually operative par excellence in the Eucharist, is the matrix from which the person comes
into being as a theological reality. Man's adoption in Christ, which as
we have seen makes no sense outside the Eucharist (see above, section 4), involves transcending all existential necessities inasmuch as
it represents the personal relationship between the Father and the
Son. Because the Son communes with the Father in freedom and love,
those who participate in the eucharistic incorporation into the human
body of the Son acquire by grace that same *personal* mode of existence
that is His.

The personal dimension of eucharistic incorporation in Maximus,
like the dimension of unrestricted and incorruptible eternal life based
on knowledge of the deifying truth of adoption in Christ (see above, section 4), is fundamental to a proper understanding of eucharistic communion and eucharistic becoming in his thought. We should say at the
outset that the reality of the person is a continuing verification of the
communion of rational beings and of their dialogical movement as gifts,
confirming that they are going in the right direction, as well as being
the fruit of that communion and movement. Eucharist is the liturgical
locus of the exchange that forms being as gift of dialogical reciprocity
between men and God. Not only God Himself but also all of us recipro-
cally distribute the gifts, as they consist in our own offerings to the community, transformed in the Spirit. So the distributed gifts are God's and
ours at the same time: Eucharist thus becomes the matrix of a universal
gift-giving and gift-sharing. A more vivid and detailed account of this

nexus of connections in Maximus's thought will be left for later chapters. Here, however, we make a preliminary but emphatic note of the clear eucharistic reference found in the fact of the person. Person is thus established upon the Eucharistic doctrine of the circulation of being as gift of dialogical reciprocity.

8. Priesthood as the "Instrument" of the Eucharist

IT WOULD BE BY NO MEANS RASH to call the priesthood, as seen by Maximus, the "instrument" of the Eucharist. Indeed, God expects the priesthood to "celebrate His love for mankind"[83] because "God ordained the priesthood and placed it on earth in His stead," and through it He Himself is "physically seen," using it to show "His mysteries to those able to see."[84] Divine love for mankind, i.e., human-divine-communion on earth, is expressed in the mysteries and as such celebrated by the priesthood, which is thus made into an instrument of sacramental cohesion and personal initiation for the body of the Church. Maximus's finest and most significant text on the priesthood is this:

> A ray of light gently draws to itself the healthy eye which delights in light, transmitting its own brightness to it. So in the same way the true priesthood, *being in everything the imprint of the blessed deity for those on earth*, draws to itself every soul that is disposed to love God and is holy, and *gives it a share in its own knowledge, peace and love*; so that when it has brought every power of the soul to the ultimate goal of its proper energy, it may present to God *those it has initiated into the holy mysteries*, deified in every way. For the goal of the rational energy in the soul is true knowledge; that of the appetitive energy is love; that of the incensive energy is peace. Just as the goal of the true priesthood is to be deified and to deify through these energies.[85]

In all respects, the priesthood exemplifies God's mode of existence among humans. It is attractive, and passes on to others the good things with which it is adorned: it passes on the universal fullness in which it abounds, characterized as it is by communion with God. It likewise passes on the fullness of the soul's rational energy as true knowledge, the fullness of the appetitive energy as love and the fullness of the incensive energy as peace. Ultimately, it passes on the existential universality that is in Christ, and unites to God in deification those it initiates into the mysteries. The term "initiation into the mysteries" or mystagogy, with its obviously eucharistic connotations, is a reference to the natural center of the priestly ministry which traditionally was, and is, the celebration of the Eucharist (indeed, because in this case Maximus is addressing a bishop, this eucharistic center becomes still more evident, given that traditionally the Eucharist celebrated by the bishop or presbyter and the profound connection between bishop or presbyter and Eucharist formed the foundation of primitive ecclesiology[86]). The mystagogical initiation provided by the priesthood, with its eucharistic foundation, is deified and deifies the fullness of the Church in the context of the Church's sacramental unity, acting in a personal way: it "assumes the sick members," as Maximus says, and heals them; and this "science of the husbandry of souls" "comforts them through payers."[87] In other words, it takes on the responsibility and labor of personally incorporating Christian believers through the Eucharist, of personally "assuming" the discrete members into the Body.[88] Thus the Eucharist is effected through the priesthood (and in this sense the priesthood is the instrument of God's eucharistic operation); the priesthood oversees the person's integration into community in God, and the Church's process of becoming in Christ.

9. The Two-Way Hermeneutical Connection between Eucharistic Theology and the Theology of the Logoi of Things

WE MAY NEVERTHELESS ASK what the eucharistic incarnation of the Word has to do with Maximus's "ontology" in the strict sense, namely the theory of the *logoi* of things. There is indeed a very interesting connection, as presented in *To Thalassius* 35,[89] where he attempts to answer the following question: "Because the Word become flesh, and not only flesh but also blood and bones; and we are commanded to eat the flesh, drink the blood, and not break the bones—I should like to know, what is this three-fold power of the Word become man?" Let us now give his brilliant answer:

> When the superessential Word and Creator of all existent things wanted to enter into being [as we know it], *He brought with Him [in His incarnation] the natural* logoi *of all that is,* all things sensible and intelligible *as well as the incompre-*

> hensible concepts of His own divinity. Of these, we say that
> the logoi of things intelligible are the blood of the Word; those
> of things sensible are the visible flesh of the Word. Therefore
> because the Word is the teacher of the spiritual logoi in both
> sensible and intelligible things, it is fitting and reasonable
> that He should give those who are worthy the knowledge con-
> tained in things visible to eat, as flesh, and the knowledge con-
> tained in things intelligible to drink, as blood. It is these that
> Wisdom mystically prepared long ago with her cup and her
> victims, speaking of this in Proverbs. But the bones, which
> are the logoi concerning the deity and surpass understanding,
> He does not give, as they are infinitely beyond every created
> nature in the same measure. For the nature of beings lacks
> the power to have any relationship with those logoi.

When the Superessential one "comes into being," this includes all the
natural principles of things intelligible and visible, in addition of course
to the incomprehensible concepts of divinity. By linking the events of
the Incarnation in this entirely natural way with the multiple eucharistic incarnations of the Word, Maximus poetically and theologically
identifies the logoi of things intelligible (which are truly "brought with"
the Logos in His incarnation) with the Blood of His eucharistic incarnation, and the logoi of things visible with the Flesh of His eucharistic
incarnation. The Word, as teacher of the "spiritual principles" of things,
provides as His eucharistic flesh "the knowledge contained in things visible," and as His eucharistic blood "the knowledge contained in things
intelligible." It is impossible to understand this passage (or what follows)
apart from its very direct eucharistic reference. The spiritual knowledge
of the inner principles which inhere in ("are brought with") the incarnate being of the Superessential, and the process of eating and drinking
Him in the Eucharist, form one indivisible reality for Maximus: this passage is certainly an excursus on his part into ontological interpretation
of the Eucharist, as well as an excursus into eucharistic interpretation of
the theory of the logoi of things.

This is no less immediately apparent further on:

> I think one would not be far off the mark in saying that the
> flesh and the blood are [respectively] the logoi concerning
> judgment and providence, because at some point these will be
> eaten and drunk; and that the "bones" are the ineffable logoi
> concerning the divinity which are concealed within them.

The sum total of the inner principles of things here (the principles of providence and the principles of judgment) are directly identified with the flesh and the blood of the Word's eucharistic incarnation, continuing the Confessor's two-way hermeneutic correlation. Immediately after this, we read:

> Again, perhaps the flesh of the Word is the complete *return and restoration of our nature* to itself through virtue and knowledge; the blood is the deification which will direct our nature, by grace, to eternal well-being; and the bones are the unknown power which draws our nature to eternal well-being through deification.

Here the well-known ontological stages used by Maximus (being, well-being, eternal well-being) are woven into a symbolic interpretation of the Eucharist: " well-being" is identified with eating the flesh, and the "eternal well-being" of deification with drinking the blood of the Word. In two other passages, the flesh and blood of the Word are respectively "true virtue" and "perfect knowledge," as well as "voluntary mortification through the virtues" and "perfection through death in adverse circumstances for the sake of truth." As we have seen already (section 7) and will show at greater length below, virtue consists in conforming to the modes of the inner principles of things, and "knowledge" and "truth" are also a profound knowledge of the inner principles; so the two-way hermeneutical connection between the theory of the *logoi* and the Eucharist in Maximus's thought is preserved here too. (In all of the above cases, the bones symbolize the ineffable and unapproachable principle of divinity in its very essence, with no reference to the Eucharist, inasmuch as they relate to the very knowledge of the uncreated essence of God who is Author of the Eucharist.) Maximus responds in the same spirit to Question 36, which is as follows:[90] "What are the bodies and blood of dumb beasts which the Israelites used in worship, eating the bodies but not the blood, which they poured all round the base of the altar?" Maximus replies that the beginner in faith (such as the ancient Israelites were) carries out the practice of virtue in obedience and faith, eating only the visible aspect of virtue, like flesh; because he is not mature enough to go further, he leaves to God in faith those inner essential principles of things which are known only to the perfect. Thus "the altar is a symbol of God, on which we all sacrifice ourselves spiritually and surrender to faith the knowledge of the things exceeding our powers, so that we may live." When Christ comes, however,

the High Priest of good things to come, and *offers the mys-*
tical sacrifice of Himself, then He gives the blood as well as
the flesh to those who through perfection keep the senses of
their soul well-practiced in the discernment of good and evil.
For the perfect person, having passed the rank not only of the
beginners but also of the more advanced, *is not ignorant of*
the reasons [logoi] *for the things he does in accordance with*
the commandment; but he first drinks these down in spirit,
and then through his works eats all the flesh of the virtues.

In this passage, it seems that beginners in the spiritual life practice virtue while being incapable of knowing the hidden reasons for it [*logoi*],
and thus they belong spiritually to the "people of old." One who is perfect accomplishes fully the eating and drinking of the body and blood of
the "High Priest of good things to come," "drinking" the inner rationales
[*logoi*] of the virtues and then going on the "eat" their flesh through his
works. Here too, we find preserved the close analogy between eucharistic theology and the theory of the *logoi* of things in the Confessor's
theological thought.

This clearly evident hermeneutic used by Maximus will lead us to
devote the next three chapters to a detailed examination of the many
different levels of meaning of the *logoi* of things in this writer. We shall
find that all the semantic-ontological aspects of Maximus's eucharistic
theology described so far can be understood only through this hermeneutic: in other words, one can rightly understand the saint's doctrine
of the Eucharist only through a knowledge of his theology of the *logoi*
of things.

Conversely—and this is not a secondary consideration—it is only
an interpretation of the *logoi* of things in terms of eucharistic theology
that can give the former its true meaning and depth.

The theology of the *logoi* of things is the key to interpreting the
Eucharist in Maximus. Once we succeed in this interpretation, however,
we will also be led *a posteriori* to discover the profound significance and
true meaning of that key. This interpretation is equally the way out of
the impasse common to students of this Father's eucharistic theology.

Notes

1. Lars Thunberg, "Symbol and Mystery in St. Maximus the Confessor,"
in Felix Heinzer and Christoph Schönborn (ed.), *Actes du Symposium sur*

Maxime le Confesseur: Fribourg, September 2–5, 1980 (Editions Universitaires Fribourg, 1982), p. 287.

2. Polycarp Sherwood, *St. Maximus the Confessor: The Ascetic Life.* The Four Centuries on Charity, trans. and annotated P. Sherwood (Westminster, Maryland: The Newman Press; London: Longmans, Green and Co., 1955), p. 79.

3. Ibid., p. 79.

4. "Inadequacy": this is how Sherwood interprets St. Maximus's humble reference to himself in the introduction to his *Mystagogy*, PG 91:660D–661A (ibid., p. 79).

5. W. Völker, *Maximus Confessor als Meister des geistlichen Lebens* (Wiesbaden, 1965), 472.

6. G. E. Steitz, "Die Abendmahlslehre des Maximus Confessor," *Jahrbuch für deutsche Theologie* 11 (1886): p. 229–238.

7. W. Lampen, "De Eucharistie-leer van S. Maximus Confessor," *Studia Catholica* 2 (1926): p. 35–54.

8. Sherwood, *Ascetic Life*, 79; Thunberg, "Symbol and Mystery," p. 287.

9. Sherwood, ibid.

10. Sherwood, *Ascetic Life*, p. 234. The fourteen passages as cited by Sherwood are as follows: *Questions and Answers* 40, PG 90:818CD (priesthood); *Questions and Answers* 40, PG 90:820A (communion); *Letter* 31, PG 91:625A (priesthood); *Letter* 21, PG 90:604D (priesthood); *On the Lord's Prayer* 48, PG 91:877C, 897A (communion); *Ambigua*, 48, PG 91:1361ff. (communion), 1364B (sacrifice), 1417C (sacrifice); *Mystagogy* 21 and 24, PG 91:697A, 704Dff. (communion); *To Thalassius* 35 and 36, PG 90:377B, 380Dff. (communion); *Explanation of Movement*, 4, PG 90:117B (priesthood).

11. Sherwood, *Ascetic Life*, p. 81.

12. A. Riou, *Le monde et l'église selon Maxime le Confesseur*, Théologie historique 22 (Paris: Beauchesne, 1973), p. 165.

13. H. U. von Balthasar, *Cosmic Liturgy: The Universe according to Maximus the Confessor*, trans. Brian E. Daley, SJ, from the third German edition (San Francisco: Ignatius Press, 2003), p. 316.

14. R. Bornert, *Les commentaires byzantins de la divine liturgie du VII au XV siècle* (Paris, 1966), pp. 107–108. Bornert's contribution is based on the fact that in the *Mystagogy*, St. Maximus comments on those parts of the rite that are apparent and audible to lay people during the service.

15. Thunberg, "Symbol and Mystery," p. 289.

16. PG 91:704A–705A. Out of this entire text, Sherwood and Thunberg refer only to 704D.

17. This has to be taken as a super-abundance of divinization and not as a rejection of spiritual knowledge as Metr. John Zizioulas seems to imply. See his "From mask to person" [in Greek], *Epopteia* 73 (November 1982): p. 958.

18. Cf. also 705A, from the same chapter. That means that this "liberation of ontology from gnosiology" is not of a Kantian type, i.e., a refusal to step out of human thought in order not to disturb God's supposed transcen-

dence, just an effort to overcome the cognitive identity between being on the one side and thought on the other. Zizioulas leaves this claim untouched. It is absolutely necessary to also add that, as we shall see later, the "gnosiological" way to God must be left open in another, "dialogical" sense, in order that God is not thought of as imposing Himself upon us, as a powerful higher Principle "dictating" our very existence to us: the danger of Monophysitism is then imminent. Knowledge here means living encounter with God, as we shall see.

19. Liturgical becoming can much more accurately be called eucharistic becoming (see chap. 4). Here we may say only that according to Maximus's teaching, in the ontological distinction between *being, well-being* and *eternal being*, the Divine Eucharist seems at first sight to have to do with the third (see, e.g., *To Thalassius*, PG 90:609A, in relation to *Mystagogy* 24, PG 91:704D and elsewhere). But because, according to St. Maximus's general principle, *eternal being* includes the principles of *being* and *well-being*, thus forming their sole meaning and their profound "cause" (*Fourth Century on Theology*, 64, *Philokalia* 2), for that very reason the development of beings toward *eternal being* is exclusively eucharistic in its character and meaning. For the present, we will use the terms "liturgical" and "eucharistic" interchangeably.

20. *To Thalassius*, PG 90:608D–609A.

21. *Ambigua*, PG 91:1193C–1196C.

22. On the relational or "communion" character of the Holy Trinity according to early Christian sources, see J. Zizioulas, "Truth and Communion," in his *Being as Communion* (Crestwood: St. Vladimir's Seminary Press, 1993), 84: "To say that the Son belongs to God's substance implies that substance *possesses almost by definition a relational character*" (emphasis original); and on p. 85 he speaks of the "relational" essence of God on the basis of Athanasius's *Against the Arians* 1.20, where it is said that without the relationship between the Father and the Son, "the perfectness and fullness of the Father's substance is depleted or eliminated." And Zizioulas comments: "nowhere in Platonic or . . . ancient Greek thought in general can we find the view that the perfectness and fullness of a substance is depleted (or eliminated), if a certain relationship is absent from it." This, according to the author, introduces "a *new ontology*" (p. 85, n. 60; emphasis original). We must first of all stress that the Cappadocians made a very sharp distinction between substance and relationship, in their works against Eunomius. Thus "Father" for Gregory the Nazianzus is "a name meaning relationship and not substance" and signifies "the consubstantiality (*homofiës* here is another word for *homoousios*) of the Bearer to the Born" (Sermon 29.16). What Athanasius wants to say here is, similarly, that the Father's substance can be fully offered and possessed by the other divine Persons and not that it consists of relationships, as Zizioulas seems to claim. Generally, "relation" cannot be identified with "substance" in patristic tradition, as Fr. Pavel Florensky claimed (cf. his classic work *The Pillar and Ground of Truth*, translated by B.

Jakim [Princeton University Press, 1997]). Zizioulas seems to follow Florensky on that point. However, the term used by the Cappadocians in reference to this "relational" mode of existence of the substance of the Trinity is, as we saw, *homoousion*, "consubstantiality." *Homoousion* refers to the "Triadic" mode of existence of the divine substance. We also have to correct Florensky here. If we replace divine substance with divine relationships, then, according to this "existentialist" perspective, we do not have real persons in communion, but *communion instead of persons*. The identification of substance with relationship is consequently followed by the identification of persons with this "relational" substance, according to Gregory's argument ("Father is a name meaning relationship"). This absolute identification of personhood with relationship forms a major problem for modern Orthodox personalism. The Greek Fathers have overcome this problem by the strict distinction between essence and its modes of existence. Consubstantiality has to do exactly with this mode of existence that (concerning the Trinity) consists in the full possession and inter-givenness of divine substance by each of the three Persons, in their own distinctive modes of existence. Thus, relationality does not replace essence, but it is the ontological indication of the way of its existence. Homoousion is, then, the revolutionary theological way of simultaneously expressing both deep otherness and deep communion. And then we really do have a new ontology. Otherwise we simply have, as we often see in Zizioulas's work, a short of radical heteronomy (person *is* relationship) instead of the patristic ontology of person as otherness in communion (cf. N. Loudovikos, *Closed Spirituality and the Meaning of the Self: Mysticism of power and the truth of nature and personhood* [in Greek]: Athens: Ellinika Grammata 1999, pp. 258–279).

23. It is clear that "Trinitarian unity" here refers not only to the personal unity, but also to the internal unity and simplicity of divine essence.

24. *Mystagogy* 1, PG 91:668BC.

25. Dionysius the Areopagite, *The Ecclesiastical Hierarchy* 3.1, PG 3:424CD.

26. *EH* 3.1, PG 3:424D. St. Maximus says the same, PG 4:136A.

27. *EH* 3.3.1, PG 3:428B.

28. *EH* 3.3.3, PG 3:429A.

29. *EH* 3.3.8, PG 3:437A.

30. *EH* 3.3.12, PG 3:444A. Cf. 3.3.13, PG 3:444C: ". . . when [the hierarch] uncovers the veiled gifts and divides their oneness into many parts, and forms those who partake into a communion, because the things distributed are utterly united with that into which they enter."

31. Thunberg, "Symbol and Mystery," pp. 305–306.

32. *EH* 3.3.12, PG 3:444AB.

33. "Symbol and Mystery," *p*. 295.

34. Ibid., p. 294.

35. Ibid., p. 295.

36. *Questions and Answers*, PG 90:820A.

37. "Symbol and Mystery," p. 304.

38. PG 91:696D–697A.

39. H. U. von Balthasar, *Cosmic Liturgy*, pp. 138–139.

40. Von Balthasar, *Liturgie Cosmique*, p. 92; cf. *Cosmic Liturgy*, p. 140: "The movement of the intellectual creature is not something removed from the realm of 'nature' and 'the world,' not a middle term between the world and God, as it is for Gregory. It is simply the consciously reflected realization of the basic structure of creaturehood itself, of its course from its origin to its goal." Von Balthasar, however, fails to seek out the ontological foundation for this movement. We shall return to this in Chapter 4.

41. Cf. *On the Lord's Prayer*, PG 90:897BC. Cf. also Thunberg, "Symbol and Mystery," 305. Thunberg goes on to make the suggestive comment that "the terminology of Eucharistic transformation (*metapoiein*) is not used about the elements but about the believers. Thus, the demonstrative power of the Eucharist, which to Ps.-Denis was linked to the distribution, is in Maximus transferred to the receiving part, and the reception of the gifts." But there is no compelling reason against accepting that both the transformation of the Gifts and their distribution, as well as their reception, form a continuum for Maximus—the single, unified, progressive manifestation, in the Holy Spirit, of the eucharistic event. Cf. D. Staniloae, *Toward an Orthodox Ecumenism* (in Greek) (Piraeus: Athos, 1976), pp. 58–59.

42. On the deifying action of the divine Eucharist, see von Balthasar, *Cosmic Liturgy*, p. 322: "The liturgy is, for Maximus, more than a mere symbol; it is, in modern terms, an *opus operatum*, an effective transformation of the world into transfigured, divinized existence. For that reason, in Maximus's view—again unlike that of both Evagrius and Pseudo-Dionysius—the liturgy is ultimately always "cosmic liturgy": a way of drawing the entire world into the hypostatic union, because both world and liturgy share a christological foundation." See also W. Völker, op. cit. 471ff., and chap. Sotiropoulos, "*Efkharistia kai Theosis kata ton agion Maximon ton Omologitin kai Nikolaon Kavasilan*," *Ekklesia* (1974): pp. 249–251, 312, 356–357. Also Staniloae, *I Poreia me ton Sotira Christo* (Thessaloniki: Perivoli tis Panagias, 1984), pp. 103–104.

43. PG 4:569CD.

44. See D. Staniloae, *Toward an Orthodox Ecumenism*, pp. 83–84. For a *summa* of patristic tradition on this point, see St. Nicholas Cabasilas, *Commentary on the Divine Liturgy* 37, PG 150:452AB, and St. Symeon of Thessaloniki, PG 155:253.

45. Cf. also John Chrysostom, *On John*, Homily 58, PG 59:269, and Euthymius Zigabenos, *Commentary on John*, PG 129:1256B.

46. *On the Lord's Prayer*, PG 90:905CD.

47. J. M. Garrigues, "Le dessein d'adoption du Créateur dans son rapport au Fils d'après St. Maxime le Confesseur," in *Actes*, 191. Further on, Garrigues regards Maximus's entire theology of adoption as an "extraordinary exposition" (*extraordinaire explication*) of 2 Tim 9–10 (p. 192).

48. J. M. Garrigues, ibid., p. 191.

49. *Ambigua* 9, PG 91:1084D.

50. *On the Lord's Prayer*, PG 90:896D–897A. This passage is cited in part by Sherwood (see n. 10 above).

51. *On the Lord's Prayer*, PG 90:897AB.

52. In this, Maximus is a representative of the Greek patristic Eucharistic tradition, from St. Ignatius of Antioch to St. Nicholas Cabasilas (fourteenth century), and St. Nicodemus of Mt. Athos (eighteenth century).

53. According to the patristic tradition, the Eucharist is the culmination and completion of all the other mysteries. St. Nicholas Cabasilas expresses the spirit of that tradition on this subject when he writes: "Therefore this mystery [of the Eucharist] is also the final mystery, because it is not possible to go beyond it or add anything to it. For it is clear that the first mystery [Baptism] stands in need of the middle mystery [Chrismation], and that in turn requires the final mystery. But after the Eucharist, there is nowhere further for us to go; here we must stand, and try to seek out how we might be able to preserve the treasure to the end" (*The Life in Christ*, Book 4.1; Nicholas Cabasilas, *The Life in Christ*, trans. C. J. de Catantzaro [Crestwood: St. Vladimir's Seminary Press, 1974], p. 114. And further on: "Because of this, it is the Eucharist alone among the sacred rites that makes the other mysteries perfect" (Book 4.3, ibid., p. 116).

54. *Various Texts: Second Century* 1, PG 90:1221A.

55. *Second Century* 2, PG 90:1221B.

56. This universality excludes any distinction of ontological type between "biological" and "ecclesiastical" hypostasis as that made by Zizioulas, in his "From Mask to Person," *Epopteia* 73, p. 960. See on this chap. 3, n. 131.

57. *Various Texts*, First Century 98–100, PG 90:1220C–1221A. Translation adapted from G. E. H. Palmer, Philip Sherrard, and Kallistos Ware, *Philokalia* II (London: Faber & Faber, 1986), p. 187.

58. For a detailed development of these views of Maximus's concerning asceticism, see chap. 3.5.

59. *On the Lord's Prayer*, PG 90:877C. This is one of the texts cited by Sherwood (see n. 10 above).

60. *Mystagogy* 5, PG 91:681C–684A.

61. Sherwood, *Ascetic Life*, p. 98.

62. PG 91:1364A–1365C. Sherwood cites only a small section of this text, 1364B.

63. Thunberg, "Symbol and Mystery," p. 290: "In other words, is the bodily eating and drinking an expression of the earlier and lower stages of spiritual perfection, or do they pertain to all or even to the last stage, and to what extent has communion thus even to do with deification?"

64. Ibid., pp. 306–308: "Through the communion man, worthily demonstrating by virtuous preparation his receptiveness, is brought by grace through the sacrament into that sphere of human spiritual development, where deification is being realized."

65. Athanasius, *On the Incarnation and Against the Arians*, PG 26:1012B. Cf. also Irenaeus, *Sources Chrétiennes* 100, pp. 947–949 ". . . to eat and drink the Word of God, the Bread of immortality which is the Spirit of the Father."

66. Cf. G. Florovsky, "The Body of the Living Christ" (in Greek) (Thessaloniki: Patriarchal Institute for Patristic Studies, 2d ed., 1981), pp. 32–34; D. Staniloae, *Yia enan Orthodoxo Oikoumenismo*, pp. 27 and 73–74; Irenei Bulovič, *To Mysterion tis en ti Triadi diakriseos ousias kai energeion kata ton agion Markon Ephesou ton Evgenikon* (Thessaloniki: Patriarchal Institute for Patristic Studies, 1983), pp. 322–333.

67. 66.Cf. Alexander Schmemann, *The Eucharist* (Crestwood: SVS Press, 1987), p. 165.

68. *Ambigua*, PG 91:1360D; a passage cited by Sherwood (n. 10 above).

69. Cf. John Zizioulas, *Being as Communion*, pp. 145–149. On 147 we read: "All this shows the early and deep connection of the idea of the unity of the 'many' in the 'one' with the eucharistic experience of the Church. . . . [I]t is certainly true that neither the identification of the Church with the Body of Christ nor the ultimate unity of the 'many' in the 'one' can be understood apart from the eucharistic word 'this is my Body.'"

70. This will be discussed at greater length in chap. 3.

71. *Various Terms*, PG 91:152A. Cf. also *Letter* 12, PG 91:468D and 469D.

72. *To Thalassius*, PG 90:440D; *Letter* 13, PG 91:524C.

73. Cf. chap. 2.5 ; 3.7; 4.2

74. C. Lévi-Strauss, *The Elementary Structures of Kinship* (London: Eure and Spottiswoode, 1969), p. 52.

75. C. Lévi-Strauss, *Structural Anthropology* (New York and London: Basic Books, 1963), p. 279.

76. G. Marcel, *Homo Vistor* (Paris, 1944), p. 23.

77. Ibid. p. 29.

78. See my *Psychoanalysis and Orthodox Theology: On Desire, Catholicity and Eschatology* (Armos: Athens, 2003), chap. 1.

79. P. Gressant, *Lévi-Strauss* (Paris: Editions universitaires, 1970) p. 68.

80. *To Thalassius*, PG 90:481C.

81. *To Thalassius*, PG 90:480A. Cf. also 480B–D. At 480CD, there is a detailed explanation of what is meant by "gifts bestowed": "One receives gifts by honoring through one's behavior the laws naturally present in existent things. I mean something like this: when the discerning mind imitates the natural law of the heavens, it is receiving gifts as it preserves within itself, smooth and unchanging, the movement of virtue and knowledge, within which the luminous and radiant *logoi* of things are set firm like stars."

82. *To Thalassius*, 477AB. Cf. also 488A, 484D–485B in the same work, and *Various Texts*, PG 90:1257B–D.

83. *Ambigua*, Epilogue, PG 91:1417BC.

84. *Letter to the Bishop of Kydonia*, PG 91:604D.

85. *Letter to Bishop John*, PG 91:624D–625A.

86. It is impossible to find in Maximus the modern almost "ontological" separation between bishop and presbyter that is found in contemporary Orthodox ecclesiological thought (see, for example, J. D. Zizioulas, *Eucharist, Bishop, Church: The Unity of the Church and the Bishop during the First Three Centuries* [Brookline, MA: Holy Cross Orthodox Press, 2001], in which a para-eucharistic teaching work is supposedly assigned to the presbyter, while the bishop is considered to be the only "natural" and direct president of the Eucharist [204ff.]). Nowhere in the sources of the first century can we find such a testimony. On the contrary, we find many texts witnessing for the opposite: that the bishop-presbyter of the New Testament was decisively the president of the Eucharist, and only as such, he also was the natural teacher of his church. The two ranks (that of the presbyter and that of the bishop) were later separated only in order for the unity of multiplied parishes to be indicated in the person of the bishop, who oversees (*epi-skopei*) exactly this unity, not by assuming all the charismata in himself, but by safeguarding the fullness of the Eucharistic unity of the parishes, where his fellow priests celebrate the Eucharist. This means that the priesthood does not belong only to the bishop; rather, all the charismata in the Church consist in special participations in Christ Himself, i.e., as Maximus insists, in "imitations," in the sense of participations in the uncreated divine energies offered to us by the Incarnation. Thus priesthood, as a charisma, is a three-fold "energetic" imitation/participation in Christ, either as bishop, presbyter or deacon, with no other "essence" than the Eucharistic one. In this way, Maximus, in his work, speaks of the unique function of "priesthood" in the Church, and not only of the bishop. "Priesthood" celebrates the Eucharist, where everyone has a special position according to his charisma. The bishop's special position consists in manifesting the unity and the safety of all the other charismata, not in replacing them with his own, or making them his own, as they exclusively belong to Christ Himself. (See my *Apophatic Ecclesiology of Consubstantiality* [Armos: Athens, 2002], pp. 30–42, 152–157, 169–172,176–188).

87. *Letters*, PG 91:625CD.

88. Concerning this unifying work of the priesthood, Maximus uses the term *mimesis* (imitation) of the unifying energy of Christ, in the sense of the human participation in it. See my *Apophatic Ecclesiology*, pp. 68–81.

89. *To Thalassius* 35, PG 90:377B–380C. Text cited by Sherwood (n. 10 above).

90. *To Thalassius* 36, 380D–381D. Cited also by Sherwood.

Chapter 2

THE BEING OF THINGS AND ITS *LOGOI*

1. Outline of an "Ontology"

A.

The *logoi* or inner principles of entities are the "ineffable and supranatural divine fire present in the essence of things as in a burning bush," which is nothing other than "God the Word (*Logos*) who in the last times shone forth from the burning bush of the holy Virgin and through the flesh held converse with us."[1] For it is the personal, uncreated, creative intervention of God the Word, by His providence and economy,[2] that constitutes the "existential depth" of creation, in Lossky's felicitous phrase;[3] or as Elias the presbyter puts it, "the foundations of the world" through the "inner essences of things."[4]

So one who approaches the mystery of creation through contemplation will come into contact with the multi-dimensional universe of God's "rational activity," and will learn

> what are the *logoi* initially embedded in the existence of each entity, in accordance with which each entity has being; [the principles] of how it naturally is, how it is formed and shaped and put together, of its ability and activity and passibility— not to mention the difference and particularity of each in terms of quantity, quality, relationship, place, time, position and motion, and habitual state.[5]

In other words, more clearly:

> what is the *logos* of the essence, nature, form, shape, compo-
> sition, and power in each thing, of what it does and what it
> undergoes; and again what is the overall *logos* which brings
> the extremes into contact with each other through a middle
> term, in accordance with the goal of each thing.[6]

It is already apparent that in regard to the existence of created
things in general, the *logoi* play a determinative role on multiple levels, defining all the orders, degrees and phases of things' existence, their
connection with each other, and their own internal structure. In this
sense, the *logoi* form the "ontological structure of reality" according
to Dalmais,[7] i.e., the "ontological expression of the divine glory" in the
words of Clément.[8] This ontogenic mode of operation of the *logoi* causes
Riou to observe that in studying them we come up against philosophical
problems, and, if it is still possible to speak of "ontology," we could do
so "in the sense . . . not of a general ontology applicable on the cosmic
level, but in the sense of a sacramental and revealed structure in the
created world."[9] Meyendorff similarly speaks of a "Christian ontology,"
and Sherwood likewise of an ontological unity-distinction between the
logoi or inner principles, and the *Logos*, the Word.[10] In fact, in the theory
of the *logoi* we observe the very first signs of a true ontology, albeit one
that transcends philosophy and is meta-philosophical—at least once
the profound contemporary crisis in ontology allows us to give the term
"ontology" a deeper and broader meaning. We will articulate this conclusion of ours in stages and in synthetic form, following a detailed and
systematic examination of the Confessor's thought. At any event, we can
use the term "ontology" for the time being, albeit with the reservation
suggested by Riou.

Continuing our effort to throw light on the nature and operation
of the *logoi* by clarifying the terminology concerned, we will look for
preliminary definitions in the writings of the main scholars of Maximus.
Thus we read in Hausherr that, in addition to the visible aspect of things,
there is also their *logos*, their "cause," in other words "their *raison d'être*
within the divine economy, their function in God's plan, their relation to
God, their capacity to reveal God, their symbolic value, their indicative
role in the spiritual ascent."[11] Riou likewise writes:

> The logoi are not God the Logos in His divine essence, who
> transcends them to an infinite degree and remains apophati-

cally unapproachable and participable; nor are they the things that form their realization. Rather, they are in some way the personal destiny of every created thing, the plan of God and in God for each thing created.[12]

Sherwood considers that:

God creates things according to their *logoi* that preexist in Him from all eternity. Nothing in God is adventitious, nothing contrary to His intent. Things are in their substance forewilled, preconceived, foreknown, and brought to being each at its appropriate time. These *logoi* as complete in God cannot suffer any increase or diminution on their realization in the created order.[13]

He also says of the unifying and bonding function of the *logoi* of entities:

The thing that binds the parts [soul and body] together is no special power inherent in either of them, but rather the creative act by which they were brought into being. This implies that composite natures are brought into being according to their respective *logoi* preexistent in God. The ultimate reason therefore of the simultaneity of parts in composite natures and these natures' character as a complete whole is the preexistent *logoi* of each nature.[14]

For von Balthasar, the *logoi* (or ideas, as he calls them) are

the basic outlines, in God, of His plan for the world, the preliminary sketch of the creature within the spirit of God, and thus something quite different, in themselves, from created universals (*to katholon*).[15]

Florovsky gives an extensive and highly comprehensive definition of the *logoi* of things in Maximus:

Maximus emphasizes the limitedness of creatures and, on the contrary, he recalls God's limitlessness. . . . The world is "something else," but it holds together with its ideal connections. These connections are the "actions" or the "energies" of the Logos. In them God touches the world, and the world comes into contact with the Godhead. St. Maximus usually speaks of divine "logoi or words." These are first of all divine thoughts and desires, the pre-determinations of

God's will—*proorismoi*—the "eternal thoughts of the eternal
Mind" in which He creates or invents the world and cognizes
the world. Like some creative rays, the *logoi* radiate from the
divine center and again gather in it. . . . And secondly, they
are *prototypes* of things, "*paradigms.*" In addition, they are
dynamic prototypes. The *logos* of something is not only its
"truth" or "sense," and not only its "law" or "definition" but
primarily its forming principle.[16]

And he writes elsewhere, "law is order, measure, harmony, coher-
ence and structure."[17] For Thunberg, there is no question of any eternal
preexistence of the *logoi* themselves within God. All things, visible and
invisible, were created "out of nothing" by the gracious divine volition
at the proper time; this happens thanks to "the existence of their logoi
within the single divine Logos."[18] For Meyendorff,

Any object receives its very existence from the *logos* that
is in it and makes it participate in God. Separated from its
logos, a creature is but non-being, *me on.* . . . The doctrine
of "natural law," considered as the proper dynamism of nature, does not mean, however, that Maximus considers creation as an autonomous entity, as Western scholasticism
was to do later. Natural movement itself requires participation in God. This participation flows from the very nature
of *logos*, which is always conceived as an action of the divine Logos.[19]

For Dalmais, likewise, "the *logoi* are the ideal principles of created
things, which exist eternally in the thought of God the Word (*Logos*)."[20]
For Lossky, finally, the *logoi* are the foundations of all things; they are
the relationships between God and the creatures He makes.[21]

This preliminary overview of some descriptive definitions of the
logoi is an initial introduction to Maximus's extremely profound teaching on the subject: we will now attempt to set out that teaching using
passages from his writings.

B.

God is hidden in the existential depth of things. Through these things,
we know Him as "being precisely the *logoi* of things which have come

into being,"[22] as Maximus boldly affirms. For "through the *logoi* in things that exist, God testifies to His existence alone; He grants to devout believers a confession and faith firmer than any proof, that He *is* in the proper sense."[23] God "confesses" and testifies to His living presence with profound clarity, and is consequently believed in as a result of the proof afforded by the reality of the *logoi* and their activity. It is in this context that Maximus interprets the passage in Dionysius (*Celestial Hierarchy*) concerning the attribution to God of the characteristics of mind and rationality, saying that "he attributes rationality to God, not because he wants to show that God is rational in the sense of participating in rationality . . . but because *He is rationality itself, being wholly* logos."[24] Being in a universal sense "rationality itself," God manifests Himself as

> the author of being and an entity transcending being; the author of potentiality and a foundation transcending potentiality; the dynamic and unending habitual state of all activity: in a word, He is the author of the beginning, middle and end of all being and potentiality and activity.[25]

The *logoi* of things, then—the specific rational actions of God—are responsible for the essence, nature, form, shape, composition, and power of things, for their activity and what they undergo, as well as for their differentiation as individuals in terms of quantity, quality, relationship, place, time, position, movement, and habitual state. Likewise, as our last quotation emphasizes, they are responsible for the beginning, middle, and end of things; that is to say, for the *logos* or principle that makes the connection between the beginning of each thing and its end point, by way of its intermediate term (as we have already seen in the *Ambigua*, 1228D). In other words, the entire existential course of a particular entity, understood in terms of providence, economy, and eschatology—i.e., in its concrete ecclesial and eucharistic context—is dependent on the *logoi*. Keeping hold of this last highly significant remark (which will be explored further later on), let us for the moment see in more detail what the *logoi* of things are as modes of God's activity or manifestation.

Difficulty 9 in the *Ambigua*[26] is a veritable gold mine for the student of Maximus's theology of the *logoi*, and we will return to it frequently. In this passage, he is interpreting St. Gregory the Theologian's words: "What is the wisdom concerning me, and what is this great mystery? Is it that because we are a particle of God that has slipped down from above, He wants us always to look to Him in our struggle and fight with the body, lest because of our dignity we should become vain and exalt ourselves and despise our Creator? Does He intend this weakness yoked to us as way of schooling our high dignity?" In addition to making a critical correction of Origenism so as to give us a profound and well-rounded theory of the movement of things, the Confessor will attempt to use the doctrine of the *logoi* to interpret the phrase "a particle of God that has slipped down from above." As he writes:

> Who can approach the infinite variety of things created out of nothing with the contemplative and questing power of the soul, and not recognize the one Word as a multiplicity of *logoi*, because He is to be discerned with and in the difference-without-division in things, through their individuality which is without confusion in relation both to each other and to themselves. And again he will recognize that the many *logoi* are one, because everything refers back to the one who in Himself exists without confusion, the essential and hypostatically existent God the Word [*Logos*] of God the Father. For He is the beginning and cause of all things, in whom all things in heaven and on earth were created, whether visible or invisible, whether thrones or dominions or principalities or authorities—all things were created from Him and through Him and for Him.[27]

In the process of interpreting the Scriptural passage to which he implicitly refers (Col. 1:16), the Confessor provides the primary ontological basis for the *logoi*: their multiplicity constantly evokes the one Word (*Logos*) to whom they owe their distribution. The two-way connection of the One with the many and of the many with the personal One, "the essential and hypostatically existent God the Word of the Father," transcends any notion of neo-Platonic emanation and allows him to go further, writing:

> He held the *logoi* of all things which subsisted before the ages, and *by His gracious will* brought the visible and invisible creation into existence out of nothing in accordance with these *logoi*; by word (*logos*) and wisdom He made, and continues to make, all things at the proper time, universals as well as particulars.[28]

In this passage, we see that (a) the *logoi* are declared to exist pre-eternally; (b) the gracious will of God is connected with the *logoi* of entities;[29] (c) there is the notion of a "proper time" for the creation of each entity;[30] and (d) Maximus is clearly talking about the existence of both universal *logoi* and particular *logoi* (as he goes on by way of explanation, "We believe that a *logos* of angels preceded their creation, a *logos* of each of the essences and powers that populate the world above, a *logos* of humans, a *logos* of each thing that has received its being from God—I will not mention all particulars individually"). For this reason, every single intelligible and rational creature "by virtue of the *logos* in accordance with which it was created, which is in God and with God, *is and is called a particle of God*. It is so called because of its *logos* which preexisted in God, as we have said."

What is interesting about this position is the clear distinction it makes both between the *logoi* and the divine Word, and between the *logoi* and the things that He created "in accordance with them."[31] Of greatest interest, however, is the underpinning of personal relationship which is clearly introduced: the "gracious will," acting with word and wisdom. This not only sweeps away the last remnants of the Origenist idea of creation as a fall, but also creates the basis for a splendid reality of participation in God:

> For because everything has its being from God, it participates in God proportionately, whether by intellect, or rationality, or perception, or vital movement, or by some essential and habitual aptitude, as the great Dionysius believes, the Areopagite who reveals things divine.[32]

The quintessence of *logos* as "participation in God"—with an emphasis on its uncreated quality—is conveyed when Maximus writes:

> [We believe that] the same [divine Word] is inexpressible and incomprehensible and *beyond any created thing* by His infinite superiority in Himself, and beyond every difference and distinction that exists and can be conceived of in creation; and as befits His goodness, this Same is manifested and multiplied in all that comes from Him, proportionately to each. And He recapitulates all things in Himself, for [all things have] *their being and their continuation* in Him, and through Him all things participate in God, both in remaining

stable as they were created and in moving toward the purpose for which they were created.[33]

The Word Himself is multiplied in things as befits His goodness, giving them their being as well as the preservation of that being, so that both their existential stability and their movement are able to participate in God through their own *logos* because they are constantly being recapitulated in the *Logos*, "so that in His love for mankind the Word who is in all, who alone is beyond nature and understanding, becomes the essence of all things," as we have heard already (Ch. 1.6), at the end of the eucharistic passage from the *Ambigua* (1364A-1365C). The eucharistic sense of the latter passage is reflected also in the expressions quoted above, making it obvious that a eucharistic interpretation of these too is to follow.

The affirmation of this profound fellowship between the Word and creation ("even to the last times"[34]) reaches extraordinary heights when Maximus writes, interpreting the Areopagite: "Because He is intellect, then indeed He thinks of entities inasmuch as He Is. *And if He thinks of entities in the process of thinking of Himself, then He is those entities.*" And Maximus continues further on: "Hence His intellections are existent things," because "when he thinks of things, He does not take prototypes from other things, because He is Himself the exemplar of things that exist." In consequence "He thinks of entities inasmuch as He thinks of Himself, and is connected to what is innate to Him; for this intellection of His is the genesis of things that exist."[35] Beyond any objective and necessary existence of *logoi*, reminiscent of the Platonic ideas, Maximus accepts the term "ideas" for the *logoi*, interpreting them as "exemplars of being," but in the sense of the "everlasting intellections" of the personal Word,[36] i.e., His "good wills" and His "divine purpose" for each separate created thing, into which He pours its "innate wisdom" and "innate life" through its *logoi*, thus demonstrating His good "preeternal intention."[37] This connection of the divine *logoi* of entities with the divine will underlines the fact that the *logoi* are not ideal individualities with their own motive force, but specific volitional manifestations of divine Love.[38] Revealing his intellectual inheritance, Maximus himself writes that "as to what I have called *logoi*, St. Dionysius the Areopagite teaches us that in Scripture they are called *predeterminations* and *divine wills*. Similarly the circle of Pantaenus, who became the teacher of the great Clement of Alexandria, says that Scripture likes to call them *divine wills*.[39] The passage from the Areopagite that Maximus is referring to is the following:

We call "exemplars" those *logoi* that preexist in God in unitary form and give things their being, which the divine word calls *predeterminations* and the divine and gracious wills which define and make entities, in accordance with which the Super-essential predetermined all existent things and brought them forth.[40]

The Platonic notion of the ideas as cut off from God and autonomous ("having substantive existence," in Maximus's terminology), together with the necessity they exert over God,[41] now belong to the past. But is that all?

C.

One enormous subject that Maximus touches on here is that of God's creating the world in freedom, which takes us beyond any pre-Platonist, Platonist, neo-Platonist, or Origenist teaching. The Platonic notion of Ideas already represents a change compared with pre-Socratic thought concerning *logos*. For Heraclitus, *logos* is "that which connects visible things to one another, which connects them as visible phenomena of one single Universe, and also what connects speech with visible things . . . *Logos* is the soul and spirit in Heraclitus's dialectic, which together with the world forms one body."[42] Ultimately, *logos* is "the structure of everything that is";[43] it is "a union of opposites and a universal bond,"[44] having "in the highest degree a transcendent indwelling" within things.[45] Like Heraclitus, the Pythagoreans and Parmenides tried to find the *logos* of things.

But in these philosophers, *logos* is not that pure operation of the mind which with inner consistency has the power to control itself and to attain to its unmoved first principle; rather, it is something that exists within things themselves and governs them. It is a substantive force with real existence which forms the initial base on which things are constructed. In the systems of Heraclitus, Parmenides and the Pythagoreans, *logos* is a metaphysical substrate which provides the foundation for the world itself as a first principle, a basic element. In Plato, by contrast, *logos* is separated from things, from actual entities; and this separation is rational and not metaphysical. In being separated from things, *logos* moves closer to its actual source, the mind, whereas in those great pre-Socratic philosophers you have the impression that logos is far away from its source and immersed in things, in nature.[46]

Thus "Plato and Aristotle, the first philosophers in the proper sense, do not direct their gaze principally at the truth of everything that exists, but subjugate the totality of being to a transcendent, metaphysical force, an Idea or divine Mind, which becomes the measure and supreme judge of truth,"[47] as Axelos writes, repeating his teacher Heidegger.[48]

Similarly, in the ancient Stoics, God is the "seminal principle (*logos*)" of the world. As Diogenes Laertius writes:

> At the beginning it existed on its own, and through air changed the whole existing substance into water. And as seed is held within a woman's body, so this seminal *logos* of the world leaves something similar behind in the fluid, thereby activating matter so as to bring subsequent things into being. Then it engenders first the four elements, fire, water, air and earth. Zeno [of Citium] talks about these in his work on the universe.[49]

In the view of K. Georgoulis, the notion of seminal principle was of the greatest importance for the Stoics, and was later used by the neo-Platonists and by Augustine. They understand the seminal *logos* as a formative force which gives rise to development. God is in a general sense the seminal principle of the world, regarded as a general force shaping the universe. In addition to this general seminal principle, the Stoics also recognized particular seminal principles for each entity that spark the development of those particular entities.[50] Furthermore, it is known that the earlier Stoics accepted ancient Greek polytheism in addition to Zeus, often identifying the various gods with the "seminal *logoi*" and calling those gods "begotten," because they are begotten together with the world and will be absorbed into the bosom of Zeus at the conflagration.[51] The important point, however, is that a fragment of the Stoics' god-*logos* exists also in man. Thus the divine *logos* indwelling man is able to know the divine *logos* at work in the world, because the one is akin to the other.[52] The pantheism of the Stoics is thus evident.[53]

Plotinus's teaching on the subject shows continuity with that of the Stoics. His well-known descending ontological scale of The One, Mind, and Soul requires the last to be divided in two, a primary soul which is close to Mind and a secondary soul which is the offspring of the first, and which he calls nature. As the higher part of the soul turns toward the intelligible world of the ideas or intellections or thought operations of Mind, it is filled through this vision with "seminal *logoi*," the "first *logoi*" as Plotinus calls them. These "first *logoi*" engender "second *logoi*" in the secondary soul, and those in turn show the active effect of nature upon matter. In this way inanimate matter in shaped, and the material world takes on the form and order in which it is manifest to the senses. Here Plotinus uses the same terminology as the Stoics: the seminal *logoi* emanate from Mind, as light does from the sun.[54] With Plotinus, the synthesis of the seminal *logoi* and ideas as thoughts of Mind, existing within Mind, represents the culmination of this philosophical tradition; this is an indication of its continuity but also, and chiefly, of its limitations.[55]

These are limitations that, it must be said, were preserved even in the Hellenic-Jewish philosophy of Philo, who also accepts the Platonic ideas, transposing them from the celestial realm to the mind of God.[56] For him, the locus of the ideas is the Logos-bond between all things,[57] a Logos that resembles the Platonic "world soul," as a mediator between the world and God, rather than with the seminal *logos* of the Stoics,[58] although it sometimes seems to resemble the Stoic concept of Destiny.[59] In addition to being the bond and "support of the world," Logos in Philo is "diffused everywhere," "continuous and undivided," "leader," "director and governor of all," "warm" and "fiery," the "law" and "fate" of everything. Elsewhere, under Platonic influence, Logos is the intelligible world, the ideal prototype of visible things, their intelligible "exemplar" and the "Idea of Ideas." There are *logoi*, as distinct from the Logos, which are the "noetic virtues" (righteousness, sobriety, etc.).[60] Thus Wolfson distinguishes (a) the uncreated Logos, which is the divine mind, the place of the ideas, and cannot be distinguished from God; (b) the created Logos, which is the unity of the intelligible world; and (c) the Logos immanent in the world, which operates within created things. In other words, according to Wolfson the Logos is divine thought, considered in itself and in relation to the world.[61] Naturally the Logos in Philo is not related to the living God the Word of the Fathers, precisely because it is not absolutely personal or uncreated;[62] and this reflects also on the ideas contained within it, making them an expression of necessity and consequently making the act of creation unfree.

The main critical conclusion of this brief overview is that in each case the "*logoi*," or "seminal *logoi*," or "ideas" of Greek philosophy are unable to comprehend either the creation of the world *ex nihilo* or (above all) the absolutely free creative activity of God. The element of necessity is self-evidently innate to ancient Greek thought: the existence of the world and the way it is formed are equally products of necessity. That means that any reciprocity or dialogue, between God and creation are totally precluded here. Nature is produced almost by necessity, without neither freedom of self-expression, nor the possibility of a free response to God. What was the fate of these teachings in early Christian thought?

The search for answers to such questions must turn first to Origen. His significance lies in the fact that he consciously undertook the task of synthesizing the ancient Greek doctrine of creation with the Judeo-Christian.[63] Philo's influence on Clement of Alexandria[64] passed to his successor as director of the school of Alexandria, Origen, who had furthermore been a disciple of Ammonius Saccas, teacher of Plotinus.[65] Of course, placing the ideas in the Logos-mind of God, as Philo does (something that influenced Plotinus and neo-Platonism in general), somewhat alleviates the problem of the necessity of creation somewhat less acute (without however solving it, because most scholars doubt the personal existence of the Logos, a non-personal Logos and especially one inseparable from God is not able to exert free choice over the existence of the ideas within it).[66] There is however the problem of the world being coeternal with God, which is unacceptable to a Christian. (Certainly Justin and the apologist Athenagoras do appear to accept that the world is created out of pre-existing matter,[67] but already in the apologist Theophilus of Antioch we find the doctrine that "God made all things, bringing them into being out of non-being, in order that His greatness should be known and understood through His works."[68] Hence it seems that by Origen's time, the question of creation *ex nihilo* had been resolved.) Origen goes back to it, expressing the view that it is impious and at the same time demeaning to God to imagine that His nature is immobile and idle, or to think that at one time His goodness was not doing good and His omnipotence had no power or authority. As one cannot be a father without a son or a lord without lordship over various entities, so it would be impossible to regard God as omnipotent if the entities over which he could exert His omnipotence did not exist.[69] So if at some point in the past entities did not exist, God's omnipotence would not have been present; He would have become omnipotent later, at the moment when things came into existence. This means that God would be passing from a state of imperfection to one of greater perfection, which is of course nonsensical. Hence God always had all the things over which He ruled and governed.[70] So, under the influence of Philo, there are two forms of creation, one is the eternal creation in the logoi as they are included in the Logos and the second is the real world, existing as a decline from the first.[71] In this way, it becomes impossible to conceive of God without the world. Furthermore, in this way it is incumbent upon God that all the fullness of His goodness and powers should be actualized eternally. Thus it is impossible for the world not to have existed: "a 'not-I' is coeternal with God and conjointly beginningless, as the prerequisite of God's very existence and life." We thus see that real otherness of creation is here precluded. The world exists in order for God to show his lordship.

Florovsky solves the problem by speaking of two different eternities in God, that of nature and that of volition.[72] Thus God freely "thinks up" and desires the world, but this is entirely independent of the "self-sufficiency" of divine life and blessedness. In consequence, besides God's natural eternity there is also a moral, free eternity, an eternity of God's free choice that the world should exist, something that nevertheless could have never happened. Following Florovsky's train of thought, Zizioulas[73] finds the solution in the identification made by Maximus of *logoi*, wills and predeterminations in God. By identifying wills and *logoi*, Maximus avoids making creation a matter of necessity. The world is created out of nothing, at the appropriate time, and is the result not of thought but of God's free and loving will. Maximus himself, being totally opposed to Origenism, writes in the fourth Century of his *Centuries on Love*[74] that "when the Creator willed, He gave substance to the knowledge of things which pre-existed in Himself from eternity and made it manifest. For in the case of the omnipotent God, it would be inappropriate to doubt whether He is able to give being to something when He wills to do so." But beyond his emphasis on the distinction between the eternal preexistence of the knowledge of things and the free act of bringing them into being within time, a little further on Maximus sets out even more clearly his opposition to Origen and the Greek philosophers, speaking of how their ideas about creation differ from his own. The philosophers essentially regard God as the creator of qualities only, whereas Maximus sees Him as creator of "the essences of things that have been created." This last point, implying creation *ex nihilo*, confirms that "created things are not coexistent with God from eternity."

Although the influence of Philo on Maximus cannot be ruled out,[75] the latter was more adventurous. Sherwood considers that the key here is the identification of the Son, the Johannine Word, with the mode of existence of the ideas-logoi, an Alexandrian tradition,[76] as found in Clement of Alexandria.[77] Beyond this, it is a fact that the key to comprehending the teaching in question is Maximus's profound

understanding of God the *Logos* as person, as the One who in a absolutely personal way contains the *logoi* within Him, identified with His
"gracious wills"[78] and "divine purpose," and His pre-eternal "good intention" which is the outpouring in love of "His divine life" (see above)
into every one of His creatures personally. Riou connects this divine
purpose with the well-known text of *To Thalassius* 60, where there is
discussion of the non-conditional incarnation of God the Word, decided upon even before the creation.[79] Given the soteriological texture
of the whole of the Confessor's theology,[80] we consider that the reality
of God's free creativity as He creates the world out of non-being cannot possibly be revealed in its full extent and significance without the
perspective of the eucharistic recapitulation of God's Providence and
Economy.[81] In fact, it is only the eucharistic incarnation that provides
constant and tangible verification of God's loving good pleasure that
the world should exist, as a treasury of the loving outpouring of divine
life, something that causes Maximus to assert boldly that "He is beings"
(see above). *A non-pantheistic interpretation of this phrase will keep
unswervingly to the path of eucharistic theology.* Without the eucharistic vision of the *Mystagogy,* when we approach the Confessor's other
texts of eucharistic theology, we cannot begin to understand how the
logoi are identified with God's wills, because those wills amount to that
which is expressed by the eucharistic communion of God and man;
and it is precisely in this that the free love of God and His willing good
pleasure are identified to the highest degree. This is the only possible
way to interpret the relation of the *logoi* to God the Word that we have
seen above (*Ambiguum* 9); this relation works as a continuous recognition and acceptance of things by their "principle and cause," with a
view to their ever-increasing participation in the divine fullness. The
creation of things through their *logoi* is free, inasmuch as those *logoi*
form the material for the eucharistic communion of the created world
with the free and personal divine Love. Just as God communes freely
with the world, so He has created it freely. Because this creative freedom of God is *absolute,* that also means that creation is *ex nihilo*: no
necessity, no entity preceded it, because the preexistence of any entity
(or of preexisting matter) would by its very existence impose some restriction on the absolute character of the personal, loving divine freedom. And furthermore: that means that creation is profoundly *dialogical* in its very essence. Creation is created for a free dialogue with God,
i.e., as a gift in itself from God that can be returned to the giver and
then distributed out of love. But, first of all as we shall see, creation is

"discussed" step-by-step between persons, and it is this "discussion" that finally produces its real "eschato-logical" being.

D.

The *logoi* of things created out of nothing are first and foremost "*logoi* constitutive of essence," according to Maximus.[82] As he writes, identifying essence and nature:[83] "Nature habitually comes into being by divine art, and the results of this divine art are plants and animals and fruits, and the change of elements into one another, and the totality of the essence *per se* of things that are, which is the principle of movement and of stability."[84] The essence of things that exist is the principle of their movement and their stability, and comes into being through divine art. As Maximus goes on:

> With candle-makers and practitioners of the plastic arts, who craft their works by hand, there has to be something that remains with the works, namely [the maker's] reasoning and mind; and so also with the nature of all things, there is something that remains with them, namely power—not a power made by hands, but *the will and devising of God*, which *like an art* serves *to bring entities into being.*[85]

This divine art is God's power, the will and devising of God, and it crafts the essence of things. "Nature does not need some elements that remain stable and others that move. For matter is that which is moved so as to come into being; and what moves it is the unmoved *logos* present in the whole, *which is the art of God.*[86] This is the fundamental definition of *logos* in Maximus: *the divine art creative of essence*. It is a definition that expresses precisely the radical nature of God's creative act and the goodness, and love of the good and beautiful, involved in it.

This is equally a definition that would seem incomplete unless we turn for our understanding of it to the other meaning of *logos* encountered in Maximus's thought, that of *logos as image*. "*Logos* is essence according to the image," he writes.[87] The notion of *logos* as image does not seem to have received any attention from scholars of the Confessor. We have already seen[88] how John of Damascus calls the volitional thoughts of God predeterminations and "images." Similarly in his treaties in defense of the Holy Icons, we read that "the first sort of image is the natural image, the Son. The second is the pre-eternal counsel in God. The third is man, created in imitation of God."[89] We regard the notion of *logos* as image of God as exceptionally important, fundamental indeed, for an understanding of the quality of that term. The *logoi* of entities as the content of the divine counsel preserve a form of image of God, different of course from the "natural" image, the Son, and from the image "in imitation," the human being. But it is nevertheless clear that this is one form in which God is imaged, and this is further elucidated by what we have seen above concerning the profound relationship between the *logoi* of entities and God the Word. This understanding of the *logoi* of entities as eternal divine wills-images of the divine nature also serves as a footnote to the eucharistic interpretation of the theory of *logoi*, because the Eucharist is precisely the place where the image of things is fulfilled, in other words the place where things *are* as God wants them to be, as we have shown in the preceding chapter. So we will return to the representational quality of the *logoi* of entities.

Maximus's understanding of things as images of the *logoi* is by now better known.[90] As he writes: "The predeterminations should be understood as divine exemplars, *of which the results of creation are images.*" And further on: "All things here are images of things there; for even the soul itself is an image and likeness of the idea."[91] Entities, then, are images and likenesses of their *logoi*. Their essence is manifested in the representational quality of their *logoi*. This allows Maximus to write, commenting on Peter's vision of the unclean animals as a special revelation from God concerned with making disciples of the Gentiles,[92] that one who frees his intellect from the sensual imagination will be able "the look upon the *logoi* of sensible things stripped of outward forms, to recognize the types of intelligible things and to learn that nothing that has its being from God is unclean." In other words, "the creeping things and animals and birds are the various *logoi* of things that exist, which to the senses are unclean, but to the intellect are clean and edible, and provide sustenance for spiritual life." One who has discovered the spiritual purity of things "has found the truth that is in the *logoi* of entities," learning that "none of the things whose *logoi* remain with [God] is altogether unclean." *The truth of the logoi is their representational texture ("the logoi remain with God") which makes their likenesses, the entities themselves, true and pure.* It is in this purity of their inner principles that God knows entities, as Maximus will says elsewhere. In *Ambiguum* 9, he refers to the question some people have as to how God knows entities. The saint responds that God does not know

> either sensible things through the senses, or intelligible things through the intellect. For He who is beyond entities cannot possibly apprehend them in ways suited to those entities. Rather, we say that He knows entities *as acts of His own will*, and we add a good reason for this: if He made everything by an act of will (and there will be no contradiction of that), and it is pious and just always to say that God knows His own will, and He made each entity willingly, then it follows that *God knows entities acts of His own will*, because He made things willingly.[93]

God recognizes entities as acts of His own will, His own words (*logoi*), images of His decisions, which are in turn an image of Him inasmuch as they are pure and genuine—inasmuch as they are, precisely, entities. Because, as the Confessor will say elsewhere, "if He does not already possess the *logoi* of any things, then nor does He recognize the making of them."[94] God creates only those things that He knows through the *logoi* which remain with Him from before all eternity. This points above all to the absolute ontological dependence of created entities upon the uncreated divine will. In other words, it means in the first place that there is an absolute ontological difference between created entities and God: entities are created out of ontologically absolute non-being, and their being is furthermore absolutely dependent on the (alone totally free) being of God. And secondly, it means that the stable existence of their being is to be ensured "by participation"—by freely dialogical participating, as we shall shortly see, in the creative and saving Word. Here we can easily make out the underlying framework behind the Confessor's thought, which is the tradition of Athanasius's theology, as well as Maximus's creative development of that tradition.

But there is also a third ontologically important consequence of the text cited above: to say that God "knows God as entities as acts of His own will" implies a radical overcoming of any separation between matter and spirit as it is widely spread in western thought, from Augustine to Descartes until our contemporary era. Matter and spirit are absolutely ontologically equal, as they are both created things by their respective divine wills/*logoi*. Both are united and conceived as one in God's providence, as we shall later see, and neither of them are superior to the other or more affiliated with God than the other; both bear God's image upon them and, as we shall see, both consist in equal eschatological vocations to be fulfilled in the spirit. As we shall also later see, the whole of creation, both spiritual and material can be said to consist of only one divine logos in God's loving will. Thus, while in Plato dualism cannot be overcome, as the "spiritual beings" (of which the human soul is the superior) possess by nature a certain kinship with Ideas or even the One, in Maximus dualism is forever overcome because both spiritual and material beings are, in their uncreated principles, ontologically equal and equally "spiritual." This is revolutionary for ancient Greek ontology.

However, because the causes of entities, namely the *logoi* of their nature, emerge "from the divine nature," it is possible for Maximus, following the Areopagite, to call that divine nature "the universal" because "everything comes into being from it" through divine will.[95] This universality of the divine nature is the fullness of being and the cause of everything that is. So here we can now see in somewhat more detail the meaning of nothingness in Maximus. Non-being, in his theology, simply means the non-existence of a corresponding *logos* in God. Because God "does not recognize the making of any things if he does not already possess the *logoi* of them"[96] nothingness for Maximus is identified with what has *not* been created, with what is contrary to God's will. The *logoi* define what is natural to the essence of things and "interpret" it in "order,"[97] because they are the *logoi* of perfect natures and not imperfect ones: "For what existence could an imperfect nature have, seeing that there is no *logos* for it?"[98] Maximus further appears to regard as evil whatever has no *logos* existing in God. Evil is groundless, pointless, undefined, artlessly made, contrary to nature and, in the final analysis, devoid of reason, *a-logo*:

> If evil is groundless, because it was not created for some purpose, it therefore naturally lacks definition. For it has no *logos* to interpret what it is, and hence of necessity it is not in accordance with nature. If then it is contrary to nature, it will not have any *logos* (rationale) in nature, just as artless construction has no *logos* (rationale) in art.[99]

Evil is non-being, "for it has no *logos* to interpret what it is."

All this leads to two highly important conclusions: First, that nothingness does not exist in God. Indeed, God is not tormented by any contrariety: His will and His good pleasure coincide. Nothingness would mean for God something not-willed, not-desired, imposed by necessity, and in Him there is no such thing. He wills and knows and loves whatever He creates, and those things alone are true entities. Second, nothingness does not exist in entities. Entities are all "perfect natures" with a causal relation to the divine universality. Nothingness is evil, irrational (contrary to *logos*), contrary to nature. Being groundless, it is devoid of purpose and hence impossible to understand in any positive sense.

The significance of these conclusions is fundamental to a critique of the philosophical tradition concerning nothingness that began at least with Parmenides. As Plato informs us in *The Sophist*, Parmenides does not accept that anyone can prove the existence of non-being.[100] In his discussion of this view,[101] Plato finally decides to attack Parmenides' position that non-being does not exist, and to show "that non-being does exist in some respect, and being conversely does not."[102] This relative existence of nothingness would remain constant throughout classical philosophy, which always brushes aside this idea of absolute nothingness, up to and including Hegel. For the latter, in his *Wissenschaft der Logik*, Being as pure abstraction coincides with nothingness.[103] The absolute is nothingness, says Hegel; and making a parallel between this and the nothingness of Buddhism—the beginning and end of all things—he regards it as the result of pure abstraction. As Hegel says:

As both, absolute and nothingness, consist in pure indeterminacy, they are at once opposites and the same. Similarly Bergson, in his *L'évolution créatrice*, calls the idea of absolute nothingness "self-destructive," "a pseudo-idea," "mere words."[104] Nor is this all: Bergson affirms that

> In the idea of an object that we think of as "non-existent,"
> there is something more and not less than in the idea of the
> object itself when we think of it as "existent," because the
> idea of the "non-existent" is necessarily that of the "existent"
> object, with the additional descriptor that this object is excluded from present reality taken as a whole.[105]

Probably the first attempt to approach the concept of absolute nothingness is that of Heidegger, who in his *Introduction to Metaphysics* considers that nothingness is nothing other than Being.[106] But here he is no longer talking about Being in the Hegelian sense of pure abstraction, but in a sense that, in the view of J. Wahl, approaches that of apophatic theology, as developed by the Areopagite and above all by Meister Eckhart, who influenced Heidegger.[107] Thus, nothingness here is not the opposite of Essence but the precondition for its manifestation: both being and nothingness belong together in Essence *per se.*[108]

Whether the notion of nothingness is relativized, or reduced to Being by pure abstraction, or denied on the basis of logic and a theory of knowledge, or indeed located within Essence alongside the notion of

Being—in all these cases, there is the latent idea of the necessity of entities: their existence is obligatory. When absolute nothingness is rejected
as inconceivable, things exist of necessity; when it is located within
Essence alongside Being, things are manifested of necessity, because
otherwise essence would never become apparent as such. In each case,
nothingness is utterly impossible to conceive of in an absolute sense by
philosophical means.[109] Such a conception is possible only in the realm
of theology, because theology alone is able to conceive of the absolute
"preontological" freedom of the personal God. It is only because the uncreated, hypostatic God is totally and absolutely free, freely giving hypostatic existence to His being, that what is not God precisely *is not*—it
is nothingness in an absolute sense. The created human being has no
intellectual or other means in his nature to conceive of the freedom of
God; there can be no philosophy of this absolute freedom. (And yet it is
in this freedom of the Father, which is identified with His love, that man
has been called, in Christ, to participate.) It is clear, then, that the notion
of absolute nothingness, stemming from the distinction between created and uncreated, requires this absolute nothingness to be beyond any
philosophical notion of nothingness. We are further taught by Maximus
that Being, which is the personal God, does not have within it anything
unwilled, any non-being. We also learn that things came into being out
of nothing, not because that "nothing" (understood of course in an absolute sense) actually existed, but because of the personal and good creative counsel of God, Who freely wills to create beings outside Himself.
With the creation of things, the absolute pre-creational nothingness no
longer coexists within them; and if it happens that some entity moves in
the direction of that nothingness, this will happen in contravention of
God's will and because it has separated itself from God.[110] The most important point, however, is perhaps that what is opposed to the reality of
nothingness is the living personal divine love, which voluntarily makes
the world absolutely living and stable, having no desire to be tormented
by the irrationality[111] of nothingness.

E.

Let us briefly complete our description of the "ontological *logoi* which
express the entire organization of reality,"[112] inasmuch as "all created
things are affirmed in every way, in respect of both their essence and
their origin, in that they are encompassed by their own *logoi*, as well as

the *logoi* of the other things around them."[113] The *logoi*, then, are additionally that which contains created things, containing and determining what pertains to their essence and their origin; at the same time they provide the basis, as we shall see in detail in Chapter Three, for communication between entities, because their *logoi* interpenetrate each other and are determined by each other. The *logos* of each entity is "threefold," because "*if entities have essence and potentiality and energy,* it is clear that in this respect they have a threefold *logos* of being."[114] Furthermore, we have *logoi* of *races, species, and individuals,*[115] *logoi* of *time and nature,* without which things could not exist,[116] and also *logoi* of *bodies and of bodiless beings.*[117] We also find a special *logos of hypostasis* (substantive existence), because "nature possesses the common *logos* of being, while the hypostasis possesses the *logos* whereby *something exists in itself.*"[118]

But let us now proceed to scan the ultimate theological horizon of the theory of *logoi,* starting with the perspective opened up by Florovsky in his study of Maximus.

For Florovsky, the central idea in Maximus's teaching is the fact of revelation.[119] The entire world is a revelation of God, grounded in His thought and will. So "this revelation is completed and fulfilled in the Incarnation." "God created the world and is revealed in order to become a Man in this world." Compared to the Apologists and the Alexandrian theologians, however, "the originality and power of Maximus's new Logos doctrine lies in the fact that his conception of revelation is developed within Christological perspectives." "It is not that Christ's person demands explanation, but that everything is explained in Christ's person." Indeed, as von Balthasar would say, "the image of Christ the Savior is at the center of Maximus's work" and "his ontology and his cosmology are an extended Christology, because the Christological synthesis is God's ultimate and first idea."[120]

So the *logoi* of entities can be looked at from the perspective of the Incarnation: "The modes of virtue and the *logoi* of things are a type of the divine good things; for in these [modes and *logoi*] God is ever becoming man."[121] So we have a series of incarnations or "thickenings"[122] of the Word, which take three main forms. The first, as we have seen, is His incarnation or thickening through the *logoi* of entities, where the Word is hidden "ineffably" beneath existent things.[123] The second, as we have already said, is His secret incarnation in the faithful through the virtues:

> The Word of God, who was born once and for all in the flesh,
> though His love for mankind is constantly being born will-

ingly in spirit in those who wish it. He becomes a babe, forming Himself in them through the virtues; and He manifests
Himself to the extent that He knows the receiver is able to
bear. . . . In this way, while the Word of God is ever manifesting Himself through the manners of those who participate
in Him, He ever remains invisible to everyone because of the
surpassing greatness of the mystery.[124]

The third is His incarnation in the Scriptures:

The Word of God is called flesh not only inasmuch as He became incarnate. He is so called also because when He is con-
templated in His true simplicity, as He was in the beginning
with God the Father, He embraces the models of truth of all
things in a distinct and naked manner, and does not contain
within Himself parables and dark sayings, or stories needing
allegorical interpretation. But when He comes among men
who cannot with the naked intellect come into contact with
noetic realities in their naked state, He converses with them
in terms familiar to them, making His won a combination
of various stories, parables and dark sayings; and in this way
He becomes flesh. Thus at the first encounter our intellect
comes into contact not with the naked Logos but with the
incarnate Logos, that is, with various sayings and stories. The
incarnate Logos, though Logos by nature, is flesh in appearance. Hence most people think they see flesh and not the Logos, although in fact He is the Logos. The intellect—that is,
the inner meaning—of Scripture is other than what it seems
to most people. For the *Logos* (Word) becomes flesh in each
of the recorded sayings.[125]

This is why Maximus calls on Christians not to become "killers of
the word" like the pagan Greeks who worship the creation more than
the Creator, preferring the letter to the spirit and not comprehending "Him who for our sake came to us in our likeness through a body,
and was thickened by means of syllables and letters for the sake of our
sense perception."[126] This is precisely why "those who live like beasts,
by sense perception alone, make the word flesh for themselves in a way
that is erroneous: they do so in the service of the passions, misusing
God's creations"; and "those who stop at the letter of holy Scripture
and dedicate the dignity of the soul to the physical worship of the Law

make the word flesh for themselves in a way that is reprehensible."[127] The killers of the word are those responsible for His false incarnations.

The incarnations of the Word in the world, to the extent that they are true incarnations, are not unrelated to each other. First of all, in the view of Sherwood, Riou, Dalmais and von Balthasar,[128] within Maximus's own theological system these three incarnations are connected with the three laws: the natural law, the written law, and the law of grace,[129] which look to the ultimate manifestation of the new world of God's Kingdom. Generally, however, the understanding of these multiform embodiments of the Word belongs to those who have comprehended the great mystery of the Incarnation of the Word. As the Confessor writes:

> The mystery of the embodiment of the Word is *the key to all the riddles and types in Scripture and contains the knowledge of created things, both visible and intelligible.* One who knows the mystery of the Cross and burial knows the *logoi* of the all those things; while one who is initiated into the ineffable power of the Resurrection *knows the purpose for which God established everything in the first place.*[130]

This passage conveys in a few lines the profound Christological basis of Maximus's theology, which is uniquely able to illumine our understanding of it, and it is clearly reminiscent of the eucharistic passage in *To Thalassius* 35, where the flesh and blood of the Word are understood as the inner principles of things perceptible and intelligible respectively. The incarnation which is the key to all riddles and types and contains all knowledge of created things visible and intelligible, and the eucharistic incarnation in the passage previously cited which contains the inner principles of things sensible and intelligible, are manifestly parallel, if not essentially equivalent in Maximus's thought; because of course "the Cross, the burial, and the Resurrection" here make up the totality of the economy of Christ, which is summed up and manifested in a real and concrete way in the Eucharist. So we can and must say that testifying to the identity of the *logoi* with the "gracious wills," "divine purpose," and "gracious intention" of God, as we have seen in the foregoing, and experiencing the eucharistic incarnation of the Word (which is the perpetual sacramental presence of His historical Incarnation) are the same thing, according to St. Maximus. In other words, to fathom the mystery of the eucharistic incarnation of Christ which reveals for us His historical Incarnation and above all His

Resurrection as God's ultimate and unconditional will for creation, and to fathom the mystery of the ultimate texture of the inner principles of things, is one and same spiritual action. Thus creation as an event of dialogically forming the very nature of things, from their origins to their ends, can be simultaneously expressed both Christologically and sacramentally. As we go on, we will see that this spiritual principle is constantly being verified.

2. Being, Well-being, Eternal Being. The Eleven Triads

SHERWOOD, IN HIS BOOK *The Earlier Ambigua of St. Maximus the Confessor,* which we have already cited, considers that there are two sorts of *logoi* in Maximus's theology. One is the basic and immutable *logos* of the essence of each thing, while the second is a distinct *logos* subject to change and perfection. The latter is the *logos* pertaining to each stage or state of existence: being, well-being, eternal being.[131] Elsewhere, the same writer recognizes the difficulty of establishing the meaning of these three states on the basis of Maximus's writings.[132]

Drawing on the Confessor's writings, we have put together a list of eleven triads of parallel terms, connected with each other by the saint himself, which elucidate his basic theological conception about the existence of three distinct existential states in spiritual life. The first and fundamental triad is that of being, well-being, and eternal being. There is indeed a principle of being, a principle of well-being and a principle of eternal being, all of which (pre)exist in God. As we read in Maximus:

> Man is a particle of God in that he exists by virtue of the *logos of his being* which is in God; and in that he is good by virtue of the *logos of his well-being* which is in God; and in that he is God by virtue of the *logos of his eternal being* which is in God.[133]

And again similarly:

> One comes into being in God through attentiveness, by not violating the *logos* of one's being which preexists in God; one moves in God by putting the *logos* of one's well-being into action through the virtues; and one lives in God in accordance with the *logos* of one's ever-being which preexists in God.[134]

Already in the latter passage we have a suggestion of the second triad, which is connected with the fundamental one: the triad of becoming, movement, and stasis.[135] We will study this triad in more detail in Chapter Three. For now, however, we will quote a short passage from Difficulty 9 of the *Ambigua*, which shows clearly how the two triads are connected:

> If rational beings had an origin, then certainly they also move, because they are in motion from a natural beginning in being to a willed goal in well-being. For the end of this movement of things that are in motion lies precisely in eternal well-being, just as their beginning lies precisely in being, which is God. For He is both the giver of being and the bestower of well-being, because He is the beginning and end.[136]

Already we can make out the third triad: nature, gnomic will, and fulfillment. Through the gnomic will, nature moves toward well-being,[137] and it "stops" in eternal well-being, experiencing the "cessation of all desire, beyond which they cannot be carried; for nor is there any other end . . ."[138] This is the state we have called fulfillment.

The fourth of our triads is provided by a passage from the *Ambigua*:

> . . . our threefold birth, i.e., the general modes of our coming into being and well-being and eternal being: one of these, through which we receive being, is *bodily;* it is one birth for both (I mean body and soul) inasmuch as these two parts co-exist with each other simultaneously, but divided into two because each part has a different mode of coming into existence. The second is *by baptism,* in which we receive well-being in abundance; and the third is *by resurrection,* in which we are reshaped by grace so as to come into eternal being.[139]

The fourth triad, then, is natural birth, baptism, and resurrection.

The fifth triad, related to the first and the others, is that of the goodness of God, the love of God, and the providence of God. As Maximus writes:

> They have quite opened up their intellect to the ultimate *logoi* of God of those attainable to humans, I mean those of *goodness* and *love;* and by these [*logoi*] they have been taught that God is moved to give being to entities and to bestow on them [the gift of] well-being.[140]

Similarly in *to Thalassius* we read:

> "The right [side]" is the mystery of the Incarnation of the
> Word according to *providence*, because this puts into opera-
> tion the deification, by grace and beyond nature, of those
> who are saved, which was foreordained before the ages. To
> this no *logos* of things can in any way attain by nature.[141]

So the being of things is due to God's goodness, their well-being to His
love and their eternal being, i.e., the deification of entities, to His providence.

The sixth triad is given to us in the *Ambigua*, 1392A:

> Those who are knowledgeable about the things of God speak
> of three modes. The overall *logos* of the genesis of rational
> beings as a whole is regarded as possessing the [modes] of
> being, well-being and eternal being: first it has bestowed that
> of being on entities *in their essence*; secondly it has given
> them that of well-being *by their free choice*, because they are
> self-moved; and thirdly it has presented them with eternal
> being *by grace*.

So we have the sixth triad: essence, free choice (*proairesis*), and
grace. In the place of free choice in another passage we find "aptitude"
(*epitedeiotis*):

> The essence possessing intelligence and intellect participates
> in the holy God both by it being and by its aptitude for well-
> being—I am speaking of [participation in] goodness and wis-
> dom—and also through the grace that gives eternal being[142]

So this is a seventh triad: *essence, aptitude,* and *grace.*

The eighth triad comes immediately afterwards, also in the *Ambigua* (1392A): "The first contains *potentiality,* the second *energy,* and
the third *rest.*" This is a triad of *potentiality, energy,* and *rest.* As Maximus explains further on:

> The *logos* of being has by nature only the potentiality for en-
> ergy . . . ; that of well-being has, through the gnomic will, only
> the energy of the natural potentiality . . . ; while that of eter-
> nal being completely encompasses those preceding it, i.e., the
> potentiality of the one and the energy of the other. It does not
> in any way inhere in entities as a natural potentiality, nor is
> it at all a necessary consequence of the desire of their will.[143]

Thus the principle of eternal being is the condition or limit that brings nature to a standstill in respect of potentiality, will, and energy, "determining all ages and times for all."[144] As Maximus immediately goes on to say, this is the "blessed Sabbath" and the "day of rest," the "eighth" and "perpetual day."

The ninth triad distinguishes between three existential "places" and states "in which human beings may be." They are *the place of the present, the place after death, and the age to come.* This triad too is directly connected with the initial three existential gradations of the *logoi.* As Maximus writes:

> There are three places or states in which we human beings may be: *this world* in which we receive our being and are born; the place *after death* where we go once we have departed hence; and *the age to come* to which we are invited with our souls and bodies. As long as we are in this world, we keep the Passover in Egypt, cleansing ourselves from the stains of sin. When we pass from this life through death, we keep a different Passover, as it were in the wilderness, *having learned to perceive the logoi of entities more plainly, in a noetic and incorporeal way, without symbols and dark sayings or the complexity afforded by sense perception. And again, in the age to come we celebrate the Passover by feeding directly on the ultimate logos of wisdom into which we are transformed when we are deified by grace.*[145]

Christian asceticism lives the experience of death before physical death, surveying the inner principles of entities and moving on toward well-being; and it is led ultimately to the eternal being of the deifying experience of the age to come.

Connected to the last triad is the tenth group of terms or ideas which we find related to each other as a triad: *practical philosophy, natural contemplation, and theological mystagogy.* By the first of these Christians are purified, overcoming the carnal mind; this is the state that corresponds to being. In the second, they contemplate the spiritual inner principles of entities, pure of every image presented by the imagination or the senses ("as if denuded of a body"); this is the state corresponding to well-being. In the third state, Christians are "are conformed to [an initiation into theology] by ineffable movements of the intellect, [knowing so far as is humanly possible] what is the breadth and length and depth and exceeding greatness of God's wisdom toward us"; this is the state corresponding to eternal being.[146]

From this tenth triad stems the eleventh and last: *practical aspect of the soul, reason (logos),* and *intellect.* Maximus writes:

> [He calls] the human being a mystical church because through the temple of his body, he makes *the practical aspect of the soul* to shine with virtue by carrying out the commandments in accordance with moral philosophy. In the *sanctuary of his soul,* he *offers to God through his reason,* in natural contemplation, the *logoi* of sense perception, once those *logoi* have undergone a pure spiritual circumcision to remove what is material. And on the *altar of his intellect,* he invokes the silence of the Godhead, which is amply hymned in the innermost recesses of the unseen and unknown utterance, [summoning It] through another silence, eloquent and rich in tone. So far as is attainable for a human being, he joins himself with that divine silence through mystical theology; he becomes such as befits one counted worthy of God's indwelling and marked by His dazzling radiance.[147]

So here are the eleven triads in summary from:

1. being	well-being	eternal being
2. becoming	movement	stasis (fixity)
3. nature	gnomic will	fulfillment
4. natural birth	baptism	resurrection
5. goodness of God	love of God	providence of God
6. essence	free choice	grace
7. essence	aptitude	grace
8. potentiality	activity	rest
9. place of the present	place after death	age to come
10. practical philosophy	natural contemplation	theological mystagogy
11. practical aspect of the soul	reason (*logos*)	intellect

So the principle of rational creatures' being brings them into existence in time through their creation and *genesis,* which is their physical *birth.* By that birth, they have been given their *nature* or *essence* as a gift of *God's goodness.* It is this essence that contains their given initial potentiality for spiritual development, and their potentiality has to do with the creature's activity in the *present place and time.* The mode whereby this potentiality will be set in motion is *practical philosophy*, i.e., the process of purification. This has to do with the *practical aspect* of the soul, and takes places through that aspect.

The *principle of well-being* is achieved through the *movement* of rational beings, when their gnomic will is oriented in the right direction; it is a gift of *God's love*, given concrete form in the grace of *baptism*. But this grace is put into *action* only through the *free choice*, which leads the creature to acquire the appropriate spiritual attitude, the *aptitude*, for that purpose. The full realization of well-being becomes possible *after death*, and hence the movement of spiritual askesis is a charismatic putting-to-death starting already in this life, a death to the world of egocentric and impassioned distortion of the truth of God's creations. Thus the believer attains to *natural contemplation* of the uncreated inner principles of entities, because the *rational power* of his soul is enlightened.

Finally, the *principle of eternal being* is actualized exclusively as a gift of God, like the principle of being; but the principle of eternal being is a "reward" for choosing and moving during the middle stage of the creature's existence. It is the *fulfillment* of his desire for God, and is given to him as a state of ever-moving *stasis* within the infinity of God's goodness, wisdom, and glory. It is the *resurrection* into the *future age* of incorruption, the age of the saints, and is an exclusive, unrepeatable and supranatural gift of *grace.* It is also the realization of God's pre-eternal *providence* for which the world was created, and its existential content is the *rest* of cessation and Sabbath rest in God. Eternal being is activated through the *theological mystagogy* that has as its instrument the highest of the soul's faculties, the intellect which contemplates God.

It should be observed that well-being is not the only possible outcome of our existential evolution: a perverted movement of the free choice will lead to woe-being. "Depending on whether the operation of the choice uses the power of nature in accordance with nature or contrary to nature, it will find that the outcome is well-being or woe-being."[148] The ultimate climax of such an evolution is *eternal woe-being.* Maximus describes with the utmost clarity the difference between eternal well-being and eternal woe-being, whereas eternal being is given by God to all:

> As to being and eternal being, God will sustain everyone [in those states] by His presence; but as to eternal well-being, he will sustain in a special way those who are holy, both angels and humans, leaving to those who are not [holy] the state of eternal woe-being, as the fruit of their own gnomic will.[149]

And so we come to the question of *apokatastasis.*

According to St. Maximus, the Church recognizes three sorts of *apokatastasis* (restoration). The first is that of each being when it fulfils the inner principle of virtue. The second is the restoration of all created nature, in incorruption and immortality, through the resurrection. The third (which Maximus thinks Gregory of Nyssa has misused) is the restoration of the powers of the soul to their prelapsarian natural state. They will lose the memory of evil, but they will not participate in God; they will not be deified. Souls will receive their original powers "in terms of understanding, not in terms of participation"; it will be clear that the Creator is not to blame for sin, and those souls themselves will naturally remain without any part in His uncreated blessedness.[150] Florovsky, in his exposition of Maximus's teaching, remarks that God will indeed return to sinners everything they had lost through sin, restoring their souls to the fullness of their natural powers and capabilities. They will "cognize" God and have a certain understanding of Him, but without participation in his blessings. Thus they will be constantly experiencing their lack of communion with Life, constantly realizing in all sorts of ways the terrible pointlessness of the spiritual path they took in rejecting God's love and making their own hell through the perverted movement of their gnomic will.[151]

All this happens on the "eighth day."

> The eighth and first day, or rather the one ceaseless day, is the unmingled and all-radiant presence of God, which comes about after the cessation of things that are in motion; when in His entirety He comes to dwell, as is fitting, in the total [being] of those who by choice have used their *logos* of being in accordance with nature, and grants them eternal well-being through participation in Himself, because He alone properly speaking *is*, and is eternally, and enjoys well-being. But to those who by their gnomic will have used their *logos* of being in a way contrary to nature He properly apportions woe-being instead of well-being, because they lack the capacity to receive well-being, having set their faces against it.[152]

There is a very important comment to be made on this passage: Maximus regards eternal well-being as that which "alone properly speaking *is*" and "alone properly speaking is eternally." We would say that eternal well-being is the conceptual and ontological center of all the existential degrees of being: it is their eschatological foundation, its ontology is founded on eschatology. It is an ontology that is not philosophical, meaning that it is not platonic, not founded on the primary "principles" (*principia*) of things, as is the archetypal and primordial way of philosophical ontology. Here we have an ontology that belongs to revelation, an eschatological ontology, founded on the truth of ultimate being, a non-metaphysical ontology of being-in-Christ (and thus *logoi* do refer to this eschaton rather than merely to the "origins" of things, as we shall see). We will reserve discussion of this subject for Chapters Three and Four, and will here confine ourselves to pointing out the central ontological and hence also semantic point of reference, which is the key to understanding the ontological gradation of the three existential levels we have described. Perhaps the clearest description of the place of eternal well-being, which is nothing other than deification, in Maximus's thought is provided by the following passage:

> This was why He made us, in order for us to become partakers of the divine nature and sharers in His eternity; and that we might appear like Him through *deification by grace. It is for the sake of [deification] that all things that are have been constituted and are maintained in being, and that things that are not are produced and come into being.*[153]

So without the prospect of "deification by grace," the entire work of creating and constituting things out of nothing and maintaining them in existence would in Maximus's view be pointless.

If we want to discover the actual way in which Maximus understands this well-being of deification, Sabbath-keeping, supranatural rest, and ever-moving stasis, we should take as our guide the idea we saw earlier, that of the mind as an "altar" and the rational "liturgy" as a *proskomide*, an act of offering the inner principles of entities to God; and also the saint's previously mentioned comment that "in the coming age of the divine promises we celebrate the Passover, feeding directly on the ultimate word of wisdom into which we are transformed and are deified by grace." With the guidance of such images, we should recall the ultimate connection of deification with the Eucharist in Maximus, as we have already described in Chapter One. For indeed, in Holy Communion we have the "communion and identity [with God] . . . through which man is accounted worthy to become no longer human, but god."[154] The Divine Eucharist, as the concrete actualization of eternal well-being, is in consequence the natural locus in which the "constituting and permanence [of entities] and the production and genesis of things that are not" find its justification, because it is the realm of their deification *par excellence*. The experience of the Eucharist, then, means penetrating into the ultimate inner principle of things, according to Maximus. For, to recall what we said in Chapter One, their eucharistic incorporation is the only possibility for them to fulfill the principle of their being, a fulfillment which thus begins even in this world.

3. According to Nature, Contrary to Nature. The Link between Ontology and Ethics: the "Internalization of Ontology"

THE *LOGOI* OF BEINGS ALSO PLAY an altogether vital role in the existential course of those beings. In Maximus's thinking, this course can be either "according to nature" or "contrary to nature." That is decided by the free movement of the will of rational beings, which may either "concur with the *logos* of nature" so that the outcome is that of their natural course, or else be "destructive of the *logos* of nature" so that they develop in an unnatural way.[155] This distinction means that there is a double free potentiality: the essential principle can either be "used well" or fall into "disuse," so that "either the essential principle natural to [the entity] has substantive existence as a result of being well used, or else the mode [of behavior] contrary to nature has a para-existence as a result of disuse [of the *logos*]; the one proclaims a faculty of choice that is in accordance with nature, the other, one contrary to nature."[156] Here, the opposite of the natural essential principle is the unnatural mode, which pertains simply as the denial of the former; it is therefore a "para-hypostasis" and not a true hypostasis, because it arises purely out of denial of the essential principle of nature. In other words, in accordance with what we have said earlier, we are dealing here with non-being, a impetus toward nothingness within creaturehood which originates in the unnatural movement of the faculty of choice: "when through weakness or lack of ability some of our natural movements err, they produce movements contrary to nature."[157] So Maximus speaks of "accomplishing the principles in accordance with nature,"[158] firmly asserting that "according to the principle of being, passion and nature can in no way coexist."[159] Passion nullifies nature and has no possible place in the essential principle of being, because "nothing natural—and certainly not nature itself—would ever resist the cause of nature."[160]

So how are essential principles "accomplished"? The remarkable linkage of ontology and ethics that we see at this point in Maximus's

theology is of exceptional significance. The essential principles are, po-
tentially, existential accomplishments of the rational being's free choice,
not mere ontological givens: the freedom of the Creator has been given
also to His creature. As the essential principles exist within God without
constraint, as expressions of His free and loving good pleasure, so man
too has been given the possibility of freely "accomplishing" and exhibit-
ing them, as well as that of morally annihilating them in a state contrary
to nature. So it is not that the essential principles simply "are": they are
also "performed," and then "the essential principle of nature becomes
the law of nature as well, when the gnomic will is in accord with it in the
way it operates the natural powers."[161] This spiritual state, in which the
essential principle of nature becomes the "natural and divine law,"[162] is
characterized by the fact that the gnomic or personal will then "operates in accord with God in all things; and this operation is a practical
disposition such as to generate virtue by the grace of Him who is good by
nature."[163] The natural movement of the gnomic will makes the essential
principle of the creature its inner law, leading the movement of the free
choice to "generate virtue" through a practical disposition inspired by
the grace of God who is "good by nature."

We have called this spiritual law an "internalization of ontology,"
in the sense (and only in the sense) that it locates the reality of the essential principle in the existential realm as a rational act of virtue, i.e., as
an internal dialogue between human free will and divine *logoi*/wills. It
would be natural for the extremely dynamic, personal, intentional quality of *logos* in God to be transferred to the sphere of the rational creature
in such a way that its realization would be predicated upon a free process
of will and a voluntary movement of the free choice—a view that leads
to the rejection of any autonomous understanding of ethics, and beyond
that to an "ontological ethics" which is what we have already referred
to as the "internalization of ontology." It is an understanding that will
certainly lead to a new interpretation of this ethic as internalized ontology: just as the natural context for gaining a profound knowledge of
the *logoi* is the Eucharist, similarly the only context in which to evalu-
ate and indeed understand such an ethic is that of the Eucharist. We
are talking about the moral action leading to the Christian's ever deeper
incorporation[164] into the Lord's Body—and for this reason, we are not
really talking about ethics in any philosophical sense of the term. It is
the movement of life, of the identification of Being with living, as this
identification functions in Maximus.[165] So for the Confessor, the *logos*
(rationale or inner principle of a creature) exerts some sort of special

vital influence on the rational being, such that the free acceptance of
that vital influence implants divine life in humans and angels, propel-
ling them toward eternal well-being:

> There are those who in all things have kept their gnomic
> will in equilibrium with nature, and have made it actively
> receptive to the *logoi* of nature, preserving in every respect
> the principle of eternal well-being, through the sensitivity
> of their will to the divine plan; and these will participate in
> all goodness according to the divine life which shines upon
> them, whether they are angels or humans. Then there are
> those who in all things have put their gnomic will into a
> state of disequilibrium with nature and have shown it to be
> actively destructive of the *logoi* of nature in every respect
> of the principle of well-being, through the antipathy of
> their will to the divine plan; and these will be deprived of
> all goodness, in accordance with the intimacy their will ex-
> hibits with woe-being. Such beings will accordingly be at a
> distance from God, because they do not have the principle
> of well-being quickened within them by the disposition of
> their will or by works of goodness, and it is in accordance
> with that principle that divine life naturally reveals itself.[166.]

As the principle of well-being is "quickened" or activated by the doing of the virtues, the divine life itself begins to be manifest. In this
sense, the essential principle of nature will be the judge of each person's own will at the Judgment, revealing what direction that will has
taken: "At the judgment, the balance-beam for each person's gnomic
will will be the logos of nature, which provides proof of the movement
of the will toward ill or well-being—that movement on which the person's participation or lack of participation in the divine life naturally
depends."[167] Maximus's direct and insistent reference to the divine life,
toward which our own essential principle and "the straight course in
accordance with the *logos*"[168] lead like a road, recalls what we have said
repeatedly about understanding this outpouring of divine life in Maximus's work in terms of eucharistic theology.[169] We see in fact that the
logos or rationale of a rational creature is the road leading it to eucharistic incorporation; it is precisely conformity with that *logos* that
leads to this eucharistically-understood incorporation of the Christian
into Christ. This *logos* is the locus wherein the divine life is manifested
and received by man; it is the locus of the existential encounter be-

tween man and God. To "accomplish" our *logos*, then, is to accomplish this encounter.

This is an "accomplishment" that, in addition to personal choice, depends on the action of the Holy Spirit:

> As God and the Spirit of God, He sustains the genesis of every being, spreading through all things by the power of His providence and stimulating the natural principle (*logos*) in each. Through that *logos,* He leads those who perceive Him to an awareness of the transgressions they have committed contrary to the law of nature—that is, those whose will is amenable to receiving the right thoughts which come from nature.[170]

The Holy Spirit stimulates the existential activity of the *logoi* or natural principles, making them a means to self-knowledge and taking advantage of the positive choice of those who have good intentions, "by the power of His providence." His providence lies in the fulfillment of His ministry of bringing things into being and holding them together, with the aid of their "straight course in accordance with *logos*" which will lead to participation in the divine life.

In the history of philosophy, as we know, ethics came to be distinguished very early as an autonomous philosophical activity and discipline. What interests us is not so much the fact that every philosophy leads ultimately to an ethics, as the fact that the need for an ethic to exist and have some foundation has always determined the character of philosophers' metaphysical concepts:[171] there is a need to raise action to the heights of thought. In this way, certain historians of philosophy consider that the survival and persistence of classical and modern metaphysics, despite the blows it has suffered ever since the Enlightenment, is due to the fact that it has to exist in order to provide a basis for the normative ethical principles that are essential for the survival of human society.[172] Ethics, then, undertakes to justify every metaphysical ontology, and of course fails, with the result that

> philosophy and ethics have always remained idealistic (in the case of the former) and ideal (in the case of the latter). Systematic ethics, with all its subdivisions, has now reached the point of exhaustion: the totality of its rules together with the basis for them has already been formulated, and is finally tending to be tangibly applied. But its commandments

have not only failed to be observed consistently, but have re-
mained altogether impracticable."[173]

This impracticability of every philosophical ethic, which in turn shakes
the foundations of whatever ontology supports it, finds an answer in the
internalized ontology of St. Maximus. The principal distinction could
be formulated in this way: Every philosophical ethic leaves man on his
own to devise ways of applying it and struggle to implement them, at the
mercy of the resistance mounted by reality, as well as various forms of
self-deception and autosuggestion operating within himself. "Ontological ethics," on the other hand, is in essence a work of Christ within man,
the instrument of which is the uncreated inner principle (*logos*) of that
particular human being which exists "with God," a work that requires
only the dialogical assent of his free choice. A healing work of Christ, a
work of restoration in the Holy Spirit to that which is in accordance with
our nature and essential principle; a work which is the spiritual process
of bringing out, through a human-divine dialogical synergy, the existential truth of the inner principles of entities, and equally a process of
giving existential reality to the ontological content of those principles.
No philosophical ethic has ever been able to acquire such ontological
weight as to become an applied ontology, an ontology put into practice,
a process whereby the world is made word (*logos*)[174] and truth. And
given the way truth is grounded in the Eucharist in Maximus's theology,
this is ultimately nothing other than "giving the world life within the
eucharistic catholicity of the ecclesial body."[175]

4. Principles of Providence and Principles of Judgment: the Uncreated Foundations of the "Natural"

FOR MAXIMUS, PROVIDENCE AND JUDGEMENT are "wings on which the
Word is borne as He lays claim to existent things unbeknown to them."[176]
In other words, providence and judgement are the two most general ways
in which God the Word mysteriously "visits" entities, both being equally
necessary to this "flight" of the Word that holds things together and constitutes them. In another allegory he uses, the Confessor expands this
interpretation:

> . . . it indicates providence and judgment: in the midst of
> which stands the Word as on a golden lampstand—[the
> lampstand being] the holy catholic Church or the soul of

each saint—signaling to all things the light of truth, because as God He embraces everything. And He reveals the true and altogether general principles according of providence and judgment that hold things together. It is according to these principles that the mystery of our salvation comes about, which was foreknown before the ages but executed in the last times.[177]

So the pre-eternal mystery of salvation, which is already being accomplished, has been constituted as a "general bond holding things together" by the principles of providence and of judgment. Their center and foundation is the Word who as God embraces everything, revealing them in the heart of the Holy Catholic Church, which is the sanctified souls of the faithful.

This holding together has to do principally with unifying the present life and the future life, with all their difference:

> . . . the principles of providence and of judgment, whereby in wisdom He penetrates both our present and our future life, as if they were different generations, apportioning to each its proper mode of activity as is appropriate.[178]

But he also refers to the cohesion of the actual ontological components of entities:

> If entities have *essence* and *potentiality* and *activity*, *it is clear that they have a threefold logos of being.* And if providence connects these *logoi* with their being, then *the logos of providence too has been established to be three-fold.* And if judgment is punitive, inflicting corrective evils in response to past, present or future abuses by creatures that deviate in any way from the aforementioned principles, then this judgement too is perceived in contemplation as having a threefold principle, according to which it continues to preserve its own indeterminacy while circumscribing the essence and potentiality and activity of things.[179]

We have seen above (Chapter 2.1) that the inner principle of the being of things is "threefold," encompassing within it a principle of essence, a principle of potentiality and a principle of activity for each particular entity. The means by which these principles are connected to the one principle of the entity's being is providence. In consequence, there is a providential principle of essence, a providential principle of potentiality and a providential principle of activity. In other words, there is a specific uncreated definition of how the strictly ontological characteristics of entities cohere together, a definition without which the reality of how actual entities function existentially cannot be understood. This definition is not an addition, but coexists indivisibly with that of the inner principle of being, rendering the latter capable of existing in its fullness. We would thus say that the principle of providence has to do with the "natural" existential functioning of the inner principles of being; it forms the uncreated foundation for them to be realized in accordance with nature. Correspondingly, according to our text, judgment scrutinizes and punishes the "abuses and deviations" of the discrete principles belonging to the threefold principle of being, having it its turn a "threefold principle"—a principle of judgment of essence, a principle of judgment of potentiality and a principle of judgment of activity, all of which are included in the unified principle of judgment belonging to the being of things. Thus the principle of judgment assists in preventing the essential principles of entities from being altered "contrary to nature," as it circumscribes the essence, potentiality, and activity of things and recalls them to the authentic interpretation of the essential principle of their being. It protects beings from the possibility of existential corruption within time, forming the uncreated foundation for them constantly to escape being annihilated in a state contrary to nature.[180]

So the principle of providence and the principle of judgment form the *sine qua non* existential and ontological context for the principle of being to exist according to nature. But is that all? What does the eternal connection of creatures' inner principles (*logoi*) of being with the principle of their providence and judgment within God the Word (*Logos*) mean for the Word Himself?[181] The western scholars of Maximus do not raise this question, just as they have not paid adequate attention to the close connection between the principles of providence and judgment and the inner principles of entities,[182] or indeed the ontological (and not simply moral) dynamics of the terms "providence" and "judgment" in the saint's writings.[183] For Maximus himself, providence is manifested "in the inexpressible mode of the Word's hypostatic union with the flesh animated by a rational soul," and judgment "in the mystery of the life-giving sufferings of God incarnate for our sake";[184] correspondingly, the principle of providence becomes accessible to the Christian through natural contemplation, and the principle of judgment through elementary practical philosophy.[185] Beyond this, however, what does creation's close connection with providence and with judgment mean for the special relationship of the Word with creation?

Certainly providence and judgment, as the Confessor sees them, have a character that is clearly ontological and not simply moral. Their purpose is to maintain things in accordance with their nature. Furthermore, they are manifestations, together with the fact of creation, of the one integral loving event of the creation of the world out of nothing; they are the expression of the Word's creative love toward created things. They are equally the expression of this love in ontological terms and dimensions. Particularly judgment, seen in this context, plays a supporting role to providence, contributing to the fulfillment of creatures' "direct course toward their *logos*." Furthermore, the unbreakable linkage of providence, creation, and judgment is the strongest possible testimony to the freedom of God as Creator. One provides only for that which one freely wills, and only then does one take care that it comes to completion in accordance with its nature. The ontological character of providence and judgment demonstrates the voluntary nature of the production of all things out of nothing, the absolute creative freedom of God. It also "proves," one could say, that creation really was "out of nothing," because it was absolutely free: if we accept the pre-existence of any created thing whatsoever, its existence would impose some necessity on this free creative and loving providence and judgment, making them subject to its own already existent laws. To be exact, we should not be able in that case to speak of providence and judgment in an ontological sense.

But there is more! The fact that the inner principles of entities cannot be understood apart from the principles of providence and of judgment is also an argument against the coeternity of the world with God as conceived by Origen. The fact that providence and judgment hold all things together means that the world willed by God does not exist in its fullness, but will exist in its perfect state in the future. But at the same time, it is certain that this future eschatological existence is the culmination of a dramatic dialogical process of cooperation between persons, (with all its possible quarrels, changes, disagreements, and complaints) in which man's free assent to or rejection of God's plan contributes to or obstructs the realization of the natural principle of creation, which is its unimpeded progress toward eternal being. If creation were in any way coeternal with God, then His providence and judgment would have no *raison d'être* in holding things together, because then creation would necessarily be perfect from the beginning, i.e., deified, because naturally God does not think of imperfect beings but (as we saw in the

first section) only "perfect natures." The fact that God thinks of the essential principles of entities inseparably from those of providence and
judgment means that He thinks of the gradual free dialogical perfecting
of the created order (through the free cooperation of God and man);
He thinks of entities in the process of their freely accomplishing the
completion which is in accordance with their nature, which of course
culminates in the eschatological fullness of eternal well-being. Thus the
essential principles of entities have a profoundly dynamic ontological
content; they are not static, perfect prototypes of entities in God, but dynamic proposals from God's personal will, we might say, toward entities,
waiting for human will/logos/response in order for creation to advance
to the eschatological fullness of the "eighth day." In consequence, "entities are not coexistent with God from eternity," according to Maximus,
precisely because the actual entities *will become in the future, freely, dialogically,* what God wills them, grounded in the uncreated principles of
providence and judgment which guide the essential principle of their
being to its possible natural realization.[186] Nature thus means dialogue
in its very essence—no part of it is left out of this dialogue, the origins as
well as the *eschata* are formed as loving proposals asking for response.

To sum up: If, hypothetically, it were the essential principles of
entities alone that existed in God, without being linked to providence
and judgment, then we could say that things were in some way at least
immutably coeternal with God; they would be created in a state of
immediate frozen perfection, because God does not create imperfect
natures. The fact, however, that the essential principles of entities are
firmly tied to the principles of providence and judgment which hold
things together means that things are not coeternal with God, because
He thinks of them in a state of a possible dynamic eschatological com-
ing-to-perfection, in their eschatological (dialogical) becoming. The
principles of their being are constantly and closely accompanied by
those of providence and judgment, and are incomprehensible without
the latter two. Many of these entities will never attain to eternal well-
being—which is, as we have seen already above (Section 2), true being
and true well-being and true eternal being—but will attain instead to
eternal woe-being; not of course by revoking the principle of their being, but by contradicting it through a negative dialogical reaction which
would be contrary to nature. And of course God does not desire this di-
saster. But neither these entities, nor the others which will freely attain
to the natural goal of eternal well-being, justifying God's providence
and plan, are coeternal with God, i.e., just "given" and frozen, because

God through His uncreated *logoi* has simply thought, prepared and proposed for them in advance precisely this potential course toward a dialogical existential perfection, together with its eschatological synergetic fulfillment in eternal well-being.

Apart from anything else, however, in the passages we have already discussed there is a very clear subtext: the eucharistic interpretation of the *logoi* of entities in Maximus. Truly the "wise economy of God's providence"[187] is manifested, as we have seen already, in the hypostatic union of man and Word in Christ, and judgment in the mystery of Christ's life-giving sufferings. As we have already said,[188] the Eucharist is for Maximus the visible and tangible summary of God's economy and providence, and both the event of the Incarnation and that of Christ's life-giving sufferings are contained in the eucharistic incarnations of the Word as part of the mystery of the Divine Eucharist. The close and indissoluble relationship between the inner principles of being and those of providence and judgment, which are accomplished within the mystery of the Divine Eucharist, are consequently an unequivocal testimony to the direct hermeneutic connection in Maximus between the *logoi* of entities and eucharistic theology. This means that the Eucharist remains the *locus par excellence* of this dialogical/synergetic encounter of human logos/will with the divine logical providence/judgment, which asks for this dialogue. Thus essential principles of entities receive even now, as a foretaste of their full actualization in the age to come, an actualisation in accordance with human dialogical consent, through the mystery of the eucharistic incorporation of the Christian into the Lord's Body; because only then are the principles of providence and judgment fulfilled, and it is they that undergird the natural completion of the principles of entities.

5. Principle of Nature—Mode of Existence. The Person in Maximus's Ontology

THE CONCEPT OF "MODE OF EXISTENCE" in Maximus's theology has decisive consequences for his theory of the *logoi* of entities; it forms, as Garrigues would put it, "the very axis of his theological thought."[189] And this because in principle, just as entities cannot be thought of apart from their uncreated essential principle, so it is literally impossible for them to exist "in the nude," without their concrete "mode of existence." So while the nature of entities that participate in the same essential principle is in some way common to them all, the mode always relates to the actual hypostasis of each creature, constituting the creature itself, the actual entity, the person;[190] it is its "personal mode of existing and realizing the vocation inscribed in its nature," as Riou puts it.[191] It is a distinction that makes Sherwood on the one hand recall the ancient Aristotelian distinction between first substance and second substance, in reference to the mode and the *logos* respectively,[192] and on the other consider the *logos-tropos* distinction as an expression of the existential antinomy of necessity and freedom which characterizes the relationship between nature and person.[193] In this case, of course, we should recall the view of Prestige, who considers that it was St. Basil who introduced this distinction into theology.[194]

St. Basil, in his discourse *Against the Sabellians and Arius and the Anomoeans*, does indeed write: "Why do you not join everyone else, and without shame confess a safe ignorance as to the mode of existence of the Holy Spirit?"[195] Or again, in a letter to Amphilochius: "the word 'knowledge' covers a wide field; something might be 'known' in the sense that we know something about its number, or size, or force, or its mode of existence, its time of origin or its essence."[196] St. Gregory of Nyssa follows him in making a similar use of the term,[197] again with a clear Trinitarian reference.[198] The term occurs in connection with the Father in Amphilochius of Iconium,[199] and in Cyril of Alexandria too it refers to the Trinity.[200] It is not our concern here to follow the rich and many-layered process of development whereby the term "mode of existence" came to include the notions of existence, otherness, and ultimately hypostasis,[201] but already in Maximus the relevant doctrine is presented as something already established. It is to Maximus himself, however, that we owe the development of contrasting pair "what it is—as it is," found in Basil and Gregory,[202] into its radical form as "principle of essence—mode of existence."[203] It is precisely the radical nature of this formulation that is St. Maximus's great contribution.

In Maximus, this distinction occurs first and foremost in direct reference to Trinitarian doctrine: "The Holy Trinity of hypostases is a unity without confusion in Its essence, and in Its simple principle (*logos*); and the holy Unity is a Trinity in Its hypostases and in Its mode of existence." It is clear in this passage how mode of existence is connected with hypostasis in Maximus's thought. [204] The Confessor brings the principle of hypostasis into his core teaching about the inner principles of entities: natures always exist as actual modes of existence, and any hint of their existence "in the nude" belongs exclusively to the realm of abstraction.

Thus Maximus transmits this distinction also to the ontology of created beings.

First and foremost, this enables Maximus to give a deeper ontological foundation to his teaching about grace and deification:

> Generally speaking, any innovation has to do with the mode of the thing innovated, not the principle of its nature. For when the principle is the subject of innovation, that destroys the nature, because the latter no longer retains the principle of its being unimpaired; but when the mode is the subject of innovation, its natural principle being of course preserved, it shows the power of the miracle, demonstrating how the nature is acted upon and acts clearly beyond its normal scope.[205]

Corruption of the essential principle would lead the entity into a state contrary to nature, whereas a change in its hypostasis by grace is the miracle of the exaltation of nature. Equally miraculous, consequently, is the manner of Christ's becoming man; Christ does not "make new" the essential principle of human nature, but its mode of existence.[206] The reference Maximus makes in some of his other writings to the pair *logos-tropos*, correlating it with the principle (*logos*) of things—mode (*tropos*) of the virtues, "through which God is ever becoming man, as he wills, in those who are worthy,"[207] also gives us an opportunity to make the connection with previous sections. The modes of existence that through the "direct course toward the *logos*" avoid what is contrary to nature and head for their natural goal of eternal well-being, at the same time justifying God's principles of providence and judgment, are the virtues, according to the Confessor. Thus the virtues are modes of authentic hypostasis—substantive existence—for the essential principles of entities. Here again ethics is absolutely linked with ontology. In a few words (and as virtues are always relational and dialogical realities), the concept of the mode of existence opens nature to a possibility of a transformation through grace.

Maximus's elaboration of his teaching on mode of existence reaches its culmination when he identifies mode of existence with the reality of the person: "Hence in the mode, the varied character of persons is made known by their action; but in the *logos*, the invariable element of the natural energy."[208] The way Maximus puts together mode of existence, hypostasis and person so clearly and so directly is one of his most valuable contributions to Christian theology and human thought, a contribution that completes the work of the Cappadocians, expressing the deepest essence of their thought on the subject with extraordinary wisdom and clarity.

However, if the inner principles of entities attain substantive existence only as concrete modes of existence, manifesting personal otherness ("the varied character of persons"), that means that personal otherness is the only possible way they can be existentially manifested. The fact of the person is thus the state in which the inner principles of entities take on their authentic hypostasis, meaning that the inner principles come to be known in person; and the knowledge of them, within the same existential dialectic, is the foundation for the fact of the person. Furthermore, the inner principles of entities are made known in the relationship that constitutes the person as otherness, which is first and foremost a relationship between man and God. So here we have the ontological foundation of the person. The fulfillment of the essential principles of entities, the realm of their natural substantive existence, is the person.

Thus we have a scale of existential steps, according to the texts we have looked at in previous sections. The essential principles of entities signal a journey toward eternal being. This course may go in accordance with nature (in which case it leads to eternal well-being; or it may go contrary to nature (in which case it leads to eternal woe-being). The principles of providence and judgment help entities to move dialogically in accordance with nature and to avoid deteriorating into a state contrary to nature. The dialogical mode of movement in accordance with nature is the virtues. All this existential mobility is included in what Maximus calls the mode of existence of the particular principles of entities. The mode of existence of these principles manifests their hypostasis (substantive existence). The supreme ontological definition of hypostasis as the mode of existence of entities is the fact of the person, so that the pair "nature—mode" ultimately amounts in Maximus's usage to the pair "nature—person." It is clear that not only the logical creatures exist in person. Everything for Maximus is personal in so far as it enters this dialogical mode of existence pertaining to logical persons. Thus Maximus introduces the person into his ontology in the most direct way possible, making it unthinkable to interpret that ontology without it.[209] If we combine all this with what we have said about a "eucharistic doctrine of the person" in Chapter 1.7, and about the communal reciprocity between man and God through the inner principles of entities, which function as gifts offered and bestowed, forming the foundation for the communion of persons between God and man, a communion ultimately expressed as a eucharistic reciprocity of "offering" and "partaking"—then we came to a deeper understanding of the meaning of the person as the nature's mode of existence. The person is the spiritual event in which the inner principles of entities are made into man's "gifts offered" to God and God's "gifts bestowed" on man, circulating between created persons, thus fulfilling their natural function, their authentic mode of existence. And, of course the only conceptual and existential framework where this can take place is that of the Divine Eucharist. The event and the mystery of the Divine Eucharist provides the authentic foundation for the personal dimension of the communal reciprocity of man and God, which makes possible the authentic existence of the inner principles of entities as the reciprocal gifts which go to make up this personal communion. We thus inaugurate a eucharistic and eschatological ontology of personal being as gift, which is to be explored.

6. The Place of the Theology of the Logoi in Interpreting the Uncreated Energies of God

WE TURN NOW TO THE RELATED SUBJECT of how the *logoi* are connected with the uncreated energies of God in Maximus's theology, a question that has been a thorn in the flesh for Western scholars of the saint. They cannot accept the distinction between essence and energies, nor, consequently, a remark such as Lossky's concerning the *logoi* or ideas of things, that

> their place is not in the essence, but in "that which is after the essence," the divine energies; for the ideas are to be identified with the will or wills (*thelemata*) which determine the different modes according to which created beings participate in the creative energies.[210]

Sherwood, indeed, directly criticizes this interpretation of Lossky's, saying that the latter "understands the *logoi* in an Areopagitic and Palamite sense."[211] Sherwood himself considers that there is no possibility of connecting the *logoi* with the relationship of nature-grace,[212] just as von Balthasar considers it pointless to look for connections between the theology of the *logoi* and the problem of natural and supranatural, or nature and grace.[213] By contrast, an Orthodox theologian such as Bulović can say that

the divine energies are the "*logoi* of things." The doctrine of
the "*logoi* of things" makes no sense and cannot stand in the
absence of the doctrine of a real distinction between essence
and energy, nature and will. And on the other hand, without
the doctrine of the "*logoi* of things" the Christian dogma of
the creation of the world would become shaky and vulner-
able, being unable to explain how it is that the world has
a beginning, while the creative power and energy of God is
without beginning. So this doctrine concerning God's "*logoi*"
and ideas is essentially identical to the doctrine of the divine
energies.[214]

Riou stands alone among the Western scholars in that, without
entering into discussion about Palamism, he simply remarks, "Maximus
himself calls the *logoi* 'divine energies' in Chapter 22 of the *Ambigua*."
No one else—not Thunberg, nor Sherwood, nor Dalmais, nor Lossky
himself, nor von Balthasar—has noticed this specific meaning in this
passage.[215]

Let us attempt a more or less systematic approach to the problem
addressed by St. Maximus. First of all, his teaching on the distinction
between essence and energy is obvious: "Man is not without a natural
energy, just as no other nature lacks [an energy] proper and essential to
it."[216] Thus

it is not possible to know the divine or human nature, even
to know that it exists or that it differs from another nature,
apart from its essential energy. For the principle of a thing's
essential force is strictly speaking the definition of that thing:
when that force is annihilated, the subject is certainly annihilated along with it.[217]

The essential energy is the expression of the subject's essential force,
defined by the very principle of its essence. The same holds true, naturally, whether one is considering a human or a divine subject.[218] In God,
the relationship between energy and force is undoubtedly based on the
understanding of the *logoi* as wills, which we have examined at some
length above (Ch. 2.1). Through the act of will, the force is put into action because "the principal and chief property of every rational nature is
movement according to its desire,"[219] a movement (or energy, according
to Sherwood) which expresses "according to desire" the "principle of its
essential force."

Every nature, then, has an energy, "the essential principle of which is spread throughout the nature." The natural energy is constituted by the principle of nature itself; it is a creature of the essential principle. As Maximus says of Christ:

> If He received the essential *logoi* of which He Himself was the hypostasis, then presumably He also had the natural animate energy of the flesh, the energy *whose essential principle is spread throughout our nature.* And if as man He had the natural energy *constituted by the principle of [human] nature,* then clearly as God too He had a natural energy, *which was manifested by the principle of the supra-essential Godhead.*[220]

The *logos*, then, also constitutes the natural energy within an essence. Furthermore, "the principle of the supra-essential Godhead" "manifests" the divine energy; the principle is the profound unity of essence and energy, as well as the absolute "legitimacy" of their co-existence. In other words, it is profound rationality, and hence also the "good reason" for the distinction between essence and energy in the unity of creatures' essential principle in God.

On the basis of these conclusions, we may now proceed to look at the text presented to us also by Riou,[221] and his commentary on it:

> . . . thus when the mind apprehends the *logoi* in things in a natural manner, contemplating the energies of God in the infinitude of those *logoi*, it reckons that there are many—or, truth to tell, infinite—variations of the divine energies it apprehends. And it will most likely find its power feeble and its method of searching for knowledge useless before Him who indeed is true, being unable to understand how God who is in truth no one of the things that exist, and properly speaking is everything and is beyond everything, is in every *logos* of each thing separately, and in all the *logoi* of all things taken together. If therefore it is true to say that every divine energy indicates through itself God, whole and undivided, [as present] in every [creature], in accordance with the *logos* of its own particular existence—in that case, who is able to understand and express precisely how God in His entirety is undividedly and indivisibly present in all things in common, and in each entity in a way that is particular, being neither subject

> to a variety of distinctions in line with the infinite variations in the things in which He is present, nor compressed into the individual existence of each one; nor yet does He compress the differences between things into one unitary totality of all things, but He is truly all things in all things, never abandoning His own indivisible simplicity?

Through His *logoi*, God is in every one of His creatures. This divine presence, profoundly mysterious and inaccessible to ordinary rational enquiry, is revealed to the mind of one who has faith in the infinitude of the essential principles that support or convey the infinitude of the divine energies.[222] Each divine energy reveals ("indicates") God in His entirety in each entity "in accordance with the principle of its own particular existence." In other words, we see the uncreated essential principle functioning as a "limit" and "definition" for the uncreated energy, not so much in the sense that it contains it but in the sense, we may say, that, as a special divine will, it takes functional "precedence" (in a purely conceptual sense, of course, and purely for the sake of our theological understanding) within God. Here we would be slightly at variance with Lossky. There is no reason to identify the uncreated *logoi* in theory with the uncreated energies, in our effort to interpret them theologically—even though the distinction between them, in God, is not an actual distinction; it is introduced in order to help us analyze the way in which they fit together. In other words, we should see this identification purely as a matter of the activity of divine will being carried out in Its uncreated energies.[223]

Anyway, we see that in Maximus the doctrine of a distinction between essence and energies in God cannot be understood without the doctrine of the uncreated *logoi* of entities in God, which in turn expresses and promotes the distinction between essence and will in God made by Athanasius and the Cappadocians. What is the significance of this functional (and not real) "precedence" of the *logoi* relative to the uncreated energies? This "precedence" relates, we think, to the fundamentally personal/hypostatic character of God[224] and the mystery of the consequent distinction of Essence and Persons/Hypostases in Him. For hypostasis or person means free will and power as a possibility of activating the personal/hypostatic essence, and ultimately energy that belongs to the essence or nature of the actual living person. In the supreme development (from a theological point of view) of the question of a distinction of essence and energies in God worked out by Gregory

Palamas, it is quite obvious that he is making use of this teaching of Maximus's, as he constantly grounds the reality of the uncreated energies in the personal/hypostatic character of the living and true God of Holy Scripture[225]—in total contrast to the philosophical and theological essentialism of someone like Barlaam, which is unable to see the reality of a living personal God Who wills, acts, and moves through His uncreated energies.[226]

The theory of the essential principles of entities in its absolute connection with the theology of the uncreated energies of God is what principally explains the "personal" character of those natural energies (not in the sense of course that they spring from persons—as they derive from essence—but in the sense that they are en-hypostatic, i.e., they express an essence that exists only as a person/hypostasis), justifying the later theories of Palamas. But there is more besides! According to what we have said in the previous section about the eucharistic foundation of the personal communal reciprocity between man and God which makes it possible for the essential principles of entities to have authentic existence, the functional "precedence" (always in a purely notional sense) of the essential principles over the divine energies also leads us to the eucharistic foundation of the theology of the uncreated energies in Maximus, as also in Palamas.[227] This means that the divine Eucharist is the existential context *par excellence* in which the uncreated energies of God are manifested as personal, deliberate, loving gifts and outpourings of divine grace to man and creation.[228]

7. The Existential Manifestation of the Logoi of Entities as Powers of the Soul

AFTER ALL THIS, IT IS ABUNDANTLY CLEAR that man's relationship with the inner principles of entities is not simply one of intellectual curiosity, even a lofty intellectual curiosity. Man is connected to the essential principles, in other words the living fullness of true being, in a way that is existential, universal and ecclesial, experiencing the fullness of the uncreated energies of God in the Holy Spirit. Thus, according to Maximus himself, "the Holy Spirit seeks and searches in us for knowledge of things that are; but He does not seek this for Himself, because He is God and beyond all knowledge. Rather, it is for the sake of us who are in need of knowledge."[229] The knowledge that the Confessor is talking about here is not the more or less intellectualized knowledge of the classical and modern philosophical gnosiological tradition, but knowledge in the scriptural sense of partaking, participation—a participation whose immediate author at every stage in the Spirit of God,[230] so that "according to God's purpose, the soul wisely traverses the sensible world through the spiritual *logoi* which are in it, and so comes to God with understanding."[231]

This existential traversing of the created world through the inner spiritual principles signals the existential manifestation of the principles of entities as *powers of the soul*, according to St. Maximus's development of the theme in a remarkable passage in *Ambiguum* 12:

> One who devoutly and through contemplation has come to understand things as they are, and by rational will has thoughtfully and rightly determined how to speak about them, and keeps judgment for himself, or rather keeps himself unswerving in judgment—such a one has conceived the totality of virtue all in one, no longer moving toward anything else now that he has come to know truth. . . . [He has] action already deep seatedly contained within his reason, without conflict, inasmuch as our intellect brings with it all the highest passionless *logoi* according to which all virtue and knowledge has its being, because *these are powers of the rational soul . . .* which do not refuse to use the body at times in order to manifest themselves, for reasons already stated.[232]

This text certainly calls to mind themes discussed above, when it connects the rational will with properly weighing one's speech; or when it recalls the way judgment functions ontologically and its direct relationship to virtue, and the relationship of virtue to "coming to know truth"; or when it refers to the internalization of the essential principles which is described as action being deep-seatedly contained within the reason (i.e., the connection between ethics and ontology, the "ontological ethics" we have already described). But it is also easy to discern here how the essential principles are existentially "incorporated" as powers of the rational soul. As the soul "steers a straight course toward the *logoi*," its powers become rational (*logikos*); they act and move in accordance with the principles of being, and gradually the *logoi* altogether "rationalize" the powers of the soul, so that in the end they are identified with them, and the *logoi* become the powers of the rational soul. In this way, "the human mind becomes like the divine Mind—it becomes a small logos as it reflects the great logos,"[233] as Florovsky pertinently observes. By participating in the essential principles through virtue, the mind makes its own a "face," "form," "character," "hypostasis," "the divinely inscribed knowledge coming from them"[234]—the knowledge of God, the presence of God which they [the *logoi*] manifest. This is the existential process of "the likeness of God," because when the human being reaches this point, according to Maximus's bold thinking:

> He has already become like God by deification, and will be permitted without suffering harm to contemplate God's creations with God, and to acquire a knowledge of them as God and not as man, possessing by grace the same wise knowledge of things that God has, because of the transfiguration of his mind and sense unto deification.[235]

What is described here is not of course the triumph of a safe and methodical theory of knowledge, but the fulfillment of the powers of the rational soul as the miracle of man's total communion with God is accomplished in our reason—the miracle of the grace and gift of kenotic divine love, the marriage of the created with the Uncreated.

The powers of the rational soul have been given to it in order to discover God, and man does indeed "find God in reason."[236] In consequence, the essential texture of the powers of the soul is *eschatological*, in that they find their true selves in being identified with the essential principles of entities, which make them into vehicles moving toward the fullness of the Kingdom of God.[237] For it is the appearance of God, His "dawning," that causes the essential principles of things sensible and intelligible to "appear with Him"; Maximus makes a direct parallel between this event and the transfiguration of Christ, thus naturally introducing an eschatological reference.[238] In consequence, the powers of the soul function properly when they are eschatologically orientated through and in the essential principles. What is also amazing, from the same perspective, is that, according to our initial text, the *logoi* as powers of the rational soul do not fail to use the body at times, in order to manifest themselves. Here we have another critical issue. For Maximus, contrary to all the Platonizing philosophical and theological traditions of both the East and the West, human essence cannot be merely identified with human soul, but it is "the whole of him." Consequently, not only the soul, but also the body enter this eschatological and dialogical ontology, simply because human psychosomatic essence is ultimately one. Divine *logoi* are thus powers of a rational soul manifested in a body, and deification concerns the whole of the human being, who bears the image of God upon him in a soul and a body, as Maximus insists. An eschatology of the human body is inaugurated in this manner.

It is easy to see now how far such a view removes us from any philosophical or psychological anthropology. For in any philosophical or psychological approach, the powers of the soul take their meaning, their ontological weight and function from the starting point from which they proceed: the unconscious psychological center (according to Freud and the psychoanalytical tradition), the thinking subject (according to Descartes), the transcendent Ego (according to Kant, Fichter, and Husserl), the *Dasein* (according to Hegel and Heidegger), etc. In Maximus, however, the powers of the soul, manifested in a body, have their very foundation in the *eschaton* toward which they are directed; only if this movement is freely actualized do the powers of the rational soul have an ontological foundation, because then and only then can they be existential manifestations of the essential principles of being. It would require a special study adequately to explore the contrasts on this point between philosophy and philosophical psychology,[239] and theology. It is already clear to us, however, that only through theology, through the eschatological (and hence eucharistic) theory of the *logoi* as powers of the soul, is it possible for psychology and philosophical anthropology to acquire an ontological foundation. As we have already said, this foundation will ultimately be eucharistic in character, in accordance with the well-known connections made by Maximus between the eschatological eternal well-being and the Divine Eucharist. The Divine Eucharist, whereby the eschaton is activated *par excellence*, is the natural framework within which the inner principles of entities become powers of the rational soul manifested in a body, which lead it to the Kingdom of God "after the consummation of existent things." This means that one truly participates in the Divine Eucharist in the degree to which the inner principles of entities become powers of one's soul. As such, the Eucharist is the ontological foundation on which the eschatological function of the *logoi* as powers of the soul can be grounded and come to fruition. Thus the Divine Eucharist becomes the ontological basis for the natural eschatological fulfillment of the powers of the soul manifested in a body, and the very proof that these powers have a true and real (i.e., incorruptible), eternal and uncreated basis which is offered to them, beginning from this life—not of course by nature, but by grace, as a gift of God's gracious providence, because He works for the perfecting of the creature by offering it true life.

As he continues to explore the existential approach to the essential principles, Maximus discusses the steps of initiation through the virtues into contemplation of the essential principles, and finally speaks of the believer genuinely approaching the "truth in all things," the universal truth of the whole world "starting from which, we will give devout accounts of the truth in many varied ways, on the basis of a wise contemplation of essences of things intelligible and sensible."[240] The ultimate prize, then, for involvement in seeking out and actualizing the inner principles of entities is the very revelation and contemplation of God's truth within things. That is to say, we make them come true by our existential participation in their ultimate truth; we are also quite literally *making them true*, in accordance with the commands of the loving and providential divine will, which seeks that Its counsels-principles should be realized in things, with the cooperation of man.

Because of this fact, the existential approach to the theology of the *logoi* of entities has enormous importance for us. It is a matter of nothing less than our personal authenticity, as a quest for the divine truth in things and surrender to that truth. In the following chapter, we will look at the highest form in which this existential psychosomatic authenticity and verification becomes a reality, as we explore the heart of the ontological and ontogenic operation of the inner principles of entities: their communal texture and action.

Notes

1. *Ambigua*, PG 91: 1148D.

2. Ibid., 1149B.

3. Vl. Lossky, *The Vision of God* (Leighton Buzzard: Faith Press, 1963)

4. Elias the Presbyter, *Gnomic Anthology* III.13; G.E.H. Palmer, Philip Sherrard and Kallistos Ware, tr., *Philokalia* III (London: Faber & Faber, 1984), p. 48.

5. *Ambigua*, PG 91: 1228AB.

6. *Ambigua*, PG 91: 1228D.

7. I. H. Dalmais, "La manifestation du Logos dans l'homme et dans l'église (Typologie anthropologique et typologie ecclésiale d'après Qu. Thal. 60 et la Mystagogie)», in Actes, p. 24.

8. O. Clément, *Theology after the "death of God"* [in Greek], (Athens: Athena-Synoro, 1973), p. 128.

9. Riou, *Le monde et l'église*, p. 55.

10. John Meyendorff, *Christ in Eastern Christian Thought* (Crestwood: St. Vladimir's Seminary Press, 1975), p. 146; P. Sherwood, *The Earlier Ambigua of St. Maximus the Confessor and his refutation of Origenism* (Rome: Orbis Catholicus, Herder, 1955), p. 180: '[St Maximus is] identifying and distinguishing the supreme Logos and the many logoi both on the ontological and on the moral level."

11. I. Hausherr, *"Philautie." De la tendresse pour soi à la charité selon St. Maxime le Confesseur* (Or. Christ. Anal. 137; Rome, 1952), p. 56.

12. A. Riou, *Le monde et l'église*, p. 56. Riou regards the term *logos* as untranslatable, and retains the Greek form. He regards the term "principe" (principle) as the best way of rendering it into French but observes that "the logos of a thing is not simply, we believe, its idea or its origin in God" (p. 54). Dalmais too ("La manifestation du Logos," p. 13) keeps the original term, attempting to translate it as "principes constitutifs" when occasion demands. He himself regards the *logoi* of things as "ensuring the stability of this world," p. 18.

13. *The Ascetic Life*, p. 46.

14. Ibid., p. 52.

15. H.U. von Balthasar, *Liturgie Cosmique*, transl. L. Lhaumet and H.-A. Prentout from the first German edition (Paris: Aubier, 1947) p. 72; *Cosmic Liturgy*, pp. 116–7. [Translator's note: The French and English versions of this work do not correspond exactly, because the English is based on a revised edition. Where this second German edition is cited, references are given to the English version based upon it. Where the French version is cited, we have given references to both the French and the English text. All translations are taken as far as possible from the English version.]

16. G. Florovsky, *The Byzantine Fathers of the Sixth to Eighth Century* (Belmont: Büchervertriebsanstalt, 1987), p. 223. Cf. also *idem, Creation and Redemption* (Belmont, MA: Nordland, 1976), pp. 61–2.

17. *Byzantine Fathers*, p. 240.

18. L. Thunberg, *Microcosm and Mediator: The Theological Anthropology of Maximus the Confessor* (Lund, 1965), pp. 80–81.

19. J. Meyendorff, *Christ in Eastern Christian Thought*, pp. 135–6.

20. I.H. Dalmais, *St. Maxime le Confesseur, le mystère du Salut* (Namur-Belgique: Ed. du Soleil Levant, 1964), p. 39. Cf. also *idem*, "La théorie des 'logoi' des créatures chez St. Maxime le Confesseur», *Revue des Sciences Philosophiques et Théologiques* 36 (1952), pp. 296–303.

21. Vladimir Lossky, *The Mystical Theology of the Eastern Church* (London: James Clarke and Co., 1957), p. 98.

22. *To Thalassius* 3, PG 90: 276B.

23. *Centuries on Theology* 1.9, PG 90: 1085C; cf. also 1.4, PG 90: 1084C.

24. *Scholia on the Celestial Hierarchy*, PG 4: 40C.

25. PG 91: 1069A–1101C. Riou analyses this text, taking it in a different direction from that of the present work (*Le monde et l'église*, p. 45ff.).

26. PG 91: 1077C–1080A; Balthasar, *Liturgie Cosmique*, p. 84; *Cosmic Liturgy*, p. 131. Sherwood examines this passage in *The Earlier Ambigua*, p. 26. He notes the influence of the Areopagite and St. Basil. He also points out the unity and distinction between the logoi and the Word.

27. *Ambiguum 7*, PG 91:1077C–1080A.

28. 1080A. Riou connects the "gracious will" of God referred to here with Eph 1:10 *Le monde et l'église*, p. 56).

29. Riou, ibid., p. 57. Cf. also PG 91: 1081A.

30. Riou agrees (ibid., p. 57).

31. PG 91: 1080B.

32. PG 91: 1080AB.

33. Scholia on the Divine Names, PG 4: 353B.

34. Cf. Scholia on the Divine Names, PG 4: 320B–D.

35. PG 4: 324A, 325AB, 353B: "everlasting intellections and logoi which make all things."

36. *To Thalassius 13*, PG 90: 296AB.

37. *Scholia on the Divine Names*, PG 4: 352B.

38. This is an essential difference between *logoi* and Platonic ideas, as we shall see later on.

39. *Ambiguum 9*, 1085A. We should note another passage where Maximus refers to Clement: in his *Scholia on the Divine Names* (PG 4: 329BC), he mentions that Clement is credited with the view that even within creation, there are "exemplars" for lower things to be found in higher things, "as the ethereal fire is an exemplar for material fire." He remarks, however, that "it is not these that the great Dionysius calls "ideas," properly speaking, but the intellections of God. For even if these could be called exemplars in creation, they are not worthy of veneration, as Moses says." It seems here that the sainted writer considers that the inner principles of entities are "worthy of veneration," i.e., uncreated.

40. *On the Divine Names 5.8*, PG 3: 824C. Cf. also Clement, *Stromatis 4.2.6*, PG 68: 1381A. Cf. also "volitional thought" (*theletiki ennoia*) in Ps.-Cyril, *On the Holy Trinity*, PG 77: 1145C, and John of Damascus, *On the Orthodox Faith* I.9, PG 44: 837A: "He saw everything—having conceived it in His mind timelessly before it came into being, each thing according to His non-temporal volitional thought, which is a predetermination and image and exemplar."

41. Plato, *Republic* I.597a–d. Cf. E. Papanoutsos, *To Threskeftiko Vioma ston Platona* (Athens: Dodoni, 1971), pp. 92, 96. Also I. Theodorakopoulos, *Eisagogi ston Platona* (Athens, 2nd ed 1975), p. 202ff.; Maximus expresses his opposition to Plato's teaching on ideas, which he regards as obscure and unworthy of God, when he takes the view, with the Areopagite, that the divine wills are defining and creative, not substantive. As he writes: "Plato understood the ideas and exemplars in a way that was lowly and unworthy of God. This Father [Dionysius], however, used the same word but explained its meaning in a godly way. He said that the divine wills are defining and cre-

ative, because on the one hand God constitutes and makes all things simply by willing them; and on the other, things come into being varied and different." And further on: "Because some have said that the ideas and exemplars are substantive, he now reproaches them for being pagans, and says: If the ideas did not exist in a way that is simple and unified, being transcendently simple intellections of the transcendently simple and unified God, then God would be composite on the basis of His own exemplar" (*Scholia on the Divine Names*, PG 4: 330D–332C). Here the nature of the *logoi* as wills and intellections of God is clarified still further.

42. K. Axelos, *O Irakleitos kai i Philosophia* (Athens: Exantas, 1974), p. 57.

43. Axelos, p. 74.

44. Axelos, p. 77.

45. Axelos, p. 89.

46. I. Theodorakopoulos, *Eisagogi*, pp. 214–215.

47. Alexos, p. 79.

48. M. Heidegger, *Platons Lehre von der Wahrheit* (Wegmarken VK, 1967), p. 142.

49. Diogenes Laertius 7. 135.

50. K.D. Georgoulis, *Istoria tis Ellenikis Philosophias*, Vol. I (Athens: Papadimas, 1975), p. 377.

51. Georgoulis, p. 389.

52. Georgoulis, p. 357.

53. G. Florovsky, "Creation and Creaturehood," in *Creation and Redemption*, pp. 61–2.

54. *Enneads* 2.3.18.

55. We should clarify here that *logos* in Plotinus' philosophy is equivalent to nature. See *Enneads* 3.8.2. 19–22: "*logos*, one might say, is immobile, while this [sc. nature] is something different from logos and in motion. But if they are referring to the whole of it [as being in motion], then that applies to *logos* too. If on the other hand there is some part of nature that is immobile, then this too will be *logos*, for nature must be form and not something composed of matter and form." Here the Platonic Idea, the Stoic *Logos* and the Aristotelian Form are all subsumed into the image of nature as the creative principle which gives shape to matter.

56. E.g., *On Providence* I.7.

57. *On Flight and Discovery*, 112: "For the logos of a thing is a bond uniting everything, keeping together all the parts and holding them tight to prevent them dissolving and coming apart." See also E. Brehier, *Les idées religieuses et philosophiques de Philon d'Alexandrie* (Paris, 2nd. edn 1925), pp. 99–100.

58. Brehier, op. cit., p. 198.

59. See M. Dragona-Monachou, "To provlima tou kakou ston Philona ton Alexandrea me eidiki anafora sto Peri Pronoias. Einai i Theodikia tou

Philonos stoiki?», *Philosophia, Yearbook of the Athens Academy* vol.s 5–6, pp. 314–5. Cf. K.D. Georgoulis, Istoria Vol. II, pp. 506–6.

60. I. Karavidopoulos, "I peri Theou kai anthropou didaskalia Philonos Alexandreos," Part II, *Theologia* 1966, pp. 248–9.

61. H. A. Wolfson, *Philo. Foundations of Religious Philosophy in Judaism, Christianity and Islam* (1948), pp. 200ff. See also Sherwood, *The Earlier Ambigua*, p. 168.

62. See N. Loudovikos, "To mysterio tou diakountos Logou kai i Orthodoxia os mystagogiki istoriki pragmatosi," *Efthyni* 180 (December 1986), pp. 608–609. An attempt at a theological critique of Philo may be found in N. Loudovikos, *Ousia kai Dynameis tou Theou kata tin didaskalia Philonos tou Alexandreos, os aphormi diakriseos tis philosophias apo tin theologia* (Thessaloniki, 1984).

63. An undertaking that caused Porphyry to write of him: "In his life Origen lives as a Christian, contrary to the law; but in his beliefs about existent things and the divine, he is a hellenizer, slipping Greek ideas into alien myths." *Apud* Georgoulis, *Istoria* Vol. II, p. 604.

64. Georgoulis, *Istoria* Vol. II, p. 600.

65. Georgoulis, *Istoria* Vol. II, p. 518.

66. See N. Loudovikos, "To mysterio tou diakonountos Logou," p. 609.

67. See John Zizioulas, "*Ellinismos kai Christianismos*," p. 552; K. Georgoulis, Istoria Vol. II, p. 586.

68. *apud* Georgoulis, *Istoria* Vol. II, p. 587.

69. Origen, *On First Principles* III.5.3, PG 11: 327B; I.2.10, PG 11: 138D–139A.

70. Origen, *On First Principles* I.2.10, PG 11: 138D–139A.

71. Metr. John Zizioulas of Pergamon, *Mathemata* II, p.7; Florovsky *Creation and Creaturehood*, p. 54.

72. Florovsky, "Creation and Creaturehood," p. 56.

73. *Mathemata* Vol. I, Addendum, pp. 65ff.

74. *Centuries on Love* 4.4, PG 90: 1048CD. 4.6 (1049A) reads: "Some say that created things existed from eternity in God, which is impossible. For how could things that are in every way limited coexist eternally with Him who is altogether infinite? This argument belongs to the pagan Greeks, who claim that God is in no way the creator of essences but only of qualities. We, however, know the omnipotent God, and say that He is the Creator not of qualities, but of the essences of things that have been created. If this is the case, created things are not coexistent with God from eternity."

75. Sherwood agrees, writing: "The direct influence of Philo on Maximus is not to be excluded" (*The Earlier Ambigua*, p. 168). H.U. von Balthasar, *Die Gnostischen Centurien des Maximus Confessor* (Freibourg-en-Brisgau, 1941), pp. 96–98, considers that in two chapters (*On Theology and the Economy* 1.83, 84) there is an indisputable direct influence from Philo.

76. Riou agrees with the Alexandrian origin of the terminology of logoi (*Le monde et l'église*, p. 56). Similarly Dalmais, *La Manifestation du Logos*, p. 13, and Florovsky, *Byzantine Fathers*, p. 216.

77. Sherwood, *Earlier Ambigua* p. 168; Florovsky, *Byzantine Fathers* p. 223; Balthasar, *Liturgie Cosmique* p. 75; *Cosmic Liturgy*, p. 119.

78. Sherwood, *Earlier Ambigua* p. 176: "The importance . . . lies rather in the union made of the logoi and the divine wills . . . In this view the logoi are not as it were, inert models, but the very creative power of God, realizing itself in the creature."

79. Riou, *Le monde et l'église*, p. 57.

80. A Radosavljević, "Le problème du 'présupposé' ou du 'non-présupposé', de l'Incarnation de Dieu le Verbe," in *Actes*, pp. 199ff. The question is discussed also by Florovsky, in his essay "Cur Deus Homo" (*Creation and Redemption*, pp. 163–170).

81. Exceptionally helpful on this point is the opinion of Riou (*Le monde et l'église*, p. 62), who considers that ultimately the theory of the *logoi* forms an "economy of blessing and recapitulation," an "eschatology of the world within the divine will," not a temporal eschatology but eschatology as a free destiny and dispensation grounded in the drama of the condescension and sacrifice of the Lamb, revealed to beings with the cooperation of the Spirit: "Thus the theory of the *logoi* constitutes Maximus's response to both the 'economic' cosmicism of Origen and the 'ontological' cosmicism of Denys. Absorbing both the Alexandrian metaphysic of emanations from the One and the metaphysic of timeless divine ideas into an economy of blessing and recapitulation, [this theory] opens up an eschatology of the world within the divine Counsel through a trans-cosmicism, beyond any pantheism and beyond development. An eschatology, which is to say an impatience, a nostalgia, certainly not for a past or for the future in the chronological sense of these terms, but for a 'what is to come' that is given as a free destiny, as a dispensation, open to the creation and revealed and accomplished in the drama of the Condescension and Sacrifice of the Lamb, realised in each being in the Synergy of the Spirit." Further on, he speaks of a "theurgic unfolding" which looks toward a "paschal renewal."

82. *Ambigua*, PG 91: 1328A.

83. *Opuscula*, PG 91: 37B.

84. *Scholia on the Divine Names*, PG 4: 296B.

85. *Scholia*, 296BC.

86. *Scholia*, 296C.

87. *Opuscula*, PG 91: 37BC.

88. See note 40, above.

89. Discourse II.19, PG 94:1340D–1341A.

90. Cf. Florovsky, *The Byzantine Fathers*, p. 223; *idem*, "Creation and Creaturehood," p. 61.

91. *Scholia*, PG 4: 352BC.

92. *To Thalassius* 27, PG 90: 353C–357D.

93. PG 91: 1085AB.

94. *Ambigua*, PG 91: 1328BC.

95. *Scholia*, PG 4: 297A.

96. *Ambigua*, PG 91: 1328BC.

97. *Scholia*, PG 4: 301C.

98. PG 91: 49B.

99. *Scholia*, PG 4: 301D.

100. Plato, *The Sophist*, 237a.

101. *Sophist*, 232a–242b, esp. 236e–242b.

102. *Sophist*, 241d.

103. G.W.F. Hegel, *Wissenschaft der Logik*, para. 87. Cf. J. Wahl, *Introduction to the philosophies of Existentialism*. Part II, chap. 3.

104. H. Bergson, *L'évolution créatrice* 4.II.

105. Ibid.

106. M. Heidegger, *An Introduction to Metaphysics*, tr. Ralph Manheim (New York: Anchor Books, 1961), p. 71: "Everything that is not simply nothing is, and for us even nothing 'belongs' to 'being.'"

107. J. Wahl, *Introduction*, op cit.

108. Ch. Yannaras, *Schediasma Eisagogis sti Philosophia*, Vol. II (Athens: Domos, 1981), pp. 42–43.

109. This weakness in Western philosophy makes it appearance somewhat peripherally in the philosophy of Sartre. His critique of the Hegelian idea of nothingness is profoundly "justified" in philosophical terms (see *Being and Nothingness*, I.1.IV–V). Nothingness cannot simply be something external to the world; it is at the same time part of everyday experience of being "like a worm within its heart." In consequence we have the process of "nihilisation"; there is the necessity for "an entity through which nothingness enters into things." The ultimate passage of nothingness into the very working of human consciousness spells the ultimate philosophical destruction of any philosophical attempt to regard nothingness as absolute.

110. This is clearly shown when, for example, Maximus writes: "Expecting that the nature of existent things would fall away into non-being, the devil strove to show man to be a transgressor of the divine command" (*To Thalassius*, PG 90: 644C). Cf. *Disputation with Pyrrhus*, PG 91: 297B: "If things come into existence out of non-being, they also possess a force that attaches to being, not to non-being. The natural property of this force is an impetus toward whatever draws together and a repulsion toward whatever causes disintegration." Similarly *Ambigua*, PG 91: 1329B: "When the genesis of things is in accordance to God's intent, their essential existence remains incapable of moving from being to non-being." And finally, *Mystagogy* 1, PG 91: 668B: "There will be a danger that their very being might fall away into non-being because it is separated from God."

111. Cf. *To Thalassius*, PG 90: 709B: "It is clear that nothing irrational [paralogon] can in any way coexist with *logos*."

112. D. Staniloae, *Eisagogi sto ergo tou agiou Maximou "Philosophika kai Theologika Erotemata,"* Vol. I (Athens: Apostoliki Diakonia, 1978), p. 22.

113. *Ambigua* 9, PG 91: 1081B.

114. *Ambigua*, 1400A.

115. *To Thalassius*, PG 90: 561A.

116. Ibid., 708B.

117. Ibid., 709B.

118. *Opuscula*, PG 91: 264AB.

119. See Florovsky, *The Byzantine Fathers*, pp. 215–217.

120. *apud* Stanilaoe, *Eisagogi*, pp. 65–66 (note 99).

121. *Various Texts* I.78, PG 90: 1211B.

122. See Thunberg, "Symbol and Mystery," p. 296: "becoming thick." See also A. Radosaljević, *To mysterion tis soterias kata ton agio Maximo ton Omologitin* (Doctoral dissertation, Athens 1975), p. 38. See also *Ambigua*, PG 91: 1129A.

123. Cf. also *Ambigua*, PG 91: 1285C–1288A. At 1285CD we read: "Having ineffably hidden Himself for our sake in the *logoi* of things, He is proportionately indicated through each visible thing as through letters."

124. *Various Texts* I.8, PG 90: 1181AB. God the Word is likewise crucified in Christians through asceticism (*Ambigua*, PG 91: 1360B), raised up through spiritual contemplation (*Centuries on Theology* 2.27, PG 90: 1137AB) and transfigured through mystical theological contemplation (*Ambigua*, PG 91: 1385B).

125. *Centuries on Theology* 2.60, PG 90: 1149C–1152A.

126. *Ambigua*, PG 91: 1129CD. Cf. Dalmais, *Le manifestation*, pp. 18–19; Balthasar, *Liturgie Cosmique*, p. 225; *Cosmic Liturgy*, p. 295.

127. *Centuries on Theology* 2.41, 42, PG 90: 1144A-C.

128. See Riou, *Le monde et l'église*, p. 63; Dalmais, *Le manifestation*, p. 19. Sherwood, *The Earlier Ambigua*, p. 35; Balthasar, *Liturgie Cosmique*, pp. 221-242 (cf. *Cosmic Liturgy*, pp. 291-314). As Balthasar writes (*Liturgie Cosmique*, p. 242): "Man, nature and Scripture are nothing other than a three-fold 'comparative', raising itself toward a divine superlative which unites the three even as it transcends them. So it is by purification of the soul, contemplation of the inner reasons of things and seeking the spiritual sense behind the letter that one directs all three toward 'the new world, the comos that is from above.'"

129. *Ambigua*, PG 91: 1285–1288A.

130. *Centuries on Theology* I.66, PG 90: 1108AB. See Dalmais, "La manifestation," p. 16.

131. Sherwood, *The Earlier Ambigua*, p. 178: "However, looking more generally on this doctrine of logos it is clear that essential and immutable logos in creatures is adequately distinguished from that which is subject to change and perfection. Maximus will even speak of a distinct logos for each state of being—being, well-being, ever being."

132. Cf. Sherwood, *The Ascetic Life*, p. 259.

133. *Ambigua* 9, PG 91: 1084BC.

134. *Ambigua* 9, PG 91: 1084AB. Cf also Sherwood, *The Earlier Ambigua*, p. 174: "Now each of these terms Maximus sets in relation with the logos of a man preexisting in God. Being is referred to the logos of being, movement to that of well-being, life to that of ever-being." Cf. also ibid., pp. 170–171.

135. Balthasar, *Cosmic Liturgy*, p. 91ff; Staniloae, *Eisagogi*, pp. 65–66 (note 99); Radosaljević, *To Mysterion tis Soterias*, p. 206ff. Sherwood writes, in full agreement with us: "He introduces . . . the triad *genesis, kinesis, stasis*. The *kinesis*, which he has distinguished from an absolutely immutable ground, is also moral movement. This distinction is complementary to those of the logos of beings, well or ill being, and ever being." (*The Earlier Ambigua*, p. 172, n. 63).

136. *Ambigua* 9, PG 91: 1073C.

137. Cf. PG 91: 1116B. Cf. also *Centuries on Love* 3.27, PG 90: 1025A.

138. *Ambigua*, PG 91: 1076D.

139. *Ambigua*, PG 91: 1325BC.

140. *Various Texts* V.80, PG 90: 1381CD.

141. PG 90: 684A.

142. *Centuries on Love* III.24, PG 90: 1024AB.

143. *Ambigua*, PG 91: 1392B.

144. PG 91: 1392BC.

145. *Ambigua*, PG 91: 1368C–1369A.

146. PG 91: 1369A–C.

147. *Mystagogy* 4, PG 91: 672BC.

148. *Ambigua*, PG 91: 1392C. (The concepts of "according to nature" and "contrary to nature" will be explored in the third section of this chapter.)

149. *Various Texts* IV.55, PG 90: 1329B.

150. *Questions and Answers*, PG 90: 796A–C: "The Church recognizes three sorts of *apokatastasis* ('restoration'). One is the restoration of each being through the *logos* of virtue, when he is restored after fulfilling the *logos* of virtue which exists for that end. The second is the restoration of the entire nature to incorruption and immortality at the resurrection. The third, which Gregory of Nyssa misuses in his homilies, is the restoration of the soul's powers, which had succumbed to sin, to [the state in which] they were created. For as the whole [of human] nature at the resurrection will receive incorruption of the flesh in the time hoped for, even so, as the ages go by, the perverted powers of the soul should put off the memories of evil instilled into the soul. And when the soul has passed through all the ages and found no place to stop, it will come to God who has no end. And thus the soul will regain its powers in terms of understanding, though not in terms of participation in good things, and will be restored to its original state. And it will be shown that the Creator is not to blame for sin.

151. G. Florovsky, *Byzantine Fathers*, pp. 244–245: "In fulfilling the fates God will restore the full entirety of his creation not only in existence but also in eternal existence. But not in good-existence, for good-existence can-

not be given without the demanding and accepting of love. God will give to sinners and return everything they lost through sin, restoring their souls in the fullness of their natural forces and capabilities. They will receive the capacity for spiritual knowledge and moral evaluation. They will cognize God. Perhaps they will even lose memory of sin and come to God in a certain understanding—*ti epignosei*. However, they will not receive communion with his blessings—*ou te methexei ton agathon*. Only the righteous are capable of savouring and enjoying. Only they receive communion with life, while people of evil will who have collapsed in their thoughts and desires are far from God, are devoid of life, and constantly decay and constantly die. They will not taste life, and will be tormented by belated repentance, by the consciousness of the senselessness of the path they took to the very end. This will be ineffable sorrow and sadness. According to St. Maximus's notions, it is not God but the sinner himself who prepares his own torment and grief on judgement day." Let us not forget that here the Confessor is also trying to correct Gregory of Nyssa's theory of *apokatastasis*.

152. *Ambigua*, PG 91: 1392D.

153. *Letters* 24, PG 91: 609CD.

154. *Mystagogy* 24, PG 91: 704D. See also chap. Sotiropoulos, "Efkharistia kai Theosis," *Ekklesia* 10 (1974), p. 249.

155. *Opuscula*, PG 91: 28D–29A.

156. Ibid., 29A.

157. *Scholia on the Divine Names*, PG 4: 304B.

158. *To Thalassius*, PG 90: 769C.

159. *To Thalassius*, PG 90: 776D.

160. *Opuscula*, PG 91: 80A.

161. *On the Lord's Prayer*, PG 90: 909C.

162. Ibid., 901D.

163. Ibid.

164. See chap. 1.6.

165. See chap. 1.5. The ethics of Plotinus are seen as being in absolute organic unity with ontology in the study by N.D. Georgopoulou-Nikolakakou, *Plotinus' Ethics of Purification* (In Greek, Athens, 1991), pp. 39ff. This is because "for Plotinus, the whole wealth of action comes about thanks to contemplation" (p. 42), and this contemplation is of course the overall ontological principle for Plotinus (p. 46). The enormous difference between this and the "ontological ethics" of Maximus lies for one thing in the fact that, as the author rightly notes, "in Plotinus it is fruitless to look for a personal God, a God of grace, and any notion of eschatology is likewise fruitless" (p. 49); but in our view, the difference lies also in the fact that in Plotinus action is always a fall—it means precisely a feeble contemplation, a "shadow" of contemplation and logos (*Enneads* 3.8.1, 15–18; 3.8.6, 1–9; 3.8.4, 31–36). In consequence, we do not think there can be any connection between the ontological ethics of St. Maximus and the ethics of Plotinus. In the Confessor, action is the path toward actualizing ontology, the natural movement

toward making entities logos by their existential incorporation into the ultimate truth of being in God. It is not a matter of a fall but of an existential and ontological elevation of entities into their true selves, which flows from a dia-logical ontology.

166. *Various Texts* 4.54, PG 90: 1328D–1329B.

167. *Various Texts* 4.55, PG 90: 1329B.

168. *Ambigua*, PG 91: 1329A.

169. See chap. 1.5.

170. *To Thalassius* 15, PG 90: 297B.

171. K. Axelos, *For a Problematic Ethic* (In Greek, Iridanos, 1974), p. 21.

172. See e.g., P. Kondylis, *The Critique of Metaphysics in Mondern Thought* (In Greek, Gnosi, 1983), pp. 24–26. On p. 26 he writes: "Basic metaphysical structures will continue to exist, regardless of how secularized they may become, as long as human beings formulate and believe in normative ethical principles."

173. Axelos, *op. cit.*, p. 26.

174. "*Logopoiisi*" ("making into logos")—the term belongs to Fr. Justin Popović. See his *Man and God-man* (Greek tr. Astir, 4th ed 1981), pp. 15ff.

175. See chap. I.5.

176. *To Thalassius*, PG 90: 517D.

177. *op. Cit.*

178. *To Thalassius*, PG 90: 681CD.

179. *Ambigua*, PG 91: 1400AB.

180. *On the Lord's Prayer*, PG 90: 873D.

181. See *Centuries on Love* 1.100, *Philokalia* II, p. 64: "When the intellect is established in God, it at first ardently longs to discover the principles of His essence, and finds no consolation in His attributes. . . . But it is consoled by the qualities that appertain to His nature: I mean the qualities of eternity, infinity, indeterminateness, goodness, wisdom and the power of creating, exercising providence over and judging creatures." (Translation adapted). Similarly in *Centuries on Love* 1.99: "When the intellect is absorbed in the contemplation of things invisible, it seeks their natural principles, the cause of their generation and whatever follows from this,as well and the providential order and judgment which relates to them." Cf. also *To Thalassius*, PG 90: 572A– 309A–C. *In Centuries on Love* 3.33 (*Philokalia* II, p. 88), we learn that the angelic powers have a more profound knowledge than humans and are able to transmit to them a knowledge "more distinct about divine providence or more precise about divine judgment."

182. Thus Dalmais and Riou have stressed almost exclusively the great significance of Providence in relation to God's "direction" of the logoi in the world. See Dalmais, "La manifestation du Logos," p. 15: "This cosmic revelation of the divine Logos in the logoi of creatures, and what it reveals to us of the Providence according to which the Creator directs them toward their goal, has hitherto never been more than outlined by Maximus." Riou (*Le monde et l'église*, p. 58) writes: "God may be called the *pronoön*, the 'fore-

seer', not by any means as the one who dominates at the top of the pyramid of hierarchies, but as the Providence that bears within it the *logos* and the *Kairos* of every being, even down to the smallest."

183. Sherwood, in his *Maximus the Confessor. The Ascetic Life* (pp. 39ff.) considers that the triad creator—foreseer—judge originates with Origen and Evagrius. Strangely, he considers (p. 39) that Maximus uses these terms more in their moral sense, not in their ontological sense as Origen does (Origen is of course giving the terms an ontological sense in order to express his heretical view that souls "fall" into embodiment, and are brought back into the spiritual realm, through judgement and providence respectively). Our view, which is clearly supported by the texts, is that Maximus preserves the ontological sense of the terms providence and judgment, but now gives it an orthodox interpretation. Sherwood (*The Earlier Ambigua*, p. 170) also distinguishes between a *logos* of essence (which he calls an "ontological order") and a prophetic *logos* (which he regards as a "providential order") relating to the "end" of the creature in either well-being or woe-being. And at this point, Sherwood finds "a basis, a hint of a doctrine of predestination" in Maximus. All our discussion of the texts so far militates against Sherwood's assertion, because it is quite clear that Maximus not only fails to make any such distinction, but to the contrary makes a profound connection between the *logoi* of being and those of providence and judgment, making impossible any sort of abstraction which would isolate some of these *logoi* from the others. It is also clear that God creates all things with the destiny of eternal well-being and none with the destiny of eternal woe-being—otherwise the ontological action of providence and judgment would have no meaning.

184. *To Thalassius*, PG 90: 681D.

185. *Ambigua*, PG 91: 1297A.

186. Already at this point, we will maintain—going against the received wisdom on the subject among western scholars—that the theology of the *logoi* has no connection with the platonic theory of ideas. And the reason lies in the fact that the theology of the *logoi* itself owes its origin to the great attachment in the Confessor's thought to eschatology and not simply to the creation-centered quest for cosmological principles or archetypes—and this eschatology is by no means teleology. It is interesting here to make use of the highly significant methodological distinction made by the distinguished contemporary historian of ancient thought W.K.C Guthrie, in reference to ancient Greek philosophy (see *The Greek Philosophers from Thales to Aristotle* (London: Methuen and Co., 8th ed. 1984). This distinction has to do with the fundamental dualism which can be applied to that philosophy: the distinction between matter and form (in which the notion of function is always included, i.e., teleology), so that ultimately we have philosophers of matter on the one hand, and teleological thinkers or philosophers of form on the other. Teleological philosophies undoubtedly begin with the Pythagoreans, who go beyond the Ionians' cosmological quest for the ultimate stuff of matter in their search for the teleology of order, proportion,

and measure—ultimately, the teleology of the structure of the world math-ematically expressed. This tendency will culminate in a judgment upon the entire philosophical tradition (the "becoming" of Heraclitus, the intellectu-alism of Parmenides, Pythagorean mathematics and Orphic mysticism) in the Platonic theory of ideas—and its subsequent development by Aristotle. The theory of ideas is strictly teleological: essences are created according to stable and static prototypes, and cannot but imitate them in their ephem-eral existence; the sensible world, shadowy and fluid, cannot but be func-tionally and teleologically centered on the ontological necessity of the ideal world, which is the only real world. Here freedom is identified with submis-sion to the absolute necessity of the given form or *telos*, meaning that it does not really exist as such. By contrast, the eschatological ontology of the *logoi* is freedom itself as an ontology, an ontology in synergy, a personal ontol-ogy, as we shall see in detail below. Here essence is called into being by the (free and loving) divine wills-*logoi*, which are not teleological prototypes but eschatological dia-logues between free persons; essence in its natural mode of existence is an eschatological formation, the outcome of a synergy of persons (God and man), as we shall see in the next section. Through His divine *logoi*, God proposes to His creatures their modes of essential exis-tence, but the final outcome depends on their responses. Thus we can speak of a *micro-eschatology*, concerning each one of God's logical creatures, who are invited to realize and fulfill their nature as a *micro-dialog*, i.e., a special and exclusive dialogue between them, as unique personal entities, and God Who thus becomes a God for "them." This was the only way for Maximus and the patristic tradition in general to avoid monophysitism or pantheism. Without this micro-eschatological micro-dialogue, beings simply mirror or reflect God's glory, energy, or logos without assimilating them. Thus they become passive surfaces of reflection instead of concrete essences-in-a-dia-logical-becoming, as we shall later see. So the gulf between the two positions is of dizzying proportions: teleology spells necessity, whereas eschatology spells freedom.

187. *Ambigua*, PG 91: 1149B.

188. See chap. 1.4.

189. J.M. Garrigues, "Le dessein d'adoption," p. 185: "The distinction be-tween logos and tropos, which constitutes . . . the very axis of his theological thought."

190. See Sherwood, *The Ascetic Life*, p. 35: "These *logoi* do not exist in the nude, but each has its certain mode of existence (*tropos yparxeos*). Whatever pertains to the *logos* of a certain nature pertains equally and in-alienably to all who partake of that nature; it is the common. The mode, however, pertains to the person and always refers to the concrete reality; it is the proper." Cf. J. Meyendorff, *Christ in Eastern Christian Thought*, p. 145: "Every being possesses in himself a pre-existent and natural law (*logos phy-seos*) but concretely it exists only according to a mode of existence (*tropos yparxeos*) proper to it."

191. Riou, *Le monde et l'église*, p. 74: "Maximus gradually sketches out, in connection with the *logos* of the creature's essence, a personal *tropos* or mode of existing and realizing the vocation inscribed in its nature." Cf. also Dalmais, "La manifestation du Logos," p. 24, who speaks of "[investigating] the interplay of *Logos* and *logoi* through the *tropos* of their existential realisation."

192. See Sherwood, *The Ascetic Life*, p. 36. Similarly *idem, The Earlier Ambigua*, p. 161: "now the distinction put in this way makes operative a whole range of Aristotelian doctrine in the service of theology." J.M. Garrigues agrees (*Maxime le Confesseur. La charité avenir de l'homme* [Paris: Beauchesne, 1976], p. 106): "[with] the irreducibility of the pair logos-tropos . . . Maximus now prefers to rely on an Aristotelian metaphysic of natures, which seems to him better to safeguard the Christian mystery of the Creation." These views, however, contain only a small part of the truth. Perhaps the most important task accomplished by Maximus work was his eschatological revision of Aristotelianism, especially on the question of "nature." Seen from the side of the uncreated *logos*, nature is now focused, as I have already argued, on the *eschata* and is by no means already a given. From the philosophical point of view, this is literally a revolution, because it dismantles philosophical metaphysics in its entirety.

193. Sherwood, *Maximus the Confessor*, pp. 81–2. This antinomy is certainly modern and cannot be found in Maximus. On the contrary, according to what we have already seen, Maximus refuses to identify nature with necessity. Nature's personal, dialogical and eschatological constitution forbids such an identification. This is why we see Maximus boldly declaring that "the nature of the logical beings is not bound with necessity" (*Disputatio cum Pyrrho*, PG–91, 293C) [Cf. my *Closed Spirituality and the Meaning of the Self: Mysticism of Power and the Truth of Nature and Personhood* (Athens, Ellinika Grammata, 1999)p. 191–204, 281–298]. The eschatological perspective can only be established upon the fullness of nature in space and time, fulfilling it in the grace of the eschatological dialog; but, in this case, we cannot identify nature with necessity any more—in order that the person should become an "ecstatic" outlet which escapes from nature! This mistake, made by some modern Orthodox theologians, turns patristic theology into bad existentialism.

194. G.L. Prestige, *God in Patristic Thought* (London, 1936), p. 245. This view is shared by Sherwood, *The Earlier Ambigua*, pp. 156ff.

195. PG 31: 13A.

196. Letter 235.2, PG 32: 872C. Cf. also Letter 38.2, PG 32: 325ff.

197. Gregory of Nyssa, *Against Eunomius* 1, PG 45: 404.

198. See Sherwood, *The Earlier Ambigua*, p. 161: "Basil and Gregory of Nyssa, seeing the positive aspect of *tropos hyparxeos*, used it only of the Son and of the Spirit, but the Father also has his mode of existence . . ."

199. PG 39: 112BC.

200. PG 75: 697D, 973D.

201. See the brief exposition in Sherwood, *The Earlier Ambigua*, pp. 155–164.

202. See Sherwood, ibid., p. 161.

203. See Lars Thunberg, *Man and the Cosmos: The Vision of St. Maximus the Confessor* (St. Vladimir's Seminary Press, NY, 1985)p.38–39.

204. *Mystagogy* 23, PG 91: 701A. Cf. also *Ambigua* 2, PG 91: 1036C: ". . . first they are illumined as to the principle of its [sc. the Trinity's] being, and thus they are enlightened as to the mode whereby it subsists. . . ." That means that the mode of existence of the Trinity is hypostatic. D. Barthrellos (cf. his work *Byzantine Christ*, Oxford University Press, 2005) criticizes my position. But if we ontologically separate essence from hypostasis, and the latter from its mode of existence, we would then have three ontological elements in God instead of two (hypostases and essence). In Maximus, it is obvious that the notion of the mode of existence refers both to the essence and the hypostases. The question is not about the person who *has* His "mode of existence," separated from Him as a third ontological attribute in addition to His hypostasis and common essence, but we rather say that He *is* His mode of existence *of* the common essence. The whole debate tends to be scholastic, but I think the patristic intention was to maintain the unity and the full reality of the person in His personal attributes, and not to dissolve it into several parts. We must not confuse logical determinations with ontological distinctions.

205. *Ambigua*, PG 91: 1341D. See also Sherwood, *The Earlier Ambigua*, p. 165.

206. See *Ambigua*, PG 91: 1344D: ". . . in accomplishing the truly new mystery of His becoming man for our sakes, he makes [human nature] new as to its tropos and not as to its logos." See also *Disputation with Pyrrhus*, PG 91: 297D–300A: "Everything natural pertaining to Christ has a supra-natural mode joined to its own principle, in order that nature may be guaranteed through the principle and the Economy through the mode." Cf. also Garrigues, "Le dessein d'adoption," p. 185.

207. *To Thalassius* 21, PG 90: 321A and 324C. Cf. also Centuries of Various Texts 4.21, PG 90: 1313A, "the spiritual logoi and modes of salvation."

208. *Opuscula*, 10, PG 91: 137A.

209. We shall see in some detail this ontology of personhood in the next chapter.

210. V. Lossky, *Mystical Theology*, p. 95.

211. Sherwood, *The Earlier Ambigua*, pp. 178–9.

212. Sherwood, *ibid*, p. 173. See similar views in J. M. Garrigues' article "L'énergie divine et la grâce chez Maxime le Confesseur," *Istina* 19 (1974), pp. 272–296. See also his condemnation of "neopalamism" on p. 296.

213. Balthasar, *Liturgie Cosmique*, p. 100; *Cosmic Liturgy*, p. 148.

214. Irenei Bulović, *To Mysterion tis en ti Triadi diakriseos*, pp. 153–4.

215. Riou, *Le monde et l'église*, p. 60.

216. *Opuscula*, PG 91: 200C.

217. *Opuscula*, PG 91: 201AB. Cf. also the passage from Gregory of Nyssa that Maximus quotes and adopts: "It is not possible for things that are divided according to the principle of their nature to concur as to the form of their energies"; and the passage from Cyril: "When the principle of *how* a thing exists is altered, then the principle of its energy in all its aspects would not remain the same either" (ibid., 284BC).

218. Sherwood (*The Earlier Ambigua*, p. 122) regards the force as a "faculty" and the energy or movement as "use of the faculty." The same author (pp. 111–2, 122) considers, on the basis of *Ambigua* 26 (1268A) that Maximus distinguishes two sorts of energy, an "immanent" energy which produces something homogeneous and consubstantial with itself, and a "transitive" energy which produces a product other than its own substance. After such a distinction, it is somewhat paradoxical that Sherwood avoids connecting the *logoi* with the divine energies. . . . On the identification of energy and force in God (in the theology of Mark of Ephesus), see the thesis of I. Bulović cited above (pp. 109ff.). This identification arises out of the synthesis of the force with the energy of God through the divine counsel (p. 113). Again on p. 114 we read, in connection with the question under discussion: "The force is a movement of God's nature toward energy, according to the bold words of St. Maximus the Confessor repeated by St. Mark, while the energy is a movement of the divine force."

219. *Opuscula*, PG 91: 56A.

220. Ibid., PG 91: 36B. Cf. PG 91:137A: "We all possess both logos and its natural energy."

221. PG 91: 1257AB.

222. According to Riou's translation (*Le monde et l'église*, p. 60): "Perceiving in a natural manner all the *logoi* which are in things, in the infinity of which it contemplates the energies of God . . ."

223. Cf. Bulović, *The Mystery*, pp. 121–123, in which he considers divine will and divine energy as a "double-in-one divine reality," according to St. Mark of Ephesus.

224. Cf. St. Gregory Palamas: "When God spoke to Moses, He did not say 'I am the essence' but 'I am He who is'. For He who Is does not come from essence, but essence comes from Him who Is. For He who Is has conceived the whole of being in Himself" (P. Chrestou, ed., *Collected Works* [Thessaloniki 1962], Vol. I, p. 666).

225. On the personal/hypostatic character of the divine energies of the Living and True God in Palamas see the cogent study by Atanasije Jevtić, "The I AM (Yahweh) as living and true God, as St. Gregory Palamas testifies concerning Him," in *Proceedings of the Theological Congress in Honour and Memory of our Father among the Saints Gregory Palamas* (Thessaloniki, 1986), pp. 111–134, esp. pp. 113–126. Specifically on how this position is grounded in the distinction of essence and hypostases in God, see pp. 125–6.

226. Jevtić, ibid., pp. 123–125.

227. For the connection between the theology of the uncreated energies and the Eucharist in Palamas, see Jevtić, "*O On*," pp. 133–134.

228. It is fortunate that some valuable studies have appeared lately which prove the personal/en-hypostatic character of the uncreated energies on the basis of Palamas' writings. One sees, however, an unease about connecting the theology of the uncreated energies with that of the uncreated *logoi*, and this despite the fact that Palamas' work offers such a possibility. But here is precisely the problem: simply proving the "personal" character of the uncreated energies is regarded as considered sufficient to save us from lapsing into neo-Platonism, into "impersonal" energies or emanations, and even the means of ecstatic participation in these which is itself regarded as "impersonal." But after the aforementioned remarks, we easily understand that by "personal" we mean nothing other than "dialogical." And this ontological dialogue between divine *logoi* and human *logoi*, accomplished in Christ, is the only natural context of the circulation of energies.

229. *Centuries of Various Texts* 4.16, PG 90: 1309B.

230. *To Thalassius*, PG 90: 612B–D.

231. *Ambigua*, PG 91: 1252B.

232. *Ambigua*, PG 91: 1108C–1109A.

233. Florovsky, *The Byzantine Fathers*, p. 242.

234. *To Thalassius*, PG 90: 773B. Cf. also *Centuries of Various Texts* 5.19, PG 90: 1356B. Cf. also *Ambigua* 12, PG 91: 1109AB: "In summary, this blessed man has been introduced through reason and contemplation to all the principles of virtue and knowledge embraced by the saints—the principles through which they first encompassed the divine form through their knowledge by an apprehension of God through contemplation, and then through the virtues prudently imprinted that form upon themselves through their reason.

235. *To Thalassius*, PG 90: 258BC.

236. *To Thalassius*, 32, PG 90: 372B.

237. Cf. *Centuries on Theology* 2.90, PG 90: 1168C: "The Kingdom of heaven is an understanding of the pure preeternal knowledge of things according to their *logoi* which are in God; while the Kingdom of God is the imparting by grace of those good things that are by nature proper to God. The first concerns the consummation of existent things; the second is a notional idea of what follows that consummation."

238. *Ambigua*, PG 91: 1156B: "When the sensible sun rises, all physical objects appear clearly at the same time; so similarly, when God, the notional Sun of Righteousness, rises in the mind, in a way known to Him such that the creature is able to bear it, He wills that the true *logoi* of all things intelligible and sensible should appear with Him. A proof of this is the shining of the Lord's raiment at His Transfiguration on the mountain, which joined with the light of his countenance in making Him known, thus bringing together with God, it seems, the knowledge of things below Him and things concerning Him.

239. On the notion of philosophical psychology see Jean Piaget, *Wisdom and Illusions of Philosophy* [Gk 153–200]. Piaget includes under "Philosophical Psychology" all psychology that is not strictly based on scientific and experimental premises: the psychology of the Thomists, dialectic materialists, phenomenologists, Bergsonists, Kantians and rationalists, as well as the whole of psychoanalysis and related schools of depth psychology.

240. *Centuries of Various Texts* 3.40, PG 90: 1277B.

Chapter 3

The Communion of Entities through Their *Logoi*

1. *The Ontological Foundations of Communion*

A.

Maximus's profound sense of the communion of beings is outlined in his remarkable comment to John Cubicularium, where speaking of love he conceives as its utmost achievement the total synthesis of beings in a single identity.[1] This phrase, which takes us directly to eschatology, is the culmination of a long journey of theological contemplation, the framework of which may be eschatological, but the development of which has obvious foundations in Maximus's theory of the *logoi*. The inner principles of entities are by no means impervious entities closed to communication, but on the contrary exist only in relationship, in a communion with each other which unifies the divisions which may appear to exist in creation:

> When the *logoi* of particular things join themselves to the universal *logoi*, they effect unions between things divided. For the more universal *logoi* encompass in a unifying way the *logoi* of the particular, and it is to these [universal *logoi*] that particular things naturally have reference.[2]

This "unitary way" in which the particular essential principles are summed up in the more general creates an ontological "relationality"[3] between the particular and the general, which is the first fundamental expression of the communion between entities. In another work, the Confessor repeats the passage just cited and then goes on:

> And also between intellect and sense, heaven and earth, things sensible and things intelligible, nature and *logos*— between these too there is a *spiritual principle of relationship giving them a unity with each other*.[4]

The "principle of relationship" referred to here, which in another of his writings Maximus will call the "principle of union,"[5] holds together the unity in communion and relationship between intellect and sense, heaven and earth, the sensible and the intelligible, nature and its essential principle. In other words, all these apparent opposites are ultimately found to be in a profound ontological communion, which gives purpose and meaning to their opposition on a secondary level: the point of the apparent contrast is to reveal more profoundly their unity in communion. Division, not having a principle of its own, is for Maximus non-being; it has to be transcended. This is the meaning of the relationality that our author sets out as a crucial ontological characteristic belonging to the very principle of the essence of things.

So Maximus discerns within things the unifying "loving affinity" which is destined to destroy the "dissension and division" which threaten them. Making a parallel between the unity of soul and body and that of things intelligible and things sensible, he speaks in general terms of the unity "of all things in each other," a unity which alone is able to preserve "natural otherness" without confusion:

> . . . in accordance with this [the divine law] *the principle of the unifying force* is implanted, which does not allow the hypostatic identity of these things based on their union to be ignored because of their natural otherness. Nor does it allow the particularity which circumscribes each thing in itself to be a force for dissension and division stronger than the *loving affinity* mystically placed in these things when they are united. The heart of this [loving affinity] is [the fact that] the cause which holds entities together has one universal mode of invisible and unknown presence in all things, being immanent in all in various ways, and making all things to be *unconfused and undivided* in themselves and in each other. And it shows that they belong to each other rather than to themselves, in accordance with their *unifying relationship*.[6]

Things belong to each other more than they belong to themselves, according to the Maximian affirmation of being as gift, the same divine Cause which holds them together being the author of this "unifying relationship." The principle of this unifying relationship is the ontological foundation for the pan-unity of creaturehood, which in its turn preserves the integrity of natural otherness by opening itself up to universal self-offering, which is the natural mode of existence for entities.

Furthermore, this is precisely God's mode of existence in creation, as Maximus tells us in another important passage:

> For having ineffably hidden Himself for us in the inner principles of existent things, He is correspondingly spelled out by each visible thing as by letters: He is wholly present in all together in the fullest possible way and completely in each individually, whole and undiminished; He is in the variety of nature, Who knows no variation and is always the same; He is in things composite, Who is simple and non-composite; He is in things subject to beginning, who is without beginning; the Invisible in things visible, the Intangible in things tangible. For us who are dense of mind, He deigned to be embodied for our sake and to be given form in letters and syllables and sounds, in order that, as we follow Him through all these means, He might swiftly gather us to Himself, unified in spirit; and might lead us to a simple and unfettered understanding of Him, having brought us close together through Himself for the sake of union with Him, even as he extended Himself for us by reason of His condescension.[7]

God's kenotic, loving "extension" or self-offering toward creation leads Him, through His uncreated *logoi*, into the differentiation of creaturehood, its complexity and its subordinate status, the lowliness of its visible and tangible nature—Him who is always the same, simple, without beginning, intangible, and invisible. The purpose of this kenotic condescension is to bring things together into unity in Him, so that when the Last Times come the richness of unity in communion will be brought to completion, "as one divine power manifests itself in all things, in a manner proportionate to each, in a distinct and active appearance, and through itself preserves the bond of union unbroken to the endless ages."[8]

This "gathering" of all creation "in ontological, not moral terms," is in Florovsky's view the essence of salvation as the healing and restoration of creation in Maximus's thought.[9] And as we have already said, the eschatological character of this gathering and communion is of course evident:

> [The result is] that the soul becomes to the body what God is to the soul, and the one Creator of all is shown to enter into all things, proportionately [to each], through humanity, and the many things that differ from one another by nature come into one, inclining together around the one nature of man. And God Himself becomes all things in all, encompassing all things and giving them real existence in Himself, because none of the things that exist any longer has a random movement devoid of His presence. It is by virtue of that presence that we are and are called *gods, and children and the body and members and a particle of God* and the like, in reference to the ultimate end of the divine purpose.[10]

In this passage, in contrast with the Platonic Origenism which takes a negative view of the material world, it seems that St. Maximus looks forward to the salvation of the entire cosmos through its inclusion into human nature, to which God in His turn gives substantive existence within Himself, so becoming "all things in all, encompassing all things and giving them real existence in Himself." The locus of the union of all things, then, is human nature, and this universal communion and relationship has an eschatological character, imaging, as we have seen above (Chapter 1.2) the very inner unity-in-communion of God in Trinity. Maximus uses here the characteristic expressions "gods and children and the body and members and a particle of God," which can receive their actual form now in history only through eucharistic incorporation as described in Chapter 1; for this incorporation stands alone as the principle image of the catholicity of the Church as transcendence of all divisions and "autonomies" within the human Body of Christ, as union of the body with the soul, the cosmic with the human, the intelligible with the sensible, and ultimately the historical with the eschatological—a union where all become reciprocal gifts of love. The Eucharist is thus the manifestation *par excellence* of this ontology of universalization, which has its roots in the fundamental relational character of entities, the uncreated principle of their union, and which receives its eschatological fulfilment as it is actualized within the eucharistic synaxis which realizes being as gift-sharing.[11] And it is precisely this eucharistic actualization of the unity of things that reveals to us the ultimate ontological foundation for their communion: it is that "unity perceived in the Trinity" which the saints "are taught,"[12] and which is realized by grace when God "in a way surpassing knowledge brings [the saints] to the unknown oneness, once they have been unified by grace and assimilated to that oneness by participation, through an identity that is so far as possible indivisible."[13]

B.

In order to appreciate Maximus's incalculable contribution on the subject of the communion of beings, we must first of all be aware that he had assimilated the ancient Greek philosophical way of thinking, and was therefore the first to recognize how far he differed from it on this point. In other words, he recognizes that according to the usual philosophical understanding, "a nature could never commune naturally with another nature; it is devoid of participation, being in essence entirely different from every other nature."[14] And indeed, on this question Plato's exploration of "communion of forms" in The Sophist[15] continues to reign supreme. According to Plato, there are three possible solutions to the problem. Either no form or substance communes with any other (Plato uses the terms metalamvanein ["to partake"], epikoinonein ["to communicate or participate"] and xynarmottein ["to fit together"]); or all things fit together and commune; or some communicate with some others, while others do not. Plato settles on the third solution, and searches for a science or an art to help him find how forms-substances-concepts communicate or fail to communicate with each other. This is the famous dialectic whereby the philosopher is able "to distinguish by classes how individual things can or cannot commune with one another."[16] We have perhaps a continuation of this problem in Aristotle's doubts about whether the generality of Being constitutes a kind. Heidegger, who notes this fact inter alia, concludes that it is consequently questionable whether particular entities can be taken as instances of Being (as "this oak" is an instance of "tree in general"). It is doubtful whether the modes of Being (Being as nature, Being as history) represent "species" of the "genus" "Being."[17] This doubt about communication between the modes of Being and Being itself leads in Aristotle to a complete "division" between them,[18] a division or differentiation repeated by Heidegger; and it does indeed require the tool of dialectic in order to bridge this division philosophically, in part at least.

So here is the remarkably bold step taken by Maximus: while he belongs to the philosophical tradition according to which substances cannot communicate, he renders them communicant and communicable through and in their inner principles—and indeed, in a certain way, totally so. For the natural state of entities is to be in communion and to make constant progress in that communion and in their communion with God through man, as we have seen in the first part of this section. Entities do not exist in the proper sense outside this universal communion ("none of the things that exist has a random movement"), because being means life, which is actualized as a communion "by virtue of which we are and are called gods, and children and the body and members and a particle of God and the like." So Maximus shows in the present case, with his theory of the *logoi* of entities, that God does not think of entities separately or individually, as single monads without windows, as Leibniz claimed. He thinks of them in communion with one another and with Him, a communion that is eschatological, providential, and ultimately eucharistic (eschatological, but having its starting point in history—whenever we use the term "eschatological" in this book, this unity of the "now" with the "ever" is implicit). So he constructs a new dialectic, a theological one this time, which we could call a *"eucharistic dialectic."* This "dialectic," i.e., the modes of the universal inter-communion of beings that makes them mutual gifts, will be the subject of the remaining sections of this chapter.

2. Providence as the Uncreated Foundation of Communion

IT IS ALREADY APPARENT THAT IN MAXIMUS'S THOUGHT, Providence plays a role in forming the union of beings into one communion and carrying out that unification. There is however no shortage of direct references to Providence in his writings, with crucial reference to its unifying operation. For "the purpose of divine Providence is to unify through right faith and spiritual love those who in various ways have been sundered by evil. Because indeed the Savior suffered for this purpose, to gather into one the scattered children of God."[19] The passion of Christ, as the culmination of His Providence, has the aim of gathering together "those who in various ways have been sundered by evil." Evil is the sundering, the destruction of communion, the failure to actualize the fullness of life in communion. The essence of salvation, by contrast, resides in the gathering together, in ontological terms,[20] of scattered beings into the communion goodness of divine love.

Having created all things by His infinite power and brought
them into existence, He sustains them, unites them together
and sets boundaries to them; and by His Providence He binds
them with one another and with Himself, both things intelligible and things sensible. Holding all things together around
Himself, because He is their cause and beginning and end,
He causes them to incline toward each other, diverse though
they are by nature, in accordance with a force of relationship
with Himself as their origin. In accordance with this force,
all are brought into an identity of movement and existence,
an identity without loss of integrity or confusion; for in a primary sense no being is in revolt against any other being, or
divided from any other, by its difference in nature or movement. Rather, everything has come together with everything
else, without confusion, through the one indissoluble relationship and protection of the only principle and cause. This
relationship makes redundant and overshadows all the relationships between entities that may be regarded as particular
to the nature of each. It does this, not by eradicating them
and doing away with them so that they cease to exist, but by
dominating and outshining them, as the whole [dominates]
the parts; or even by manifesting itself as the cause of the
whole, by virtue of which both this totality and its parts naturally exist and appear, because they have their cause in its
totality shining over them. Just as the sun outshines the stars
in both its nature and its strength, so in the case of the parts,
which are effects, their cause veils their existence. For it is
natural that as the parts are known from the whole, so things
caused should literally have their being and be known from
their cause, and should hold their individuality in abeyance
when they are encompassed by their reference to their cause,
and take their quality from the single force of relationship
with that cause, as we have said.[21]

As we study this comprehensive passage, we find first and foremost that
the act of creating out of nothing is fulfilled and brought to completion
in the "binding together" of all things into communion with one another and with the Creator, as a manifestation of His providential power
and the culmination of His work of "sustaining," "uniting together," and
"setting boundaries for" created things, which secures them against fall-

ing back into non-being. In the second place, we observe that the way in which God brings together things that are "by nature diverse" is the unifying force of the common tendency or "inclination" of beings toward Him. As entities incline toward God, they are unified—this is an inclination toward God as cause, beginning, and end. This inclination is a "force of relationship" according to St. Maximus; and here we have another version of what we encountered in the first section of this chapter as a "relationality" of entities through their essential principles, a version that explains the ontological importance of that relationality. The result of this providential "binding together" of entities produced by the "force of relationship," the inclination toward God, is that they progress toward an identity of existence and movement which is on the one hand indissoluble but also preserves otherness; it is "without confusion." This identity transcends all differentiations of essence and movement thanks to an "indissoluble relationship" so profound as to be ultimately a "growing together," albeit "without mingling." In other words, as Maximus insists, the particular essences are not eradicated or done away with, but like a sun the supranatural divine cause of all veils the distinct individual beings, manifesting first and foremost the communal truth of the whole on which the parts literally depended for their existence. So the result of Providence among entities is to bring out their communal unity and their universal inter-communion; to emphasize the communal whole, not at the expense of the parts, but by preserving and giving universal fulfillment to their otherness; by universalizing the parts in a personal way, we might say, in the ontological context of "growing together without mingling." By the action of His Providence which effects communion, God reveals Himself as a "fathomless depth encompassing all things"[22]—encompassing them "by Providence . . . when all have been converted to a state of changelessness by their union with God."[23]

So the life of communion with God and intercommunion among creatures is the life of "changelessness," of incorruption by grace for which the Father "is working till now" as is the Son, as Maximus tells us. In a passage from *To Thalassius*, he tells us that in addition to sustaining the created order, God also effects, through His Providence, the increasing similarity of particulars to universals, until He unites the drive for independence of the particulars to the natural general principle of the rational nature through the movement of those particulars toward well-being, and makes them to be united among themselves and with the whole and to share the same movement, so that the particulars do not have a difference of will from the universals. But *one and the same logos will be seen to pertain to all,* not divided up according to the modes of the things to which it is predicated, and *thus it will show that the grace which deifies all is at work.* It was in reference to this grace that God the Word made man said, "My Father works until now, and I am working": the one works by His good pleasure, the other by doing the work Himself, and the Holy Spirit essentially fulfils both the Father's good pleasure regarding all things and the Son's activity, that through all and in all God in Trinity may be one, manifest in all in a way corresponding to the grace in each of those who are worthy, just as the soul inheres by nature in the whole body and in each of its parts, without suffering diminution."[24]The movement of particular entities toward well-being leads to their universal unification, a state in which "one and the same *logos* will be seen to apply to all," and in respect of that *logos* the various states and orders of entities will be seen as mere modes of existence. Maximus's vision is truly remarkable: the variety of created natures reaches such a communion and union among themselves that, by the operation of the Providence of God in Trinity, the many inner principles of entities become "one and the same *logos*" obviously corresponding to the character of creation as ultimately *one* gift from above. This is brought about, according to the Confessor, by the "grace which deifies all"; it is the deification of entities receptive of deification, "all joined to God and to each other through the Spirit."[25]

So the Father is well pleased, the Son is author of the communion of entities as mutual gift-giving and the Holy Spirit activates this communion; that is to say, He leads entities to deification, including the entire created order in human nature and directing it toward the life-bringing call to communion issued by the Father in Christ. To say that God acts through Providence means that His action is life-giving, providing ever deeper contacts with the life in Christ activated as communion; it is this life alone that makes things truly to be, because true being and communing are now manifestly connected.[26]

This is precisely why Maximus connects Pentecost with the actualization of this ontological communion in accordance with God's Providence. As he writes: "Pentecost [is] . . . the beginning and end of things, and the *logos,* through which all things are by nature composed."[27] In this profound statement, the culmination of divine Providence in which the many principles of entities are brought together and "composed" into one is connected with Pentecost, the universal outpouring of the Spirit, the eschatological event *par excellence* because it is the "beginning and end of things."[28] "The mystery of Pentecost is the direct union with Providence of things which are subject to Providence; that is to say, the union of nature with its *logos* according to the purpose of Providence."[29] Pentecost is, then, an image of the eschatological fact of the full "restoration" of entities in accordance with God's Providence for them and, consequently, the perfect union of natures with their essential principle, the complete "logification" of things, which in turn is identified with their perfect communion in the one "*logos* through which all things are by nature composed." The image of Pentecost, as the eschatological realization of Providence, with the communion of entities in their inner principles refers us directly to the eucharistic recapitulation and realization of this Providence, as we saw in Chapter 1. Precisely because divine Providence works to increase the communion of entities in the Spirit, and the Eucharist is the inexhaustible manifestation of this Providence, the Eucharist is also the supreme realization within history of this communion between beings and God.

3. Christ as the Mystagogue of the (Eschatological) Union in Communion

AT THE CLIMAX OF HIS HIGH-PRIESTLY PRAYER before the Cross, where Christ is praying for all the faithful, He beseeches the Father:

> . . . that they may all be one; even as Thou, Father, art in me, and I in Thee, that they also may be in us, so that the world may believe that Thou hast sent me. *The glory which Thou hast given me I have given to them,* they that may be one even as we are one, I in them and Thou in me, that they may *become perfectly one* [lit. "be perfected in one"], so that the world may know that Thou hast sent me and hast loved them even as Thou hast loved me. (John 17:21–23)

Here the Lord connects perfection with unity,[30] a unity that stems from the fact of the glory of adoption as sons, which Christ grants also to the faithful, in other words the Father's love for the faithful, which is that love with which He loves the Son. This unity in communion, the image of the unity between the Father and the Son, is contrasted with "the world"; but the world, mired in division and discord of every kind, is able through the unity of Christ's disciples to discern in Him the deity of the Son, His mission from the Father. This unity among the Lord's disciples is fulfilled, i.e., their adoption in the Son is completed, when, in Christ's words, He lives within them ("I in them"), while the Father rests in Him. This is the mystery of the "truth" of which the Lord speaks a little earlier (vv. 17 and 19) ("sanctify them in Thy truth," "for their sake I sanctify Myself, so that they also may be sanctified in truth"). So Christ reveals the truth of beings as it exists in the Father, bringing about the adoption of the faithful and, as an expression of that adoption, their unification in communion. The truth of God is manifested in the communion that Christ forms with His friends and brethren in the world.[31]

Maximus does not refer directly to the passages of John just quoted. But the way he develops his thought looks like an exegesis of these passages, and certainly presupposes that the writer has assimilated them. We will look at an extended passage from the *Ambigua* in which Maximus presents the destiny of man as communion and the unifying work of Christ,[32] "in order to recapitulate all things in Himself and fulfill the great counsel of God the Father."[33]

Five great divisions, then, cut through the nature of things. The first is the division between uncreated nature and created nature "which has received its being by becoming." The second is the division within created nature between the intelligible and the sensible. The third is the division of sensible nature into heaven and earth. The fourth is the division of the earth into paradise and the inhabited world. And the fifth is the division of man himself, that "most comprehensive workshop," into male and female. Man wields the "power to unify" the five rifts, and his mission is "through himself to make manifest the great mystery of the divine purpose," as he proceeds step by step, "in an upward movement," toward unifying "the near with the far and the lesser with the greater," a process which is "brought to completion" in God. This is the reason why man is introduced into creation last, "as a sort of natural bond mediating between the extremes of the whole through the parts of which he is composed, in his own person bringing into one the multiplicity of things which are by nature separated from each other by an interval." Man's destiny is gradually to remove the ontological dichotomies "in sequence and in order," starting with removal of the division between male and female through an "utterly dispassionate relationship," by acquiring "perfect knowledge of the *logos* according to which he exists." Next comes the unification of paradise and the inhabited earth through "saintly conduct," followed by the union of heaven and earth, in which the entire sensible creation becomes "one and undivided"; this is attained through "a life in every way identical to that of the angels in virtue." Next he unites things intelligible with things sensible

by becoming equal to the angels in knowledge, in order to
make the entire creation into one creation; for in him, the
science of knowing the *logoi* of entities is not divided between knowledge and ignorance but is equal to [that of] the
angels, not falling short in any way. This is the "science of
knowing" whereby the abundant outpouring of true wisdom
comes upon one in its pure form, so far as is permissible, and
without intermediary bestows on those who are worthy the
unknowable and inexplicable understanding of God.

We see in this passage that knowledge of the inner principles of entities
makes man equal to the angels; and this is the way in which the unity of
creation is restored, because the latter is no longer divided into knowable and unknowable but becomes transparent in its entirety, intelligible and sensible together, once the inner principles which animate it are
known. And finally man unifies created nature with uncreated: "through
love" he makes them "one and the same by virtue of his habitual state of
grace," when, in Maximus's daring words,

in his entirety he co-inheres wholly in the whole of God, and
he becomes everything that God is apart from identity in essence . . . he has acquired as his one and only prize God Himself, who is the end of the movement of all that moves and
the firm and immovable stasis of all who are brought to Him.

Instead of uniting things divided, however, man used the power
given to him for that purpose to deepen the division, "and thereby very
nearly risked pitiably relapsing into non-being." And so God became man,

in order to save man who was lost; to unify in Himself the
natural divisions of the entire [created] nature, *to reveal
those universal* logoi, *expressed in particular things, whereby
the union of things divided naturally takes place,* and so to
fulfill the great counsel of God the Father, recapitulating all
things in heaven and on earth in Himself, in whom also they
were created.

In this passage, we see that the salvation of man is identified with removing the divisions in nature, and that this in turn, being the "recapitulation of all things in Christ," constitutes the "great counsel of God
the Father." What is very significant in this passage, however, is the quite
clear identification made between unifying the divisions in nature and

joining together the particular inner principles of entities, the essential principles through which alone things divided can be united. When
Maximus speaks of unity-communion among entities, he means communion and unity through their essential principles.

By the very fact of His birth from a Virgin, Christ overcomes the
dichotomy between male and female. After "living on earth in a way
befitting man" and enduring His Passion, He rises and by "eating with
the disciples after His Resurrection from the dead" reveals the union
of paradise and the inhabited world, while by His Ascension He unites
heaven with earth, showing that "the entire sensible nature is one according to the universal *logos* in it, eclipsing in Himself the property
of division which sunders it." Next, with His soul and body He passes
through all things sensible and intelligible and unifies the entire created
nature, "showing how the whole creation converges into one in Him in
accordance with its absolutely primary and universal *logos*, which is entirely without division or conflict." And at the end of all this, Christ appears before His Father as man,

> having fulfilled as man in deed and in truth, in unfailing obe-
> dience, all that He Himself as God had ordained to happen,
> and accomplished God the Father's entire plan on our behalf,
> because by misuse we had ruined the faculty given to us by
> nature for this purpose.

The ultimate destiny and plan and Providence of God, the universal unification of all things, is the work of Christ, who is thus the mystagogue
of this eschatological fulfillment of God's Providence. A Providence of
unification, revealing creation as "one," "according to the one, simple,
unbounded and undifferentiated concept of its creation out of nothing,
according to which *all creation can admit of one and the same inner principle, altogether undifferentiated,* as one single gift from God, and one
single gift offered by men back to God, because its nonbeing is tempo-
rally prior to its being." By analogy with the singular call that brought
creation into being out of non-being, the entire creation ultimately
admits of one singular essential principle, without any differentiation
as regards the particulars. The connection made between the absolute
unity-in-communion of the created order and creation *ex nihilo* demonstrates precisely, once again, Maximus's extremely profound understanding of unity. Nothingness is absolute non-coherence; and it is for
precisely that reason that it is non-being. Being is constituted as such
through and in the communion of the particulars with the universal

and in the closing of rifts, as a progress in the communal life of entities ending ultimately in the "altogether undifferentiated *logos*" of creation. Thus we see that Maximus prefers speaking always in ontological language when he speaks of Christ's work and Christ's Cross. A "moralistic" or "legalistic" language concerning "reconciliation" between God and humanity is absolutely strange to him: his own way is to prefer ontology to the legalistic drama of forgiveness, and this is perhaps a paradoxical tendency for his western readers. However, this is the way, as we shall see again later, the Greek patristic tradition perceives not only the Cross, but also the ascetic life in general, i.e., as the *tropos* or the way of achieving the unity between the "meanest" and the "most honorable" things in ontological and not merely moral terms.

As Maximus explains, "To tell the truth, all things coincide with each other"; all those things that have been created by God out of nothing are related and commune and "are identified,"

> and not even the meanest of things is abandoned and left altogether devoid of connection with those that are by nature most honorable. For all things which are distinguished from each other by their particular differences are united by the general identities which they share on the universal level, and are thrust together by some general principle nature so as to become one and the same with each other.

The meanest of entities commune with the most honorable so as to become identical with them, "thrust together" toward "one and the same" general principle of nature. In this respect, that entity in which all the individual entities are joined together is general and one.

At this point the Confessor explicitly reveals his Areopagitic background, referring to Dionysius's treatise *On the Divine Names* and quoting the passage, which he expounds in connection with the participation of the multiplicity of entities in the one, because "there is no entity that does not participate in some way in the one."[34] Balthasar rightly insists that, notwithstanding the use of these texts of Maximus by Scotus Eriugena to support his essentially pantheistic system of emanations, the Confessor himself remains within the bounds of the Council of Chalcedon, rounding out the Alexandrian doctrine of deification with his own doctrine of synthesis.[35]

In what immediately follows, it becomes abundantly clear how the "without confusion" and "without division" function in Christ's work of unification. Just as all the principles of the particulars are contained within the principles of the "universal and general," it so happens that these general principles are held together by wisdom, and the particular principles by "prudence" (*phronesis*). The latter principles open out into the "symbolic variety" of things, and then "are unified by wisdom, receiving the natural union with the general principles which leads to identity." This "natural union" of entities precludes any natural participation in it on the part of the Divine *Logos*; it is a natural union of the nature of creaturehood only. Here we have the "without confusion." The "without division" appears immediately afterwards:

> The wisdom of God the Father and His prudence is the Lord
> Jesus Christ, who holds together the universals of entities by
> the power of wisdom, and contains their component parts by
> the prudence of understanding (*synesis*), because by nature
> He is Creator of all things and exercises providence for all
> things; who also through Himself brings together into one
> things that were divided, putting an end to the warfare which
> exists among entities and binding all things into a peaceable
> friendship and a concord without division, things in heaven
> and things on earth, as the divine Apostle says.

The Lord "brings together into one things that are divided" through Himself; in His providence He "tightly binds" things with wisdom and prudence, without division and equally without confusion, uniting them among themselves and with Himself;[36] He leads them to "peaceable friendship and concord without division," celebrating the mystery of the universal unity of things, their elevation to the glory of adoption by the Father, in Him, which is enjoyed by His friends.

This precisely is the foundation of Maximus's doctrine of deification: that human nature is assumed into the one Hypostasis of the Word, without confusion and without division, and—as a consequence of this assumption—the rifts in nature are closed. This assumption of human nature makes possible the saving work of the Church. The rifts now become reciprocal gifts: male thus become a gift to female, paradise to world, heaven to earth, intelligible to the sensible, uncreated to created, and vice-versa. The Church (which in the fifth chapter of the *Mystagogy* is seen as a type and image of the soul) becomes the bride of the Word, whereupon "that mystery of the unity past words and understanding is accomplished. In this mystery, God will become one flesh and one spirit with the Church, the soul, and the soul with God."[37] At that point, then, as far as the Church-soul is concerned "the *logos* that

conceptually divides it into many will no longer exist, because its head
will be crowned with the first, only and one *Logos* and God."[38] When the
deifying marriage[39] takes place, it does away with notions of divisions of
every kind, as the Church-soul is led through the *logoi* to the "blessed
and all holy marriage bed" of the Word.

Our study so far has made it possible to examine briefly the question of whether or not the Incarnation of the Word was unconditional,
a question that has somewhat divided scholars of Maximus. The discussion centers primarily on the well-known passage in *To Thalassius* 60,[40]
in which the Incarnation of Christ is described as "the goal planned in
advance, for the sake of which everything [exists], whereas it does not
itself [exist] for the sake of anything else." Thus:

> looking to this goal, God brought forth the essences of ex-
> istent things. (. . .) For the union of limit and limitlessness,
> measure and measurelessness, finitude and infinity, creator
> and creation, stability and movement, was presupposed be-
> fore the ages; and this union came about in Christ when He
> appeared in the last times, through itself giving fulfillment to
> what God had foreseen.

Aside from this text, where the doctrine of the non-contingent Incarnation of the Word comes across clearly, there are also other texts from
the saint that support the same view,[41] as well as texts maintaining that
the Fall of man and the need to "save nature" was the precondition for
the Incarnation.[42] Of the scholars in the field, Balthasar considers that
Maximus favors the non-contingent Incarnation of the Word.[43] Similarly, Sherwood seems to incline to the same view,[44] as do Riou[45] and Dalmais.[46] Florovsky, in a meticulous study devoted to this question, also
comes down in favor of this view,[47] as does Radosaljević.[48] Essentially
the only directly dissenting voice is that of A. Theodorou, who considers that, because the idea of a non-contingent incarnation is not purely
scriptural, it is not possible that Maximus should maintain it.[49]

According to the passage of St. John's Gospel quoted at the beginning of this section, only the indwelling of the Divine Word in the
faithful can provide the foundation for their adoption as sons and their
perfection through unity and in unity (which is also a unity of the entire
world, within human nature, as we have seen above). For Maximus himself, only the unconfused and undivided union of God the Word with
created human nature is able to unify creation in its totality and bring
it to the Father; and this union is celebrated, as we have seen, as a mar-

riage between Christ and the Church which unifies and deifies the latter ("the *logos* that in thought divides it into many will no longer exist"). So it is only Christ, as God-man, who elevates the communal character of human nature into an instrument and means of closing the various existential gulfs;[50] only in Him does human nature exist in its authentic ontological form as a "mediator."[51] Consequently, in Maximus's perspective, the very interpretation of the Gospel passage already cited is an indirect yet clear commentary on the presence of the Son and Word of God, as the sole mystagogue of the deifying and unifying communion of entities "in their *logoi*." And this means that without the perspective of a non-contingent incarnation of the Word, the work of divine Providence in effecting communion would make no sense and would be impossible from the start, because (to speak hypothetically) Providence would have to be able to accomplish this task even without the Incarnation, which is, as we have seen, the "ontologically essential" foundation for this providential activity.[52]

At this point, we should further note that according to Maximus, Christ is known precisely in and through the communion He creates. Christ, as the truth of existent things, is their "unification by wisdom," the "peaceable friendship among all things," the "concord without division of things in heaven and things on earth," the mystagogue of communion as well as that communion itself, in other words "our life," as the Apostle says.[53] This "hidden" life which will appear at the end of the ages, and appears already in the Church, "in the breaking of bread"[54] at the Eucharist, is Christ as communion; it is the communion which the Son "Himself effects," while "the Holy Spirit essentially fulfils both the Father's good pleasure regarding all things and the Son's activity, that through all and in all God in Trinity may be one."[55] The cooperation of the Spirit in fulfilling the Son's work of communion provides a crucial link between Christology and Pneumatology, and between both of these and ecclesiology;[56] and this leads us on to a discussion of communion as love in Maximus.

4. Communion as Love. Eucharistic Love

A.

FOR ST. MAXIMUS, THE COMMUNION OF ENTITIES in Christ reveals their true nature; it allows the natural referential character of the inner principles to actualize the "principle of union," revealing in this communality the dimensions of the mode of existence natural to things. Furthermore, the removal of divisions means participation in the life of Christ, in whom and through whom alone are ontological rifts abolished in the Holy Spirit. In "fulfilling" Christ's work of unification and salvation, the Spirit is at the same time constructing Christ's Body, the Church, the place in which God works the union "of the essences of entities, without confusion"[57] and makes the faithful "conjoined and unified with one another" despite the "many and untold differences" between them.[58]

In offering us this authentic, unified world, Christ offers Himself, because He is the incarnate unity of all, and any participation in this unity is a participation in His Body, an experience of being incorporated into the Body of the Lord, that Body which alone is the actualization of the communion of God, man and creation which lives to all ages. And this is a personal communion, in that the Lord is the communion of creaturehood and God within one and the same Person—because God the Word takes human nature into His Hypostasis, His Person, and through human nature the entire creation, according to Maximus. This is why, as we have said before, it is precisely this hypostatic unity of created and uncreated in the one Person of Christ that is transmitted through the Eucharist, by grace, to the entire churched creation. And it is precisely this personal aspect of the union-in-communion of all in Christ that reveals love as the ultimate essence of unity.

> For the most perfect work of love and the ultimate goal of loving activity is to make the properties and names of those bound together in love fitting to each other, by a mutual exchange: to make man God, and to have God called man and manifested as man, through a single identical purpose and movement of the will in both.[59]

Love, having its ontological grounding in the relationality and connection among the *logoi* and the connection of the *logoi* with the one *Logos* of God,[60] is manifested according to Maximus as an absolute coincidence of the movements of the will of rational beings, within the wider existential context of the communion of God and man. For, as Maximus says, "I believe as I received and was taught, that God is love; and that as He is one and never ceases to be one, so He unites into one those who live according to His love, bestowing on them one heart and soul even though they are many."[61] Love, then, is the essence of unity and is a movement of assimilation to God, the will being the instrument by which it acts.

For love persuades the faculty of will to go along with the principle of nature "according to which we can have one mind and one will with God and with each other, just as we have one nature, being in no way at variance with God or with each other."[62] Unity of mind leads to the "simplicity and identity" of communion, through which "they have all been made one with all, and with God even more than with one another, because they possess in their nature and will nothing but the one principle of being shining through them, and the God who is perceived by the mind in that principle."[63] From this last passage we understand that love is that mode of existence which is man's natural movement, a movement in a straight course toward *logos* (his inner principle), authenticated in the profound relationship-in-communion and union of rational beings among themselves and also with God, who is "perceived by the mind"—manifested—in the single principle common to these unified beings.

This supreme manifestation of God in the unity in Christ through love[64] leads Maximus ultimately to identify love with truth, so that love is elevated into the supreme path to knowledge of the "unapproachable beauty of the holy and royal Trinity." Indeed,

> the way of truth is love: the Word of God gave that name to Himself, and those who travel by this way He presents to God the Father purified from all manner of sins. This is the door by which one enters into the Holy of Holies, and is made worthy to behold the unapproachable beauty of the holy and royal Trinity.[65]

In this highly significant passage, Christ is presented as the truth precisely because He is love—which is thus the essence of truth as communion and hence to the only path to knowledge, to "vision" of the truth of the Holy Trinity. Love is the door of entry into the Holy of Holies of the truth of the royal Trinity, precisely because the Holy Trinity "is love."[66] And this vision of God, proceeding from "loving the Lord your God with all your heart and your soul and your might, and your neighbor as yourself,"[67] leads to "being identical with God in goodness insofar as that is attainable for man"[68] and to God "being formed" in each believer.[69]

This is the "regeneration and re-creation in the Spirit,"[70] as the Confessor calls it, which is worked out in the Church as a communion of love at once eschatological and historical—the Church, where historicity becomes the locus of a foretaste of the eschaton and exists as such, so that the eschaton becomes its ontological center without however being identified with it. A regeneration that is worked out as authentic life, a life of being "conjoined and united"[71] in communion and love, in contrast to the danger of separation from God and "falling away into nonbeing." This is made possible by the profound identification of love with Christ,[72] such that

> He is all in all, who encompasses all things within Himself by a simple and infinitely wise power of love, like a central point from which straight lines radiate as from one simple and unified cause and force. . . . The purpose of this is that the creatures and artifacts of the one God should not be in any way alien or hostile to each other, lacking a focus for showing friendship and peace and identity with one another, so that their very being would risk lapsing into non-being because it was separated from God.[73]

For Maximus, lack of communion between entities is identified with their separation from God and return to nothingness. Refusal of communion, then, is non-being, and communion is the only possible way in which being can be actualized, while love as a good and infinitely wise power is the quintessence of the life of beings, actualized as it is in communion.

Love is the reason why communion among entities is the only possible way for them to exist: it is in other words their truth,[74] their true, authentic, and sole mode of existence. It is for precisely this reason that in Maximus, the entire ascetic struggle has as its goal the acquisition of the love[75] that saves and preserves the truth of creation:

> all forms of virtue are introduced, complementing the power of love which brings together things that are divided and re-creates man so that he has one *logos* [for the whole of human nature] and one mode [of being].[76]

The acquisition of love is equally the goal of Christ's commandments: "The entire purpose of the Savior's commandments is to free the intellect from dissipation and hatred and lead it to love of Him and of our neighbor."[77]

The great barrier to actualizing through love the true, communal mode of existence for beings is self-love; this is the "prime sin" according to St. Maximus, the first offspring of the devil and mother of all the passions.[78] Self-love, being antithetical to love, is antithetical to communion, antithetical to truth, antithetical to life. It is the refusal of communion, the lie, death. It is the self-annihilation which stems from ignorance of God and manifests itself as pride, envy, conceit, vainglory, irascibility, murder, anger, deceit, hypocrisy, mockery, malice, greed[79]—the full tragedy of the total division of a being, the multiple fragmentation which annihilates it, casting it into the falsehood which is refusal of communion. Self-love attacks beings using the deception of individual pleasure;[80] it separates people from each other and from God through differences of mind and opinion, divides nature up, distorting its natural mode of existence,[81] produces ignorance of truth and anger toward one's fellow-men,[82] and is supremely and comprehensively summed up in an impassioned and senseless love for the body.[83] Thus self-love is the cause of division in the one essential principle of nature,[84] whereas "perfect love does not divide up the one nature of human beings according to their differences of mind and opinion; but keeping its attention always on that one nature, it loves all people equally."[85] In combination with self-restraint, love[86] and prayer[87] overcome self-love, leading to "unity with God and with each other"[88] as the fullness of life. This practically means that one can love himself only *with* the others and not without them. One can love himself only as a gift to the others as well as he loves the others as gifts to him.

B.

At the beginning of Chapter 13 of John's Gospel we read, by way of introduction to the Last Supper, that the Lord "having loved His own who were in the world, loved them to the end." So the Last Supper (and ultimately the Eucharist) is the completion, the fulfillment of Christ's love, according the Evangelist—of that love which was the essence of His entire work, for the sake of which He now offers His very Self, the Self which "is love." The Eucharist is the end, the *eschaton*, in other words the manifestation (already, and not yet) of the Kingdom of God's love in Christ, the love through which the world was created and in which it finds the fullness of its life according to nature, its ultimate truth. The eucharistic table gives definitive "solidity" to this love; the Eucharist is its ultimate and essential manifestation, the inexhaustible and uninterrupted reality of God's absolute communion in love as gift sharing with the whole world.[89] In Maximus, this evangelical truth is presupposed where he refers to voluntary death "for each other" as the essence of "divine solicitude" and consequently also of human love for each other. Maximus understands love as the sacrifice that makes me a gift for the other:

> To deify us by grace in the same degree that He became man by nature according to His dispensation, in order that we may not only learn to cleave to one another naturally and love each other as ourselves spiritually, but even to care more for each other than for ourselves, which is divine; and to prove this love of one another by being eager to accept voluntary death for each other through virtue.[90]

Christ was the first to offer His life willingly, and this sacrificial and loving divine solicitude resulted in "making peace through the blood of His Cross between those in heaven and those on earth."[91] The peaceable communion of all is due to Christ's sacrificial love and is made a reality "by His blood." And this because the sacrificial outpouring of His blood is the gateway to His Resurrection by which the nature of the created order is made new. This connection with the blood of the Lord Jesus' Cross as an outpouring of His pacific love leads Maximus ultimately to relate the peaceable and joyful communion of all in Christ to the Divine Eucharist: by His precious blood, Christ "showed that there is one festive gathering of the earthly and heavenly powers for the distribution of the divine gifts."[92] The distribution of divine gifts (*theia dora*—this eucharistic expression is a *hapax legomenon* in Maximus's writings) is the "dwelling place" of the festive synaxis of the powers of earth and heaven, the locus of their supreme communion in the Cross and Resurrection, the place where being as gift is ultimately realized, as here it is mystically revealed that "*logos* is the union of things divided, while irrationality (*alogia*) is the division of things that were united."[93] The joining and incorporation of things in eucharistic communion in Christ is thus shown to be the quintessence of their very ontological texture, precisely as participation in the divine life, in the unity-in-communion of the Trinity. "The Lord imparts a share in divine life by making Himself our food . . . ," Maximus continues, still in the same passage; "so that by tasting this food we truly become aware that the Lord is Christ. For by the quality of divinity He changes those who eat of it, deifying them, because He clearly is and is called the bread of life and of power."[94]

In the passages just quoted, it is amazingly clear how Eucharist and communion, Eucharist and love as gift-sharing (in an ontological sense) are linked together in this Father's thought. In His sacrificial love, the Lord goes on to unify through His blood those that were divided, in a communion that belongs to His Resurrection. His eucharistic Body and Blood constantly activate and preserve the communal, "festal" unity of all as an expression of His sacrificial love, proving that the universal reciprocal offering of entities as gifts is the quintessence of the one uncreated inner principle of the creation, in contrast to the "irrationality" of division. When the Lord is distributed and shared out as food in the eucharistic gathering of the faithful, they are being given a share in divine life; they are being introduced to the "divine quality" of God's mode of existence of communion as sharing-in-being,[95] as a process of deification and adoption in Christ.[96] Maximus's ontology is eucharistic, comprehensible sense only through and in the Eucharist: the Eucharist alone causes things to be, because it is the living and active actualization-in-communion of being as the *synaxis*, the gathering of entities by God in the risen Christ, a gathering characterized by mutual love and adopted sonship. It is the very love of God as the eucharistic Body and Blood. In order to distinguish this love of God in Christ, to show its profoundly ontological character in comparison with all the other possible forms of love, we call it "eucharistic love."[97] The love of our Lord Jesus Christ is His eucharistic Body and Blood, and His eucharistic Body and Blood are His love, whereby He maintains the one inner principle of the creation as a communion of love as gift-sharing and Grace, in the likeness of the divine unity.[98]

It was this eucharistic love that we had in mind principally when we spoke above of a "eucharistic dialectic." The "eucharistic dialectic" is eucharistic love in the following sense: just as the "eucharistic dialectic" underlines the fact that God thinks of entities not individually and separately, but in a universal and absolute communion with each other and with Himself, so eucharistic love is the mode of precisely this universal communication between entities, the mode whereby they commune ontologically, incorporated into the ecclesial-eucharistic synaxis. It is the way in which they participate in the eucharistic gifts of the sacrificial love of God in Christ. Through the Eucharist the *logoi* of beings are fulfilled as gifts, in the deep mutuality of reciprocal circulation that confirms their deep communion in Christ. Christ's Eucharistic love makes everything a gift, offered in Him to the Father, and returning, circulating in a manner such that, ultimately, everything becomes God's gift to everyone. Therefore, the whole being is a dialogical/circulating gift, elevating to the Father, descending from Him and being distributed to everyone. This circulation is expressed by what we previously called the "Eucharistic illumination" concerning God's very mode of Trinitarian union.

Thus love for one another is articulated in the Church as participation in the love of Christ, the love manifested in His sacrifice and Resurrection,[99] a love given substance in the eucharistic Gifts. It is kenotic, selfless and sacrificial. At the same time it has a profoundly ontological character, in the sense that it is (exclusively!) the natural flower of the Christian's eucharistic incorporation in the Body of the Lord: it is a eucharistic love, an eschatological event of communion "breaking into" history through the eucharistic synaxis. This love is the "communion of the Holy Spirit" which is constantly "fulfilling" the Body of Christ, His Church, according to the good pleasure of the Father.

At the same time, this is the explanation of Maximus's concept of "eternal well-being" which we encountered in Chapter 2.2: "eternal well-being" is "the only real being," "the only real well-being" and "the only real eternal being." Eternal well-being is the ontological center and ultimate existential basis for all the gradations of being, precisely because it is the *eschaton*, the state of the fullness and fulfillment of the love of God in Christ, the love which is incarnate in the Divine Eucharist as eucharistic love and so enters even into the present age as an eschatological communion between created and uncreated in Christ. Eternal well-being is the perfect eschatological communion of love between created and uncreated, thanks to which things move and have their being even in the present age.

5. Asceticism as the Existential Foundation for Communion

AS WE HAVE ALREADY SHOWN, the aim of the spiritual life is to defeat the all-embracing passion of self-love and acquire the love which, as we have seen, is "the door through which one enters into the Holy of Holies," and leads to "being identical with God in goodness insofar as that is attainable for man." Thus the primary definition of asceticism according to Maximus is the obedience of man's gnomic will to the loving call to communion addressed to him by Christ, as He celebrates the mystery of gathering into His Body those who were divided, through His sacrificial love.

The most comprehensive passage that I know of on the subject in Maximus is as follows:

> The human self-love and cleverness which has led people to reject each other and circumvent the law has fragmented our single nature into many particles. It has introduced the insensibility which now pervades human nature, arming nature against itself by means of the gnomic will. Hence anyone

who by sober reasoning and nobility of mind has succeeded in destroying this anomaly of nature has shown mercy first of all to himself. For He has made his gnomic will accord with nature, and through his nature has joined himself to God in his gnomic will. He has shown in himself the mode whereby the principle of being in the divine image [is realized]; he has shown how in the beginning God fittingly created our nature to be like Himself, as a manifest image of His own goodness, and made it at one with itself in every way—a stranger to strife, peaceful, free from factionalism, tightly bound together both with God and within itself, by a love whereby we cleave to God in desire and to each other in fellow-feeling.[100]

To the extent that people's self-love has fragmented human nature into many "particles," introducing at the same time the "insensibility" of indifference to this division, it has turned our nature against its own self by means of the gnomic will. The ascetic is one who has "sober reasoning and nobility of mind," and whose aim is to use these qualities to destroy this "anomaly of nature." So he brings the gnomic will into harmony with nature, thus allying himself with the will of God who created human nature and manifesting the mode of existence natural to the principle of our nature, which means being "in the divine image." That means manifesting a spirit of communion "alien to strife, peaceful and free from factionalism" which, as a fundamental ontological characteristic based on love, is the natural state of beings inasmuch as it "tightly binds" our nature within itself and to God, unifying it and making peace. The work of love is to preserve communion, because it generates "desire" toward God and "fellow-feeling" toward each other. Thus it changes persons into reciprocal gifts.

Asceticism, therefore, is for Maximus the existential personal foundation of communion. Through it, the human being joins himself to the loving communion of the risen Body of Christ, and by the virtues makes his gnomic will one with God's good pleasure for the world. The ascetic's basic *modus operandi* is to rid himself of "the desire for pleasure and the fear of pain,"[101] because "we love the passions on account of pleasure, and we avoid virtue on account of pain."[102] Pleasure and pain, according to Maximus, constitute "evil self-love" and must be transcended in order for the Christian to attain to "good and spiritual self-love," a state separated from affection for the body in which "we never cease to worship God, seeking from God the sustenance of our soul."[103] The ascetic goes beyond the "surface" of things;[104] he wants to see the inner principles of things actualized in accordance with their nature, seeking to establish the powers of his soul in accordance with the inner principles of entities that are in God.[105]

Asceticism is grounded in the help of "the grace of the Holy Spirit" and "one's own toil and diligence,"[106] and proceeds by "joining and interweaving"[107] the intellectual operations of the person (joining "rationality with intellect, prudence with wisdom, action with contemplation, virtue with knowledge, faith with enduring knowledge"). It unifies the soul by bringing it into the unity of all things in Christ and leads to ever deeper union with God, "the true and good and one and only,"[108] in the ecclesial body of Christ. The important point here is that the ascetic—the Christian—acts in total obedience ("joining himself to God in his gnomic will"), so imitating the obedience of Christ and joining to his own individual will to God's will. For Maximus, there is a concrete ontological framework for asceticism. Asceticism is the route whereby (by realizing God's divine *logoi* in his life as personal acts) one personally becomes part of the universality of being as gift which is in Christ through acquiring selfless eucharistic love; it is the existential method of being personally incorporated into the Body of the Lord, inasmuch as only what can be assumed by the Lord is valid and true.[109] Christian asceticism, then, is profoundly communal;[110] it is quite literally valid only as an existential foundation or precondition for communion, inasmuch as any spiritual act within the Church body is valid only to the extent that it can be incorporated by Christ and "transferred" by Him "into the place of that part [of the Lord's Body] which has been spiritually eaten [in the performance of that act], according to the harmonious disposition of the body,"[111] preserving and reinforcing the harmonious communion of the members of the Body.

Through his obedience, the ascetic removes himself from the immediacy of the surface of things in order to fulfill God's good pleasure for the world, which is for it to be given life within the eucharistic universality of being as gift of the ecclesial body. Asceticism is the longing to acquire personal universality by participating in the "eucharistic love" of Christ.

6. Cosmological Unity

WHAT IS THE EXTENT OF THE CHURCH'S TASK and, in consequence, what are the limits of Christ's eucharistic love according to Maximus? The Confessor's interest in cosmological interconnections between Church-

God-world and man is very intense, and certainly not confined to his *Mystagogy*. This is quite natural because, as we have seen above, the inner principles of entities have an innate "relationality" which leads them to ever greater "unions," where the "more specific" species are contained within the "more general" until the one unitary principle of creation appears, because "all creation can admit of one and the same inner principle, altogether undifferentiated."[112]

This last can come about, however, only in Christ and through Christ, and indeed only through the human nature of Christ. Indeed, as we saw above, Christ is able to accomplish the healing of the five natural rifts because He *also* has a human nature:

> Because He has a body and senses and a soul and an intellect like us, and through these parts of Himself has reconciled each extreme to that part to which it is related. . . . In a manner befitting to God He has recapitulated all things in Himself, showing the entire creation to be one, like another [sort of] human being.[113]

Christ works through His human body, His senses and His soul, using these to make the corresponding parts of creation His own and ultimately recapitulating all things in Himself. The phrase Maximus uses is characteristic: Christ unifies the entire creation; He makes it one "like another sort of human being." The unification of creation, then, is identified with a certain sort of "humanization," in the sense that "the many things which differ from one another by nature converge around the one nature of man."[114] The whole of the rest of creation converges on man and is contained in him; through his mediation,[115] and specifically by his soul becoming for the body, and by extension for the world, what God is for the soul, God proceeds to sanctify the entire world through man's soul and body.[116] Thus by taking flesh, the Word has literally "encompassed all things and given them real existence in Himself," because "God Himself has become all in all,"[117] precisely through the true and full human nature which he assumed. This was man's original goal, in which he failed and to which he was restored in Christ:[118] it was for this "microcosm"[119] to make the world into a "macroanthropos,"[120] enhypostatized in the Word. In unifying the world through his love and bringing it to God in accordance with His Providence, man would fulfil God's will in the world, leading the world to its eschatological fullness; thus the micro-eschatologies of the little things are fulfilled.

When the body will be like the soul and things sensible like
things intelligible in beauty and glory, with one divine power
manifesting itself in all as a clear and active presence, proportionately to each, and through itself preserving the bond
of union unbroken to the endless ages.[121]

The comparison and parallel between man and the cosmos is certainly not original; as Riou says, it is already a commonplace in the time
of the ancient philosophers.[122] And indeed, we think that for Maximus
its interest lies not so much in the philosophical value of such compari-
sons, but rather in the theological foundation they provide for a cosmological communion mediated by man. We saw above (Chapter 3.5)
that communion is the fruit of an ascetic obedience to God's calling, in
Christ, to communion in the Eucharist. In Maximus, then, cosmological unity is something that occurs exclusively and solely in and through
Christ; and in consequence, man is brought into play in this process
exclusively through ascetic obedience to God's good pleasure, according
to which the world is to be given life within the eucharistic universality
of the ecclesial body. In consequence, cosmological unity is both the
fruit of our personal ascetic journey toward becoming part of this universality in Christ and the framework for that journey. This amounts to a
universal "personalization" of the cosmos, as we shall see in the following section, because the unity of things is possible only when they are
totally offered to God by man the priest, within a nexus of relationships
of communal reciprocity.

7. The Person as the Locus and Mode of Communion among Entities

MAXIMUS HAS ASSIMILATED the identification of hypostasis and person
found in the Trinitarian theology of the Cappadocian Fathers;[123] and this
leads him, in our view, to a profoundly significant theory of the person
as the authentic locus and mode of existence of the entire cosmos, and
thus ultimately of its salvation in Christ. We have already seen this Father applying the universality of the Church to the concrete existential
structure of each Christian, in Chapter 4 of the *Mystagogy*; in Chapter 7
of the same work, we saw the cosmos as "macroanthropos," and man as a
"microcosm" which effects the salvation of the world when he brings it as
a priestly offering to God. From the Cappadocians doctrine of "person"

in Trinitarian theology we pass on, through Maximus, to a heightened
emphasis on the significance of the Person of Christ for the salvation of
the world; for the person of Christ is the locus, existentially and ontologically, of the mystery of *Enhypostatization*.[124] Indeed, Christ assumed
human nature into the Hypostasis of the Word, into His Person; and as
we saw in the previous section, through human nature He also assumed
the entire creation "like another sort of human being." The incorporation of the entire cosmos, *via* human nature, into the mystery of the
hypostatic union of man and the Word[125] makes it "one in hypostasis"[126]
with the Word, giving it a place in the existential framework of the personal communion of man and Divine Word in the person of the Word.
This is of course the ultimate fulfillment of the communality of the inner
principles of entities with each other and with the Divine Word in that
it heals the rifts and divisions in nature, as we saw earlier. The Person
of Christ, then, is the *locus* of the healing of natural divisions, and in
hence the *locus* whereby the inner principles of entities achieve fullness
and exist according to nature. For because things possess a mode of existence as well as an essential principle, their authentic mode of existence
is given them in the mystery of their enhypostatization in the person of
God the Word *via* His human nature.

As we have seen above, the mode of existence of the Divine Word
incarnate is expressed as free, selfless and sacrificial love, out of his filial
loving obedience to the Father, through which He refers everything to
Him—a love which makes peace among divided beings "by the blood
of His Cross" and secures for all ages the "festival" of this union through
the "divine gifts" of the Eucharist. Through this sacrificial and kenotic
love of His, the Person of Christ, the incarnate personal Divine Word,
thus becomes also the *mode* of authentic communion among beings,
their "way," by grace, to the unity-in-communion of the Trinity.[127] Thus
Christ, through His love, is the truth and the life of the world and the
sole *mode* whereby the universal union-in-communion of all things as
gifts is fulfilled in His Church.[128]

In the degree to which man aligns himself, through his ascetic obedience, with the will of God as Christ reveals it in action in the universality of His ecclesial Body—to that degree he is incorporated into the
Body of the Lord and by grace enjoys the personal communion with God
the Word which makes him a person, within a relationship of true reciprocity in love. For Christ gives the Christian, by grace, His own mode
of existence as son of the Father, through the mystery of His hypostatic
union as it is extended by grace to man and the creation through the

Church. Man becomes a person, then, inasmuch as he in turn is formed into the likeness of Christ, the locus and mode of communion among entities—that is to say, a personal being. This process begins of course with baptism, the mystery of new birth,[129] of man's adoption by God, which gives him a new hypostasis, according to the spiritual logos of his biological nature[130]—this is his personal incorporation in the Body of the Lord.[131] Thus man participates by grace in the personal mode of existence of God the Word. This participation by grace in the mode of existence of the human nature of the incarnate Word makes man the locus in which "the many things that differ from one another by nature converge around the one nature of man."[132] But in order to receive, express, and preserve this personal existence voluntarily and by his free will, man needs to participate in the sacrificial personal love of the Lord, a participation born of his decisive victory over self-love and adherence to Christ's kenotic mode of existence. Thus the Christian's participation in Christ's personal mode of existence is completed by grace, making him into a personal, i.e., ecclesial being, the locus and mode of authentic existence for the entire cosmos, the minister of the profound communion between creation and God which is inaugurated by Christ. Man is then doing Christ's work in the world, a work accomplished "with the Holy Spirit essentially fulfilling both the Father's good pleasure regarding all things and the Son's activity."[133] That is to say that man participates through askesis in the eucharistic love of Christ, being made into a person through his partaking by grace, in the Holy Spirit, in Christ's mode of existence.

The reality of the person is and will forever remain altogether inaccessible to philosophy,[134] however much there have been brilliant premonitions of it at various times in the history of human thought. It is a reality that is profoundly ecclesial, eucharistic. It is hardly possible, then, to produce a philosophy of the person, a (more or less metaphysical) Christian personalism.[135] The person can be approached only within the experience of participation in the eucharistic love of Christ, the eschatological communion of gift-sharing in the Holy Spirit; only the divine love of Christ, as it is preserved in genuine ecclesial experience, is able to reveal the reality of the person. The person exists within the eucharistic synaxis and, as we have said earlier,[136] constitutes the spiritual reality in which the inner principles of entities become "gifts offered" by man to God and "gifts bestowed" by God on man, and things thus fulfil their natural function, their authentic "mode of existence." This is precisely what is meant by universal "personalization" of the world within the ecclesial-eucharistic experience: entities become part of a relationship of loving personal/dialogical reciprocity between man and God (and among human beings themselves) by becoming reciprocal gifts, which form precisely that reciprocal personal relationship of love which preserves the "supreme union" of entities with God—or, as Maximus says, the simultaneous "identity and otherness"[137] of persons.

So the existential manifestation of the inner principles of entities as powers of the soul,[138] an eschatological reality, finds its fullest ontological definition in this process whereby man becomes a person. The faculties of the soul find their ultimate truth and are "socialized" when they are identified with the inner principles of entities, precisely through the Christian's ascetic obedience to the will of Christ which leads him to acquire by grace, through the Holy Spirit, the personal mode of existence of the Lord. So for man to be made person means that he is "made *logos*" in the image and likeness of God, in the sense we have seen above. Christ is the beginning and the catalyst for communion in creation, the well-spring of communion, its only ontologically absolute definition—the being-as-gift of entities is profoundly and absolutely Christocentric. Personal communion exists exclusively in Christ, who is in personal communion with the Father and the Spirit. The Christian's progress in the Spirit toward the personal mode of existence proper to Christ—his gradual incorporation into the body of the Lord—is his deification, his "perfecting without end" as a participation by grace in the personal, loving and living communality of God in Trinity.[139]

Notes

1. PG 91, 404B. Cf. John Chrysostom, PG 62:16A, where God's renewal of all things is equated with "uniting all things."

2. *To Thalassius* 48, PG 90:445B.

3. Cf. *Mystagogy*, Summary, PG 91:708B: ". . . the ingathering and relation of the many different *logoi* to an entirely comprehensive *logos* . . ."

4. *Centuries of Various Texts* 2.64, PG 90:1244C.

5. *Opuscula*, PG 91:108C.

6. *Mystagogy* 7, PG 91:685AB.

7. *Ambigua*, PG 91:1285D–1288A.

8. *Mystagogy* 7, PG 91:685C.

9. G. Florovsky, *The Byzantine Fathers*, p. 236: "St. Maximus explains Christ's redeeming work as the restoration, the gathering of all creation in ontological, not moral, terms."

10. *Ambigua*, PG 91:1092C.

11. Although Balthasar sees that "the Body is only unified through the Eucharist" (*Cosmic Liturgy*,Communio-Ignatius, p.324), he seems to fail to see how the latter is intrinsically linked to the very ontology of the communion of things.

12. See above, chap. 1.2.

13. *Mystagogy* 13, PG 91:692CD.

14. *Opuscula*, PG 91:108CD.

15. *The Sophist*, 251B–254B.

16. *The Sophist*, 253E.

17. M. Heidegger, *Introduction to Metaphysics*, p. 68.

18. Aristotle, *Metaphysics* XII.vii, 1027ab: "It moves in this manner: the object of desire and of thought causes motion: it causes motion without being in motion. . . . That the final cause may apply to immovable things is shown by the distinction [of its meanings]."

19. *Centuries on Love* 4.17, PG 90:1052B.

20. The phrase is Florovsky's: see above, note 9.

21. *Mystagogy* I, PG 91:664D–665B.

22. *Mystagogy* I, PG 91:665C.

23. *To Thalassius*, PG 90:625C.

24. Ibid., 272A–C.

25. *To Thalassius*, PG 90:272D.

26. Cf. John Zizioulas, *Being as Communion*, p. 105, where the author claims that ultimately "communion becomes identical with being." We consider that in Maximus there is a connection of being with communion. However, this does not mean that we do not also have an emphasis upon the otherness of entities. We must be very careful when we identify, as Zizioulas does, being with communion, as we shall later see. According to Maximus, we cannot say that being *is* communion, but rather that being is *in* communion. The difference is enormous, as we shall see. This latter aspect also involves "becoming" in ontology; only in this way communion is something freely achieved, step-by-step, in space and time, and not something dictated or imposed upon beings. When we identify being with communion, as if being automatically reflects its heavenly archetype, we lose all the existential dimension of this possible achievement, and we also lose the way of a possible verification of it.

27. *Various Texts* 5.46, PG 90:1368C.

28. On the connection of Pentecost with eschatology and with unity see John Zizioulas, *Being as Communion*, p. 112: "Through the outpouring of the Spirit, the 'last days' enter into history, while the unity of humanity is affirmed as a diversity of charisms." And he continues: "The objectivisation and individualization of historical existence which implies distance, decay and death is transformed into existence in communion, and hence eternal life for mankind and all creation." On the connection between Pentecost and eschatology, see John Zizioulas, *Dytiki Theologia* (notes from the supplementary course, 1986), p. 47.

29. *Centuries of Various Texts* 5.49, PG 90:1369A.

30. In its literal sense, of course, this has to do with perfecting the unity of the faithful. But this perfecting of unity is an indication of perfection, because it expresses the fullness of Christians' adopted sonship in Christ.

31. Cf. Heb 2:11–12: "For He who sanctifies and those who are sanctified have all one origin. That is why He is not ashamed to call them brethren, saying, I will proclaim Thy name to my brethren, in the midst of the congregation I will praise Thee."

32. See Balthasar, *Liturgie Cosmique*, pp. 203–208; *Cosmic Liturgy*, pp. 271–5; Riou, *Le monde et l'église*, pp. 146–159; Garrigues, «Le dessein d'adoption», p. 185; Florovsky, *The Byzantine Fathers*, p. 230; Meyendorff, *Christ in Eastern Christian Thought*, pp. 142–143 and 138. L. Thunberg deals with the question at length in his *Microcosm and Mediator*, pp. 373–427. See also I. H. Dalmais,"La fonction unificatrice du Verbe Incarné dans les oeuvres spirituelles de Saint Maxime le Confesseur," *Studia Patristica* 14 (1962), pp. 445–449, and I. Hausherr, *Philautie*, pp. 163ff.

33. The text comes from the *Ambigua*, PG 91:1304D–1313B. All the quotations that follow, up to the next reference to the works of Maximus, are taken from this passage.

34. The text, as quoted by Maximus, is as follows: "For there is no multiplicity that does not have some sort of participation in the one: for that which is many in its parts in one in the whole; that which is many in accidental qualities in one in subject; that which is many in number or in its faculties is one in species; that which is many in species is one in genus; that which is many in its processions is one in origin—there is no entity that does not participate in some way in the one." *On the Divine Names* 13.2, PG 3:980A.

35. Balthasar, *Liturgie Cosmique*, p. 207; *Cosmic Liturgy*, pp. 274–5: "In this way, Maximus has built the Alexandrian doctrine of divinization into his own theory of syntheses by removing its Neoplatonic and spiritualist sting. In the form in which he presents it, there is not the slightest danger of pantheism. It is of course true that Scotus Eriugena must have built his own system directly on texts such as this. But the pantheistic tones that he added to it through his theory of four natures are not present in Maximus. The East's instinct for divinization is held in check here by the Chalcedonian term 'unconfused' (*asynchytos*)." Cf. Riou, *Le monde et l'église*, p. 149: ". . . a hierarchical vision of the connections between the world, man and God is replaced by a scheme of *perichoresis* rooted in Chalcedonian Christology." Balthasar (ibid.*)* finds in the Alexandrian theology of the Areopagite and Evagrius Ponticus Maximus's main teachers for his view of the synthesis of ontological distinctions in Christ (in relation to Evagrius, this was first noted by M. Viller, "Aux sources de la spiritualité de saint Maxime: les oeuvres d'Evagre le Pontique," *Revue d'Ascétique et de Mystique* 2 (1930), pp. 156–184, 239–268). Meyendorff, however, regards Athanasius as the direct precursor of Maximus in this instance (*Le Christ dans la théologie byzantine*

[Paris: Cerf, 1969], p. 194). Cf. D. Staniloae, *Eleftheria, Prosefchi, Agiotita* (Athens: Leimon, 1980), pp. 105ff.

36. Cf. the parallel passage in *To Thalassius*, PG 90: 436AB, where it is said that Christ "showed the nature of things generate to be one, mystically conjoined according to some *logos*," by progressively healing its divisions, and then "united created nature with the uncreated according to a *logos* and a mode surpassing nature."

37. PG 91:681A.

38. PG 91:681B.

39. PG 91:681B. Cf. G. Florovsky, *The Byzantine Fathers*, p. 243.

40. PG 90:621BD.

41. See *To Thalassius* 22, PG 90:317B–321C; ibid. 54, 532AB; *Ambigua*, PG 91:1097A–D.

42. *To Thalassius* 63, PG 90:692B. Cf *Ambigua*, PG 91:1040B, etc.

43. *Cosmic Liturgy*, pp. 271-2.

44. Sherwood, *Maximus the Confessor. The Ascetic Life*, p. 72.

45. Riou, *Le monde et l'église*, pp. 92ff.

46. I.H. Dalmais, *Introduction*, p. 14.

47. G. Florovsky, "*Cur Deus homo?*," in *Creation and Redemption*, pp. 163–170.

48. A. Radosaljević?, *The Mystery of Salvation*, pp. 181–196. See also *idem*, «Le problème du 'présupposé'», in *Actes*, pp. 193–206.

49. A. Theodorou, «*Cur deus homo?* Unconditional or Conditional Incarnation of the Divine Logos» (A commentary on the theology of St. Maximus the Confessor), *EEThSPA* 19 (Athens, 1972), pp. 297–340.

50. Cf. G.M. Garrigues, "Le dessein d'adoption," p. 189.

51. Cf. A Riou,. *op. cit.*, p. 158.

52. We do not of course think that this means that there are after all two conflicting views in the Confessor's writings, as the majority of scholars would have it. Careful study of the texts quoted convinces us that the non-contingent Incarnation of the Word does not at all preclude the idea that the Incarnation takes place because of the need to save the world. We have seen in the texts that the task of eschatologically joining entities in communion was entrusted to man. Man's failure leads God the Word to take on this task Himself. This allows Maximus to speak of God's intervention in order to save creation. On the other hand, however, the ultimate aim of creation and its sole ontological justification is its hypostatic union with the Divine Word through human nature (because it is precisely this hypostatic union that is "passed on" by grace to the created order as well through the Church by means of its Mysteries, especially the Eucharist)—whether this takes place through direct human initiative or through Christ. So when the Confessor has in mind this absolute "necessity" for the Incarnation, he speaks of a non-contingent Incarnation of the Word. When he is attributing the particular way in which the economy of the Incarnation took place to man's failure to accomplish Christ's work himself, by closing the ontological gulfs and

becoming one with the Divine Word so as to be deified, he talks about God's intervention "to save nature." The two positions are complementary to each other, but that of a non-contingent Incarnation is the foundation for eschatology.

53. Col 3:4: "When Christ who is our life appears, then you also will appear with Him in glory."

54. It is characteristic that in Acts 2:42, the communion ("fellowship") of the faithful and the eucharistic breaking of bread are placed side by side: "they devoted themselves to the Apostles' teaching and to the fellowship, the breaking of bread and the prayers."

55. See above, p. 20.

56. Cf. Riou, *op. cit*, p. 127: "Thus the Spirit is creation in God in the body of Christ."

57. *Mystagogy* I, PG 91:668C.

58. Ibid., 667D.

59. *Letters*, PG 91:401B.

60. See Staniloae, *Eisagoge*, p. 23.

61. *Letters*, PG 91:613A.

62. *Letters*, PG 91:369C.

63. *Letters*, PG 91:400B.

64. Cf. *Letters*, PG 91:400CD: ". . . having in view the altogether unique *logos* of our nature which has to do with unchangeable likeness, the *logos* in conjunction with which we know that God appears . . ."

65. *Centuries of Various Texts* 1, 37–38; PG 90:1193A.

66. 1 Jn 4:8: "He who does not love does not know God, for God is love." Cf. G.M. Garrigues, *Maxime le Confesseur. La charité avenir divin de l'homme*, pp. 185ff.

67. *Letters*, PG 91:401C.

68. Ibid.

69. *Letters*, PG 91:401B.

70. *Mystagogy* I, 667C.

71. *Mystagogy*, 667D.

72. cf. N. Matsoukas, *Kosmos, Anthropos kai Koinonia kata ton Maximo Omologiti* (Athens: Grigoris, 1980), pp. 255–259.

73. *Mystagogy* 1, PG 91: 668AB.

74. In this way, love enters the field of ontology. This ontological dimension of love is essentially absent from the works of the some of the most important Maximian scholars, such as Riou, Thurnberg and Balthasar. This dimension is missing even in Sherwood's aforementioned work *St. Maximus the Confessor: The Ascetic Life.The Four Centuries on Charity*, although he claims that "charity for Maximus is as catholic as the Church" (p. 97).

75. On this point, Radosaljević agrees (*To Mysterion tis Soterias*, p. 130): "For St. Maximus, then, love is the key to all the problems of his ascetic doctrine." It is essential to note here that this connection of love with askesis is usually missing in the works of modern Orthodox eucharistic theologians.

Maximus obviously takes a different path. Without askesis no eucharistic illumination can occur as askesis is exactly the expression of our free and loving will, as we shall shortly see.

76. *Letters*, PG 91:400A.

77. *Centuries on Love* 4.56, PG 90:1060D.

78. *Letters*, PG 91:397C. Cf. G.M. Garrigues, *Maxime le Confesseur. La charité*, pp. 176ff.

79. *Letters*, PG 91:397CD. Cf. Hausherr, *Philautie*, p. 10.

80. Hausherr speaks of the law of self-love, which is dependent on pleasure divorced from God (*Philautie*, p. 86).

81. Cf. Hausherr, ibid., pp. 88ff.

82. *Letters*, PG 91:396D–397A.

83. *Centuries on Love* 3.8, PG 90:1020A. But for Maximus there is also a "good self-love." See next chapter.

84. *To Thalassius*, PG 90:725A.

85. *Centuries on Love* 1.71, PG 90:976B.

86. *Centuries on Love* 3.8, PG 90:1020A. Cf. G. M. Garrigues, *Maxime le Confesseur. La charité*, p. 180.

87. Hausherr, *op. cit.*, pp. 104ff.

88. *Letters*, PG 91:397C.

89. Cf. A. Schmemann, *The Eucharist*, p. 213.

90. *To Thalassius*, PG 90:725C.

91. *On the Lord's Prayer*, PG 90:877AB.

92. Ibid., 877B.

93. Ibid., 877BC.

94. Ibid., 877C.

95. On love as an "eschatological birth in Trinitarian life" see G. M. Garrigues, *Maxime le Confesseur. La charité*, p. 195. Here, however, the eucharistic-ontological approach is absent.

96. See chap. 1.4, above.

97. This essential dimension of love, which makes it an ecclesiastical charisma, is almost completely absent from the works of Maximian scholars.

98. How long will our usual hasty reading of the text be able to scan with the dispassionate eye of the biblical scholar explosive lines such as those of John 6:47–58, in which the Lord offers Himself as eucharistic bread? St. Maximus, like all the holy Fathers, reads existentially, with his entire being. Here faith is the action of eating the Bread-Christ. Eating is eternal life when what is eaten is He who gives Himself "for the life of the world." Christ is the life of the world because He is the God and Son of man who offers Himself out of love. Because He loves the world with perfect love, He is the supreme gift to it: its real food. The food of the world is love, the love of the living Father which gives life to the Son, the love of the Son which gives life to the world: "As the living Father sent me, and I live because of the Father, so he who eats me will live because of me" (v. 57). In order to live, the world feeds

eucharistically on the love of Christ, on Christ-love. What more can one say about the profoundly paradoxical verses 54–56? No natural experience of nourishment or super-nourishment could be life eternal if that nourishment were not love as gift-sharing, meaning the only eternal love of the Father in Christ. This is why the Confessor's spirit-filled reading of Scripture (which in this case conflates the Areopagite and Gregory of Nyssa, broadening the horizon all the time) does not see in the Eucharist an impersonal, albeit supranatural, relationship of feeding (i.e., something mechanical or magical), but precisely the most rational, the most personal thing there can be: a realized ontology, a rational, free communion of love with love, of freedom with freedom, of gift with gift, of person with person. Only as a deiform person can one truly partake, and indeed one constantly become more profoundly a person. Only thus can one commune as a psychosomatic unity, in freedom and truth, with the supreme uncreated love: here and here alone is the place of ontology, here is the foundation of the theory of the *logoi*. This is why, in Maximus's thought, the eucharistic relationship with the Lord is a "eucharistic enlightenment," an existential experience of the "unity perceived in the Trinity" in the Person of the Father. As an altogether natural consequence, this relationship presupposes also the theory of the *logoi* which are fulfilled, authenticated, actualized in the light of this relationship, as gifts, bestowing on the world a true ontology which, as we shall see below, flows from the very mode of being of God in Trinity as it is offered to us by grace when we receive adoption as sons in Christ.

99. *Opuscula*, PG 91:140AB: "Like the Maker and Master of all, our Lord Jesus Christ, so too His disciples and apostles, and then the holy Fathers and teachers and the martyrs were offered as a sacrifice through their own deeds and words, their struggles and sweat and toil and blood and finally by their terrible deaths, for the sake of our catholic and apostolic Church, the Church of those who believe in Him . . ." The sacrifice of giving themselves over, as a personal act of love, to toils and labours and death itself is the mode of existence of the Saints, in imitation of the Lord.

100. *Centuries of Various Texts* 1.46, PG 90:1196BC. As we clearly see in this text, Christian asceticism aims at the restoration of nature and has nothing to do with any sort of disdaining it. Here a serious question can be raised: how can those aforementioned Orthodox personalists who despise nature, identifying it with blind necessity, understand asceticism in the way Maximus does? We do not overcome or escape from nature—we only restore it in the order of Grace, where it already was.

101. *Centuries of Various Texts* 1.50, PG 90:1197AB.

102. *Centuries of Various Texts* 1.50, PG 90:1197C.

103. *Centuries of Various Texts* 1.50, PG 90:1197B. See Hausherr, *Philautie*, pp. 60–64. Hausherr seems not to have noticed the distinction between good and bad self-love in Maximus.

104. On the distinction between the "surface" of things and their *logoi* or "inner essence," see *Centuries of Various Texts* 2.6, PG 90:1224A.

105. See *supra*, chap. 2.7, 7. *The existential manifestation of the logoi of entities as powers of the soul.*

106. *Mystagogy* 5, PG 91:677CD.

107. Ibid.

108. Ibid.

109. See chap. 1.6.

110. Cf. A. Schmemann, *The Eucharist*, Gk 160–1.

111. See chap. 1.6.

112. *Ambigua*, PG 91:1312B.

113. *Ambigua*, PG 91:1312AB.

114. *Ambigua*, PG 91:1092C.

115. See Riou, *Le monde et l'église*, p. 158; Thunberg, *Microcosm and Mediator*, p. 28.

116. *Ambigua*, PG 91:1092C: ". . . that the soul becomes to the body what God is to the soul, and the one Creator of all is shown to enter into all things proportionately [to each] through humanity." Cf. also Staniloae, *Eisagogi*, p. 198 note 64.

117. *Ambigua*, PG 91:1092C.

118. *Ambigua*, PG 91:1092BC.

119. See Thunberg, *Microcosm and Mediator*, p. 28; Florovsky, "The Byzantine Fathers," p. 225.

120. See Riou, *Le monde et l'église*, p. 158: "But in rooting this comparison in the mystery of the Hypostasis, Maximus turns it around, so that it centers on the vocation of the new Man to achieve unity and synthesis, because he is a mediator called to make the world into a 'macrocosm' enhypostatized by the Word." See also Thunberg, *Microcosm and Mediator*, pp. 140–152; Balthasar, *Cosmic Liturgy*, pp. 173–177.

121. *Mystagogy* 7, PG 91:685C. Cf. Riou, *Le monde et l'église*, pp. 158–159.

122. Riou, *Le monde et l'église*, p. 158.

123. The first to introduce the term "person" into theology in this sense was Gregory of Nyssa. See K. Oehler, *Antike Philosophie und Byzantinische Mittelalter* (München: Beck-Verlag, 1969), p. 25: "What is said only implicitly in Basil becomes explicit in [Gregory of Nyssa]: the notion of *hypostasis* becomes more clearly defined through its assimilation to the notion of *prosopon*." See also Gregory the Theologian, Hom. 39.11, *On the Holy Lights*: "When I speak of God, you should be illumined with one light and with three: with three according to the properties or hypostases, or *persons* if one wants to call them that (let us not quarrel about names, so long as the words bear the same meaning); one according to the principle of the essence or Godhead." Likewise Basil, *Letter to Amphilochius of Iconium* (Letter 236.6): "So that throughout, the unity is preserved by the confession of one Godhead, and the particularity of the persons is confessed by the definition of the specific properties understood of each." Basil also writes, in his *Canonical Letter*: "This term corrects the evil of Sabellius, for it removes the [notion of] identity of hypostasis and introduces the perfect concept of the persons."

See also John Zizioulas, *Mathemata Christianikis Dogmatikis* (Publications Department, University of Thessaloniki), Supplement to Part I, pp. 1–32.

124. The theory of the *enhypostaton* is developed by Leontius of Byzantium (see *Against the Nestorians* 2.5, PG 86: 1544B; 2.13, PG 86: 1561B). In Christ two natural hypostases, the divine and the human, were united to form one person. In reality, however, the human natural hypostasis never existed as an independent entity—in that case, it would naturally have included sinfulness and the legacy of the Fall—but existed from the beginning in union with the divine nature as *enhypostaton*. So after the Third Ecumenical Council, the Fathers no longer speak of a human *hypostasis*, but of a human *nature* in Christ. This nature was united with the one Hypostasis of the Word before it began any sort of "individual" development; it is therefore neither a person nor a hypostasis but an *enhypostaton*, i.e., a hypostatic element which never had any existence outside the Hypostasis of the God-man. Cf. P. Chrestou, *To Mysterio tou Anthropou* (Thessaloniki: P.I.P.M., 1983), p. 45; also Balthasar, *Liturgie Cosmique*, pp. 175–182; *Cosmic Liturgy* pp. 237–245.

125. *Opuscula*, PG 91:152B: "A hypostatic union is one that brings and binds together two different essences or natures into one person and one and the same hypostasis."

126. *Opuscula*, PG 91:152A.

127. See chap. 3.4.

128. It is at this point that we could speak of Maximus extending, or rather deepening, in the Chalcedonian way, the Areopagite's thought. Here the cosmological frame of reference of being, culminating in God the Word who rules it, opens up more clearly into Christology through the mystery of enhypostatization: it opens into this hypostatic Christology in which, through the mystery of Christ's person, the "transmission" that saves the created order will be able to take place. Through Christ, the personal mode of existence of God's Trinitarian Being will be "transmitted" or "transferred" to creation through its adoption by the Father in Christ. But this is not a reversal of the Areopagite—it is a matter of assimilating his thought in a living theological way, correcting and developing it further, or even clarifying its deepest intentions. We should also lay particular stress at this point on the sacramentally-centered and ecclesial character of this "transmission" to creation of the hypostatic union of the two natures in Christ, a transmission which has the character of an eschatological ontological foundation for creation. On this point there is a possible difference between Orthodox and Western theology. For Orthodox theology still preserves today the direct connection between bringing creation into hypostatic union by grace and the fact of the Church, and especially the Eucharist. Thus Riou, who correctly understands that Christ effects a hypostatic union with our humanity "with a view to recapitulating the whole universe in His person, to enhypostatizing the world" (*Le monde et l'église*, p. 103), is unable to identify this fact with the Church and the Eucharist—he is unable to see it in its eschato-

logical ontological dimension, as a process of the ecclesial transfiguration in which the world's being is transformed, even now, into the being of Christ. Here is seems that we have two differing ecclesiologies. There is an "ontological" ecclesiology according to which the "Christ event," as Church, is even now continuously being realized sacramentally, waiting for its fulfillment in the end times; and there is a rather "institutional" ecclesiology, in which the view of the Church as a place where creation is being led by the Spirit, by grace, into the mystery of hypostatic union is regarded as a confusion between Christ and the Church. Here the Church is the (institutional) "sign" and "instrument" of salvation; the Church saves in the name of Christ, but He does not act hypostatically within it! Thus many Western theologians seem to be reluctant to comprehend the very core of Maximus's ecclesiology, because he sees the Church as precisely the event whereby the created order is ontologically "enchristified," an event eschatological and eucharistic in character. This is why—to return to the texts—Riou, who has written one of the most important recent books on the Confessor, can go so far as to say that "the Church enhypostatizes all creation" (*op. cit.*, p. 140) and that "the Church is henceforth the hypostatic, iconic presence of God in the world" (*op. cit.*, p. 141); but in subsequent pages this insight begins to slide away, so that "iconic" ends up being understood as "symbolic" (p. 145). What Riou ultimately extracts from Maximus is a pneumatological Church (which is what he wants), a perfect instrument for the salvation, enhypostatization etc. of the world, but without Christ. Christ Himself is not ontologically active in the Church, enhypostatizing creation in His Body; the Church is a splendid mechanism for salvation in place of Christ, or in the name of Christ but not, in a way, Christ Himself acting in the Spirit.

129. "Regeneration." See 1 Pet 1:3, 23.

130. J. Zizioulas, in his "From *Prosopeion* to *Prosopon*," pp. 950ff. see also note 41, p. 959, insists that this new hypostasis is "not dependent on the necessity of biological nature." As we have already seen, this way of understanding nature does not belong to Maximus, who never identifies nature with necessity (nor personhood with freedom) as many modern, theological or not, existentialisms or personalisms do. On the contrary, nature is, for Maximus, an uncreated call for freedom already (in God's respective logos of each being). It is exactly this call that is fulfilled in Christ's Incarnation in a participational way. The new mode of existence thus given by Baptism is exactly the fulfillment of the uncreated principles of nature, now understood as existential ways, as we have seen above (Chap. 2.3). However, if nature is definitely bound with necessity, then what is the need of the Incarnation and what is the meaning of the Resurrection? The very ontological meaning of Incarnation is that nature is naturally open to its supernatural cause; it is, in its very essence, a call for deification, in the sense that it can be only fulfilled in God, when it is deified. Thus this new hypostasis given by Baptism is not against the "biological" (or, better, natural) hypostasis of man, but it is

given in accordance to its uncreated logos, which calls him to deification. It is exactly the biological that finds his truth in becoming ecclesial.

131. We recall that Cabasilas in his *Life in Christ* calls Baptism, Chrismation, and the Divine Eucharist "mysteries of incorporation."

132. *Ambigua*, PG 91:1092C; see chap. 3.6, and note 115.

133. *To Thalassius*, PG90: 625. See chap. 3.2.

134. Nicolas Berdyaev agrees on this point: *Five Thoughts on Existence*, (Koinotita, Athens) p. 194.

135. Here we disagree with Berdyaev and his disciples. The person in its original depth belongs to the mystery of the age to come; it is ultimately an eschatological, eucharistic reality, and for that reason a kind of scandal to any usual philosophical approach. If the person is to form the basis of an ontology, that ontology would be eschatological and eucharistic. We are talking about the very experience of the Saints; the person marks the entry of the *eschata* into history, and as such it judges philosophy, revealing the reason why philosophy cannot present the ultimate truth of things.

136. Chap. 2.5.

137. *Opuscula*, PG 91:145B: the supreme union and identity also embraces otherness. Cf. *Mystagogy* 7, 685AB: ". . . in accordance with this [the divine law], the principle of the unifying force is implanted, which does not allow the hypostatic identity of these things on the basis of their union to be ignored because of their natural otherness."

138. See chap. 2.7.

139. In this sense, the person is shown to be "image" fulfilled in "likeness." In saying all this, however, we do not wish to overlook the primarily "iconic" character of the person in man. Indeed, man is above all personal in the image of God: man's fall and debasement do not expunge the personal character of his existence in the divine image, but rather obscure it. Even then, man is still personal; this signals the profound existential tendency for the image to be fulfilled in the likeness, although that tendency may follow unnatural paths. We should therefore distinguish at this point between what we describe as "personal" and what we call "person." However much man has fallen from his original dignity, he remains naturally and effortlessly an image of God, which is to say that he is "personal" what psychology and educational theory like to call a personality or what philosophical calls a (metaphysical or knowing) subject, basically individualistic in character. (Here we are not unaware of the whole corpus of non-transcendent, worldly mysticism of the "personal": from the idealistic and phenomenological transcendence of the ego to kern's meta-psychological Freudianism and the meta-biological Self [in Popper-Eccles], or even the transformation of fevered scenes drawn from the ego in surrealism and post-modernism. Everywhere we find, as in the Jungian clinical myth of "individuation," the archetypal deiform quality of the personal, sometimes in a quest for its uncreated ontological horizon.) When we interpret Maximus's thought in terms of man becoming person, we are referring precisely to the natural,

i.e., eschatological fulfilment of the "personal" in the "person," of the image (which is preserved, albeit corrupted), in the likeness. Both existentially and ontologically, the demand for, or the reality of, the "personal" as expressed in the image is quite a different matter from the eschatological actualization of the person in the likeness of God within the Church. It is in reference to that actualization that we speak of the ("personal") human being becoming a person—meaning that the eschatological eucharistic ontology of the person is truly actualized in the context of his regeneration in Christ. The image is preserved only in the likeness, because the latter—and here we come to the heart of Maximus's thought—is ontologically prior to the former: in the Confessor's eschatological ontology and in total contrast to any sort of philosophical ontology, the ontological foundation of the person lies in the *eschaton* (and not in his "beginning"), which is to say that it lies in the likeness it is thanks to the likeness that the image exists and has ontological justification. That is why failure to achieve likeness quite literally shakes the very ontological foundations of the image. For when it is not eschatologically grounded in the likeness, the person in the image of God quite literally tends to non-being (according to the spirit of Maximus's thought). Surely this has a bearing on the antinomic experience of hell as described by Maximus, as a knowledge of God "by a certain understanding, but not by participation," i.e., "personally" but not "as person."

Chapter 4

The Becoming of Entities through Their *Logoi*

1. *The Philosophy of Movement in St. Maximus*

ACCORDING TO MAXIMUS, the created character of things entails their being in motion. The saint constructs a peculiar "philosophy of motion,"[1] completing his ontological theories in a similarly fruitful way: "For nothing that has come into being [is] altogether motionless according to its own inner principle, not even something inanimate and tangible."[2] A further formulation explaining this ontological property of motion, which as we see applies to all created things without exception and not only to rational beings, is as follows:

> For everything that comes from God and is subsequent to Him undergoes motion, inasmuch as these things are not in themselves motion or power. So they do not move in opposition [to their nature], as it has been said, but through the *logos* creatively placed within them by the cause which framed the universe.[3]

Things do not move "in opposition" to God but in accordance with His will, with the uncreated essential principle of their nature which pre-exists in God. Their motion is "creative"; according to Maximus, it has to do with the Economy concerning them, not of course with the stability of their essence which is a given:

> According to the *logos* of their substantive existence and being, all things are entirely fixed and motionless; but accord-

ing to the *logos* of their circumstances, that *logos* according
to which the Economy of this whole is established and un-
folds, it is clear that everything is in motion and not fixed.[4]

This movement, the writer explains, does not have to do with the mutability or change or corruption of things, but is an ontological property
belonging to them.[5] Maximus distinguishes sharply between the "irrational impetus toward non-being" which he calls "unstable behaviour
and a terrible disordering of soul and body" and again "deliberate inclination toward the worse";[6] and on the other hand "positive movement"[7]
as a property of the inner principle of the creature's nature. The latter is
the creature's "ascent and restoration" (due precisely to the natural operation and power of things consequent upon their essential principle)[8]
to its "divine goal."[9] And precisely by reason of the supreme goal of this
movement, "nothing originate has ever halted in its motion, nor has it
attained the lot appointed to it according to the divine purpose."[10]

  Maximus regards motion, then, as a "natural faculty" of beings
who press ahead toward their goal, a "passion" of nature leading nature
to dispassion, or an "active operation" of beings directing them toward
the completely perfect—it takes place "in a straight line or a circle or a
spiral,"[11] and, of course, in time and space.[12] The goal—dispassionate,
completely perfect, uncreated, unmoved, perfect, complete, beyond
quantification and without beginning[13]—is God. For He is "the principle
of the becoming of things that move, the author of their existence,"[14]
according to Maximus; because for all God's creatures, intelligible and
sensible alike, "becoming precedes motion."[15]

  It is well known that Platonism and Origen[16] regard motion as preceding the genesis of the world: the created spirits which were at rest
in God experienced *koros*, satiety with God, and fell away or "moved,"
with the result that the world came into being and some of those spirits
were imprisoned in bodies, by way of punishment. Salvation consists in
the liberation of souls from the body and the world and their return to
God, from whom they had fallen away. This myth was quite widespread
in Maximus's time, and a philosophical expression of it is to be found in
the Origenist triad of *motion, becoming* and *fixity (stasis).*[17] Maximus
does not change the terms, but he does change the order of the first two,
so that the triad becomes "becoming, motion, fixity,"[18] in the light of the
Alexandrian doctrine of the Logos.[19] The creation of the world is a result
of the free, loving will of God; and so motion, which is ontologically
inherent to the created world, is not evil in itself. Everything that is cre-

ated is necessarily movable; and its movement is a "passion," as we have seen, which is to say that it is something passive: creation is subject to the necessity of motion by its very nature. The impassioned state which follows that fall is of course connected with the passivity which characterizes the motion of creaturehood; but as we have seen, such a state is a perversion and destruction of motion.[20] In other words, the only possible meaning of motion is for it to be directed toward the unmoved, uncreated God, who is unmoved in the sense that He is not subject to precisely the passivity characteristic of creaturehood's motion, because there is nothing higher than Himself toward which He could move.[21] This free movement[22] of things "originate" ends in fixity, when they "pass over things that have come to an end" into the divine "infinitude," where God appears as the "Horizon" of all movement, its end, precisely because He is its beginning.[23] In consequence, "God is the beginning and end of all becoming and movement in entities, because it is from Him that they have come into being and through Him that they move, and in Him that they will attain their final fixity"[24]—a fixity that is not a natural operation of movable things, but "the goal of the faculty or operation that tends to that end."[25]

In order to understand this teaching of Maximus, the reader should refer back to Chapter 2.2. There the triad "becoming, movement, fixity" is connected with ten other triads of terms, which literally contain the essence of this Father's theology of a progressive "process of becoming"[26] which completes God plan for creation, in such a way that it becomes self-explanatory. The partial connection made by other writers, who link this triad with one or two others, is inadequate to explain the Confessor's doctrine on this point precisely because it is partial. So for example Balthasar is content to link the triad "becoming, movement, fixity" only with that of "being, well-being, eternal being,"[27] while Sherwood adds the triad "substance, power, operation."[28] In the above-mentioned chapter, we identified in addition to those two triads nine others: (1) nature, gnomic will, fulfillment; (2) natural birth, baptism, resurrection; (3) goodness of God, love of God, providence of God; (4) essence, free choice, grace; (5) essence, aptitude, grace; (6) potentiality, activity, rest; (7) place of the present, place after death, age to come; (8) practical philosophy, natural contemplation, theological mystagogy; (9) practical aspect of the soul, reason, intellect. We therefore refer the reader to the detailed exploration of the connections between these triads in Chapter 2.2. In light of our present discussion, we will say only that the notion of *becoming*, i.e., the movement of the created order toward a

goal and indeed the highest possible goal, God Himself, as a fundamental ontological characteristic of created being, is the essential existential
precondition, the natural "middle term" justifying the genesis of things
within their fixity in God,[29] their eternal communion with God through
man in Christ. In this section of the book we will look at the movement
or becoming of entities as the "middle term" which allows them to commune with each other and with God, precisely joining their creation out
of non-being with their eschatological restoration.[30]

2. Will and Movement. Personal Movement and Prayer

THE CREATION OF THE ENTIRE INANIMATE PART of the cosmos took place
simply by the divine word, which is to say that inanimate creatures did
not receive something of God's inner life; whereas the creation of man in
the image of God causes him to have a free and conscious life. In consequence, man's movement toward spiritual communion with God is the
expression of this freedom and consciousness of his: as Maximus says, it
is a "movement of free will," and that capacity of free will (*autexousion*)
is identified in his writing with man's will (thelesis).[31] Free will is defined as "lawful dominion over actions within our power, or unimpeded
dominion over the use of things within our power, or unenslaved desire
for things within our power."[32] "Deliberation" (*vouli, voulesis*) is "a appetite in search of its desire, applied to some action that is in our power,"[33]
while "we deliberate about those things that are in our power and can be
brought about through our agency";[34] and "it is said that *gnomê* is our
innate appetite for things in our power."[35] Furthermore, "we deliberate
with authority,"[36] as Maximus says in defining the free will of the movement of the *gnomê*. The very close connection between will and free will
becomes apparent when he defines will as "the appetitive faculty of the
being in its natural state, which holds together all the characteristics
essentially proper to our nature";[37] the free will has ensured that this faculty is "unimpeded" and "unenslaved," making it possible for it to exist.
And Maximus goes on, speaking of the will:

> Being naturally held together by this [the will], the essence
> desires to have being and to live and move, both physically
> and intellectually, longing for the fullness of its own natural
> existence. For nature has been made so as to will itself, and
> whatever gives it its natural constitution; for through its ap-

petitive desire, it is dependent on the *logos* of its being, in accordance with which it exists and came into being.[38]

Nature desires the fullness of its existence, reaching out to the inner principle of its essence and through it to everything that goes to make up its natural mode of existence. So the will is an expression of the life of an essence and its movement toward achieving the fullness of that life. This natural will is formed as a movement of the particular person through the *gnomê*, which is our "innate appetitive desire for things in our power, the basis for our choice."[39] The *gnomê* gives rise to choice, once the act of willing and its elaboration (deliberation) and judgment have taken place.[40] And of course it is "with authority" that we exercise choice, i.e., with free will, and in general "it is with authority that we deliberate and judge and exercise choice, and initiate action and use what is in our power."[41]

The distinction between natural and gnomic will in man is fundamental for Maximus. The gnomic will alone can actualize the natural will's "desire for whatever is naturally constitutive" of us as a "self-chosen impetus and movement,"[42] i.e., one that arises from choice and free will. If then "willing" is a property of nature, "how to will"—the way "willing" is put into practice—is a characteristic of the hypostasis[43] or person, according to the Confessor. It follows that the gnomic will makes use of the energy of the natural will,[44] as a personal movement of nature toward the fullness of its life. Without the natural will movement cannot exist, because that will is "the first and foremost of natural properties and movements, an innate faculty,"[45] a faculty that is given by God[46] and holds together the "essential properties of the nature."[47] But movement is equally unable to exist without the "mode of movement"[48] the process whereby movement is activated in a free and personal way through the *gnomê*. Movement can only be personal, and in order to exist it requires natural mobility and a mode of movement, i.e., a natural and a gnomic will.[49]

If this personal, gnomic activation of our natural movement is not to be "a perversion and a downward slide,"[50] then it has to take place "in accordance with reason (*logos*),"[51] in harmony with the essential principle (*logos*) of our nature, which ultimately means in harmony with the will of God. This is what Maximus calls an "agreement of wills" between God and man. And this comes about because

One single thing is willed both by God and by the saints, namely the salvation of those who are being saved. This is a divine purpose, devised before all ages to be the goal of all things. On this matter there will be agreement in will both among those who are being saved, and between them and God who saves.[52]

The wills of the saints coincide among themselves and with God: they are not identical, but they agree, they go hand in hand, they move in step around the one common desire for salvation, which is God's purpose for man, devised in advance, and the shared longing of the saints. For "one purpose was appointed for both, namely the salvation of all—a purpose proposed by God, and freely chosen by the saints."[53] The saints choose salvation voluntarily and in free will, and move toward it in a personal way through their gnomic will; and that salvation is the will of God, a will with which their own gnomic will coincides exactly. Far from doing away with free will, according to Maximus this is the natural state of man's free will, stable and unchangeable. Yet more graphically, he calls it "cession of the *gnomê*," a yielding of our will to God according to the example of Christ and St. Paul.[54]

This mode of personal movement among the saints is seen by Maximus as an "imitation" of the motion of God's "will which is good by nature."[55] And the way we actualize this harmony through imitation, this coincidence of the wills of God and man, is by prayer, according to this Father. Prayer is the mode whereby we personally fulfill the divine will, because "one who has mystically offered worship to God with his rational faculty alone . . . has fulfilled the divine will on earth and has in all things become a worshipper on a level with the angels."[56] The will of God, with which the personal gnomic movement of Christians must be harmonized, is unceasing worship:

> He reveals this when He says to the great David, What is there for me in heaven, and what have I desired of thee on earth? Nothing is brought to God by the holy angels in heavens save rational worship. Asking the same from us, He taught us to pray saying, "Thy will be done on earth as it is in heaven."[57]

When the Christian asks for God's will to be done on earth, he is worshipping God like the angels. Furthermore, this will of God's, according to Maximus, is the salvation of man—i.e., exactly what man himself truly wants. So the coincidence of God's will and man's (and of human wills among themselves) is uniquely manifested in the prayer that asks, as an act of worship, for God's saving will to be done on earth. So when the soul receives the radiant inner principles of divinity which are accessible to creatures, just as the angels do, and learns to sing in ceaseless Trinitarian praise of the one Godhead in concert with the heavenly powers, then it is brought to the adoption which has been bestowed upon it and to the likeness by grace which is the seal of adopted that :

> Through this [adoption] the soul, after prayer, has God alone as its mystical Father by grace, and will be gathered to the oneness of His hidden presence, ek-statically separated from all things. And it will be undergo divine things rather than knowing them, to such an extent that it will no longer wish to belong to itself, nor will it be able to be known in itself either by itself or by anyone else, except for God who in His entirety has in His goodness taken it up entire.[58]

As this passage clearly shows, prayer is the motive force by which one who has come to know God by faith and been enchanted by His beauty, and spends his life singing God's praise unceasingly like the angels, enters into the innermost sanctuary of the divine unity and rests there, thus fulfilling his ek-static personal movement. Through prayer, he shows precisely that "he does not wish to belong to himself," but to God who has "taken him up" in his entirety.

Prayer, then, is that mode of personal gnomic movement which leads to "agreement," to the harmony and coincidence of human free will with the divine will which is good by nature, a coincidence which alone is able to secure a favorable outcome to man's natural movement. Through man, all inanimate things become part of this relationship of prayer and participate in a "cosmic liturgy," a truly cosmic movement of worship whose goal is the participation of creation in the "joy of the firstborn,"

> in which we shall become children of God, all of us carrying within us in all purity Him who is the Author of this grace and the Son of the Father by nature, in His entirety yet without His being circumscribed: it is from Him and through Him that we have and will continue to have our being and movement and life.[59]

Through the ontological connection between will and movement, and the distinction made between natural and personal will, Maximus also stresses the close connection of gnosiology to ontology in spiritual life. Spiritual life and human relationships are thus not unconscious, as

Zizioulas seems to claim, as if relationship with or participation in God should preclude any connection with human natural or gnomic will.[60] On the contrary, interiority, as the locus of the free gnomic will, forms the cornerstone of Maximian "spirituality." Zizioulas is much too afraid of any kind of interiority as he always sees a kind of psychologism behind it. One can find a great quantity of evidence in the patristic tradition making clear that interiority should not be identified with any kind of psychologism, as it forms an ontological part of human being. Zizioulas thus fails to realize that without this kind of ontological or existential interiority (and consciousness) any sort of relationship, knowledge, or participation leads us to a sheer heteronomy.[61]

3. Movement as Ek-stasis. Ek-static Love

WE HAVE SEEN IN AN EARLIER CHAPTER[62] that God has a free and personal relationship with creation through His uncreated energies—a relationship which is the product of will and love, as the theology of the uncreated *logoi* of entities shows us. But how does Maximus reconcile the movement entailed by this relationship between God and creation with the immobility proper to God as Uncreated? The Confessor's answer is that God is said to be in motion in that He moves things toward Himself, calling them by their naturally mobile essential principles:

> Thus the divine, which is altogether unmoved in its essence and nature, being infinite, boundless and limitless, is said to be in motion, like some innate intelligent principle in the essences of things, when by His Providence He moves each thing that exists according to the *logos* whereby it naturally moves.[63]

This immobility of God's uncreated nature does not conflict with His personal, willed, and loving relationship with created things, which is a relationship not of essence but of energy.[64] The main contribution on this subject comes from the Areopagite, who further calls this movement on God's part a movement "outside Himself," an "ek-static superessential power."[65] This "ek-stasis" on God's part causes Him to be called not only "longed for and beloved" but also "intense longing and love," according to the Areopagite.[66] Maximus starts by adopting this Areopagitic distinction in the best known and most substantive text he has given us on the subject:

> As intense longing (*eros*) and love (*agape*), the Divine is in motion, while as the longed for and beloved He moves toward Himself everything that is receptive of intense longing and love. To put it more clearly: He is in motion in that He creates a relationship of innate *eros* and love among those receptive of these [emotions], while He causes motion in that He is by nature attractive to the desire of entities that move toward Him. And again: He moves others and is in motion in that He thirsts to be thirsted for, and longs intensely to be longed for, and loves to be loved.[67]

The loving movement of God is one that "draws upwards,"[68] creating a relationship of *eros* and *agape* in "those receptive of these [emotions]." It is a movement that moves humans' desire toward the Desired, a movement expressing His love of being loved and thirst for being thirsted for, as Maximus says, adding his own contribution to the Areopagitic text.[69] So the Divine moves within rational beings, according to the Confessor, and moves beings through their inner principles. It is precisely this movement of God's that then stimulates the ek-stasis of rational beings toward Him, as He "draws them to Himself and moves them to spiritual erotic union, and He is productive of movement in that He moves every one (of His creations), through its own *logos*, to return to Him."[70]

This theory of ek-stasis shows God creating a stable relationship of love outside Himself. So this is not some neoplatonic emanation, but first and foremost a relationship, created by God, with a conscious otherness outside Himself that responds to His call to this relationship.[71] In this way, of course, we are taken beyond the notion of a God petrified in immobility, like Aristotle's "unmoved mover,"[72] and also see a greater emphasis on the personal character of the movement of rational beings, as a conscious and deliberate response to the divine calling. This response makes the rational being likewise ek-static, in that it is responding to God's love of being loved by wholly attaching itself "to God alone in an ek-stasy of intense longing."[73] In principle, this involves a transformation of man's natural incensive power and desire. Desire is changed by the contemplative intellect into "the unmingled pleasure of the divine *eros*, and immaculate beguilement," and the natural incensive power transformed "into spiritual ardor and fervent perpetual motion and sober madness."[74] It was in reference to this sober madness, says Maximus, that Paul was told, "Paul, you are mad" (Acts 26:24). Paul himself speaks of it to the Corinthians: "If we are beside ourselves [*exestemen*], it is for God;

if we are in our right mind, it is for you" (2 Cor 5:13); "and it is evident that he is using the term 'ek-stasis' [literally, 'being beside oneself'] to mean the sober madness in God; for this 'madness' causes the mind that experiences it in sobriety to be transported outside existent things."[75]

This sober madness or ek-stasis is a condition experienced by the whole being; it is by no means an exclusively intellectual or emotional construct. It is not simply a movement of the intellect, the incensive power or the desire, but *eros*. Here is the most characteristic passage:

> If an intelligent being moves intellectually, in the way appropriate to it, then it certainly also has an intellectual perception. If it perceives intellectually, then it certainly experiences intense longing for what it perceives. If it experiences longing, then it certainly undergoes ek-stasis toward that object as its beloved. And if it undergoes [this], it is obvious that it presses on eagerly. And if it presses on eagerly, it is certainly increasing the intensity of its motion. And if it increases the intensity of its motion, it does not stop until it is wholly contained in the whole of the object of its love, and is entirely embraced by it.[76]

The movement of the intellect leads to *eros*, and that in turn causes ek-stasis toward its object. The experience of ek-stasis makes the movement urgent and unrelenting until lover and beloved finally embrace. Ek-stasis is the vehicle of *eros:* it is the erotic movement, as Maximus says, a movement of the whole being which will ultimately lead that being to take on the quality of the beloved, so that it no longer wants to be known by itself but rather by the beloved in whom it is contained, "circumscribed," as air is contained within light or the iron within the fire.[77] This state of "partaking in the good" God is the destruction of death, according to the Confessor. As the entry of death through our free will caused corruption to have dominion over us, so the willing and total surrender of our free will to God (what Maximus calls "cession of the *gnomê*," as we saw above) makes us refrain from willing what God does not will. This is Christ's state of obedience to His Father; it is the state St. Paul is in when he says, "it is no longer I that live, but Christ lives in me." It is also the state of the image that has measured up to its prototype and been conformed to it, and consequently has nowhere else to go, nor can it move anywhere else—or rather, it would not even desire to want anything of the sort, because it has already been deified. Then at last there is "only one energy [operating] through all things, that of God and those who are worthy of God—or rather, that of God alone, because in accordance with His goodness He has wholly interpenetrated all those who are worthy."[78] This energy of God's is His love, His loving will that offers His beloved ones participation in the infinite, divine, delightful and incomprehensible knowledge of things and of His wonders.[79] The content of infinite love is infinite knowledge.

When the reasoning brain and the intellect,[80] the faculty of desire and the incensive faculty are brought together and united "around things divine," their offspring is love, "whereby we inscribe in our memory the beauty of the divine comeliness . . . and possess . . . the blameless longing for divine love."[81] The mode whereby the faculties of the soul are thus brought together and united is the virtues: prudence, courage, sobriety, and justice make up the two comprehensive virtues of wisdom and meekness (the one being the perfection of knowledge, the other the perfection of action[82]). Again, these two comprehensive virtues are brought together "in the most comprehensive virtue of all, by which I mean love: this produces ek-stasis in those who begin with it, draws those motivated by it and unites those who have ended in it, and above all it effects deification."[83]

The personal movement activated by his gnomic will becomes ek-stasis when the faculty of deliberation is identified with love. Just as the personal loving will of God creates the world out of nothing, moving His uncreated energies through the uncreated inner principles, so also human movement becomes personal ek-stasis when man's gnomic will attains to love through the virtues. It is love that introduces a being into the mystery of constant mindfulness of the ineffable divine beauty, as well as mindfulness of all things in their unity in Christ. This is to be connected with what was said about prayer in the previous section: the mystery of prayer is the mystery of love; prayer is the love that surrenders the human will to God. Love, as the essence of Christian prayer, makes that prayer communal. We are talking about prayer "in person," i.e., "for the whole world," not about the prayer of individual (narcissistic) piety. Even when the Christian is praying for himself, he experiences the consubstantiality of the human race. Ek-stasis, then, makes no sense unless the person penetrates, through the movement of his gnomic will, into the love which it by nature ek-static, and is ultimately identified with that love. Furthermore, it is love that makes this free human movement supremely personal. Love is the ek-stasis which makes the rational creature a person, i.e., deifies it, according to Maximus, identifying it in the perfection of its movement with the "divinely perfect *logos* according to which it is and has come into being,"[84] a *logos* or principle that by nature "goes outside itself so as to be deified."[85] Hence ek-static love at once "draws" and "unites" those who are motivated by it and reach final perfection in it. As we have seen already, this attraction and unification images the Trinitarian unity of God; it is empirical knowledge of the unity-in-communion of the Holy Trinity.[86] Ek-static love is the means, the path to this knowledge, which is a gift of God and, as we have said, infinite and eternal, at the same time extending throughout the "essential being of things, the what and how and wherefore of their existence."[87] Ek-static love leads to knowledge-through-participation[88] of the communal mode of existence of entities, of their truly natural existence as it appears solely and exclusively in the mystery of communion between God and man, which is the mystery of man's deification. For when a human being is deified, as the completion of the free movement of his ek-static love, that deified person is in a state of "affectionately loving and embracing the aforementioned *logoi* which pre-existed in God, or rather God in whom the *logoi* of good things are firmly established . . . honoring them as such and acting in accordance with them."[89] The ek-static movement of love in harmony with the loving will of God is the "straight course toward the *logoi*" of things, because those inner principles are God's wills; it promotes the truly natural mode of existence of the entire cosmos, through man.

Ek-static love is the movement whereby man transcends his comprehensive self-love and unites himself to the sacrificial eucharistic love of Christ. Self-love is transcended because achieving love is a matter of asceticism and kenosis; ek-static love is the path to communion, and consequently demands true self-denial in accordance with the Lord's example. That is why man's personal ek-stasis toward communion with God through love cannot be accomplished without the help of the Holy Spirit.[90] Indeed, as Maximus testifies, "from the natural movement of beings we learn of the indwelling life of that being, the life-giving force in beings which is the Holy Spirit."[91] This life-giving activity of the Spirit is manifested when He acts by "permeating all things providentially by His power and stirring up the *logos* in each according to its nature," because He "holds all things together and exercises providence and stirs the natural seeds within them."[92] Hence the "stirring" of the principles in things, that which awakens them to their truly natural mode of existence, comes from the Holy Spirit. It is He, as the "indwelling life of beings," in Maximus's bold phrase, that directs the natural motion of beings in accordance with Providence, toward their adoption in Christ.[93]

When this movement in a particular human being acquires the character of personal ek-static love toward God, this is due, according to Maximus, to "the grace of the Holy Spirit overcoming him, and showing that God alone is actively working within him."[94] The Holy Spirit "overcomes" the human being, meaning that He destroys its narcissistic self-love and leads the human will to loving submission to the will of the loving God, so that there is only one "active operation" or energy, that of God and those worthy of God; or rather, that of God alone, because "in accordance with His goodness He has wholly interpenetrated those who are worthy" and embraced them in their entirety.[95]

The Holy Spirit supports, holds together and directs the ek-static love of humans as a journey toward the eschatological universality of mutual loving personal communion between God and man in Christ (who is the perfect communion of God and man unto all ages), in opposition to the self-love and multifarious divisions and rifts resulting from the Fall. In other words, the Holy Spirit establishes and directs the "Christonostalgic"[96] impetus in created things. In this sense, the Holy Spirit "constitutes" the body of Christ, His Church, by directing the loving movement of rational beings toward Christ.[97] This role of the Holy Spirit is clearly apparent in the Divine Eucharist. But this will be discussed in the next section.

4. Ek-static Love as Becoming-in-Communion. Eucharistic Becoming

A.

THE TRUE DESTINY OF MAN is to commune freely with God,[98] because communion with Him who provides our being bestows the gift of "true being" on His loved ones.[99] Man's "irrational" movement is "intense longing for nothingness"—the destruction of the love which "we owe to God alone,"[100] separation from God and "lapsing into non-being,"[101] death. For Maximus, as we have seen, death is removed when man achieves "yielding of the gnomê," i.e., the free surrender of his free will to God in imitation of Christ; when he experiences ek-stasis toward God in love by the grace of the Holy Spirit[102] and progresses, though prayer toward his adoption, by grace, in Christ.[103] Maximus identifies man's adoption in Christ, which is "union and familiarity and divine likeness and deification,"[104] with the way in which all things "universally relate to [the

Church] and come together" in His Church, where all are "conjoined and united to each other."[105] The Church is the locus in which death is gradually transcended through the communion of man and God; which comes about gradually as man deliberately and freely "goes outside himself," i.e., outside his narcissism, moving toward God through love. This movement on man's part is existentially valid to the degree that it involves a continuous series of progressive increments in his communion with God. It is a "becoming"[106] which is successful when it forms a progressive approach to an ever deeper communion between created things and the Creator who exercises Providence for them, and also among created things themselves. The example of a circle as used by Maximus is well known: God is the center from which the existential courses of existent things radiate, and to which they return. He Himself works toward this end, "circumscribing their ek-stases in a circle and drawing to Himself the distinctions among entities, of which He is also the Author."[107] Progress toward God in this personal ek-static becoming is a continuous progress toward achieving the unity, the love (and the knowledge engendered by it) and the reciprocity-in-communion of humans and God.

Maximus certainly includes the entire creation in this becoming: "The world needs man in order to find its Creator again," as Meyendorff puts it so beautifully.[108] Indeed, as we have seen earlier,[109] the world is recapitulated in the person of Christ "like a sort of human being," by means of His human nature. God in Christ holds together and unites and circumscribes things sensible and things intelligible, holding them fast around Himself who is their Cause, their beginning and end: all the things that are by nature separate from one another He causes to converge with one another, making their relationship with Him the fundamental dynamic principle of the relationship between them.[110] God brings all these entities into an "identity of movement and existence, an identity without loss of integrity and without confusion."[111] Here we have a unity of natures without confusion and without division; a unity in the process of becoming, in a becoming-toward-God that preserves and supports the "unmingled union" of their unity-in-common, in precisely the same way as this unity, the "indissoluble relationship" between entities, supports and authenticates their becoming-toward-God. For He alone is "the cause of wholeness, by virtue of which both the Whole and the parts of the Whole naturally exist and appear."[112] He is the dynamic and personal cause of the wholeness of entities, which does not admit of division or confusion, and only in this way does the continuous becoming through Him and toward Him ensure that this free communal "wholeness" of things is manifested and preserved.

The quality of movement in the finite space-time of the created world is "different" precisely "because of the finite fixity of the world and the disintegration through change wrought by time."[113] This movement comes to an end with the appearance of the "infinite fixity,"[114] the ultimate uniting of what is "in accordance with its own principle" in movable nature with God's ultimate Providence for the created order, which is uncircumscribed because uncreated, and naturally altogether immovable.[115] So our nature will then "come to be in God . . . and have an ever-moving fixity, and a stable motion-in-sameness as it is eternally centered on that which is the same and one and only."[116] Let us recall here what we said earlier about the ontological action of Providence in bringing to completion things' truly natural mode of existence,[117] as well as what we said about Providence as the uncreated foundation for the communion of things.[118] The ultimate fulfillment of entities' truly natural mode of existence is the fullness of their communion in God and with God: this is the eschatological fulfillment of the work of Providence in respect of creation. The person who reaches this point has made God Himself, by grace, the "quality" and "mark" of his or her existence, as Maximus boldly says: that person has been deified and consequently transformed, "receiving an ever-moving fixity which is the boundless enjoyment of things divine, and a movement in fixity which is the insatiable appetite for those things."[119]

We see, then, how deification as a profound and ineffable communion of man and God has as its ultimate characteristic ever-moving fixity and fixed motion (or fixed motion-in-sameness). Implicit in the first case is that rest in the highest Good which contains within it motion as constant enjoyment of God (ever-moving fixity). Implicit in the second case is the movement of insatiable appetite for the uncreated beauty of God, which however constantly takes its fill and rests in His bosom (fixed motion, or fixed motion-in-sameness). In consequence, it is clear that in the state of the deifying full communion between created and uncreated, in the state of "eternal well-being" which is the eschatological sabbath rest and cessation[120] in the "face to face"[121] reciprocity of loving communion between man and God, a transfigured and deified "becoming" continues to exist. *A becoming which keeps the communion of God and man living, real and personal,*[122] overcoming Origen's "satiety," which is ultimately precisely the eschatological absence of personal becoming-in-communion and relationship between created and uncreated. It is this eschatological communion that motivates becoming, causing entities to penetrate ever deeper into it and experience it in infinite modes of fullness; becoming is what enriches this already all-rich and infinite personal communion with constantly new divine delights.

B.

The end of all things ("of knowledge and of things known") is called by Maximus "truth." Entities move toward truth, "drawn together" toward it "by some general principle"; truth prevails as the beginning and end of things, and draws to itself the "movement of things that come into being."[123] Since the Fall, the meaning and truth of things is hidden in their end, according to this holy Father.[124] That end is the incarnate, personal God the Word who draws all toward Himself, "both our thoughts and our words concerning flesh and soul and the nature of things."[125] God the Word draws all to His truth—or as Maximus says, following Ecclesiastes (Eccl 1:5), to His place:

> For as Ecclesiastes says, He draws them there and draws them
> to His place: clearly this refers to those who follow Him as
> the great High Priest who leads them into the Holy of Holies,
> whither He has entered bearing our nature, as a Forerunner
> on our behalf (cf. Heb 6:20).[126]

Here we have a highly significant aspect of the way in which the becoming of existent things is interpreted: becoming is a sacred rite in which Christ the High Priest presides, and which leads those who follow it to the truth, in other words to the eschatological place of Christ the High Priest, the Holy of Holies of His session at the right hand of the Father (i.e., the total deification of human nature), where he has entered as our Forerunner.

It is this liturgical dimension of becoming that Maximus wants to present, among other things, in his *Mystagogy*. In Chapter Five of that work, where the Church is presented as a type of the soul, he teaches that the evolving movement of the faculties of the soul is identified with the movement of existent entities toward their ecclesial assembly in Christ. Thus when the soul moves in this way, like the Church, through virtue and knowledge, it goes beyond the bounds of creaturehood by grace and attains to the "marriage bed of God, surpassing truth and goodness . . . in which blessed and all holy marriage bed that terrible mystery of the unity past words and understanding is accomplished. In this mystery,

God will become one flesh and one spirit with the Church, the soul, and the soul with God."[127] According to Maximus, the reality of this union is preserved tangibly and visibly in the mystery of the divine Eucharist, of the Church, because

> the holy Church of God . . . gathers all things together for the mystery accomplished upon the divine altar; one who is able to be initiated into this mystery with prudence and wisdom through the rites celebrated in the Church makes his soul truly a Church of God, and divine.[128]

The way the soul achieves this liturgical becoming and follows Christ the High Priest into the Holy of Holies of deification is, according to Maximus, by being initiated "with prudence and wisdom" into the "mystery accomplished upon the divine altar," the Divine Eucharist. The "rites performed in the Church," culminating in the Divine Eucharist, are for Maximus the "direction"[129] guiding the soul's liturgical becoming toward deification. Still further: this personal becoming succeeds and achieves its goal when it is incorporated into this one unique ecclesial becoming which culminates and is confirmed in the Divine Eucharist. And further yet: the Divine Eucharist forms the heart and essence of ecclesial becoming, because in it "everything is gathered together," and here, "through partaking of the pure and life-giving mysteries," the "communion with God and identity with Him through likeness which is possible by participation" is made manifest; "the communion through which man is accounted worthy to become God rather than man."[130] In other words, we have a manifestation of the fulfillment and completion of the whole purpose of ecclesial becoming, in the profound eschatological communion of God and man, which has even now begun. We consider, then, that according to Maximus the becoming of things within the Church is and has to be a eucharistic becoming, in the sense given above.[131]

So in order for personal liturgical becoming to succeed, the movement of the Christian's personal ek-static love toward God has to be incorporated into the eucharistic becoming of the Church. For this incorporation alone is able to lead to that personal becoming, to a becoming in communion with God, because the Divine Eucharist alone is the real, ontologically real, incorporation of the Christian into the Lord's Body[132] and communion between God and man. Eucharistic becoming, then, is the inescapable ontological precondition for every particular personal becoming, if the latter is to lead to communion with God.[133] Furthermore, we must recall here that this personal becoming takes place in Christ, as an ascetic practice of obedience to the will of God's love, which is to give life universally to the world in His Church; that is to say, it is a denial of our narcissistic self-love in all its forms, through participating in the kenotic love of Christ as manifested in the Cross and Resurrection). Here we should remind ourselves of what was said in Chapter One (section 8) about the guiding role of the priesthood, which is God's instrument in the personal liturgical incorporation of the faithful, those who have been ontologically initiated into the life of Christ's Body. So self-denial, in order to overcome the boundless self-deceptions of narcissism, has to have this concrete, material character of obedience to the spirit-filled authority of ecclesial "direction"—it must take the form of "cutting off the will" (which is not a negation of natural human will, but a cure of the gnomic will's illness, that is, self-love) as enjoined by our neptic tradition, a free action before the spiritual father, in order for the Christian to pass from his (always narcissistic) individuality to the personal-hypostatic dimension of eucharistic incorporation, which expresses Christ's mode of existence for the created being. This is how the "cession of the *gnomê*" (of which we have spoken often enough already) is to be understood, the cession of man's free will to God which ignites the Christian's ek-static movement of love toward Him. In surrendering his will to God, man surrenders himself so as to be incorporated, "initiated" as Maximus says, into this ecclesial, dialogical eucharistic becoming which leads to the absolute communion of man and God as gift-giving and gift-sharing. This is also why the communal prayer "in person" of which we spoke earlier has its basis, according to the Confessor, in liturgical prayer. Liturgical prayer is the locus where individual prayer becomes personal, ek-statically going out of itself toward the ontological communion of things in Christ.

In the light of the above, it becomes easier to understand what was said in the previous section about the role of the Holy Spirit in generating ek-static love in humans and guiding that love in its becoming toward God in Christ. The changing of the Precious Gifts (that means not of their essence, which remains the same—that is, created essence—of course, but of their mode of existence) takes place "in the Holy Spirit": the Holy Spirit is the author of eucharistic becoming, and in consequence He naturally also guides and assists the effort of Christians to incorporate their personal movement and journey into this eucharistic becoming, through asceticism, prayer, and participation in the sacramental life "performed in the Church." There is something more that

we might add: by this becoming, under the authority of the Spirit, communion between beings and God, as well as between beings themselves,
is not something imposed upon or dictated to them, which then remain
passive, but a dialogue, i.e., a whole course of mutual proposals and responses, which truly involves history, as a gradual process of a possible
participation and incorporation in the Body of Christ. What we have here
is dialogical reciprocity as a gift which man is offered by God. That is to
say, man is offered the possibility, not only to have an otherness offered
by God, but also to give otherness *to* God, to address God, to talk with
God, to present God with created nature, so that created nature is not
only something given by God, but is also as a gift of man to God. Without
this becoming, being conceived as communion risks to be understood
as a direct reflection of the Kingdom to come, an unavoidable mirroring of Divine Glory upon created beings, while these beings lose their
essences and energies as they are simply flooded by the innovating God.
"Being as communion" has thus to be immediately corrected as "being
as becoming-in-communion," if we do not want to ultimately conceive
of the Church as an automatic institutional reflection of the Kingdom of
God above history, i.e., without the failing or unfailing human struggle
to gradually participate (and here we have again the existential mystery
of the Cross) personally in God's gift, which is His very life outpouring
on His world. We shall discuss this issue in the next chapter.

Notes

1. The phrase is Sherwood's (*The Ascetic Life*, p. 49). See also Balthasar,
Cosmic Liturgy, pp. 137–154.

2. *Ambigua* 9, PG 91: 1072B

3. *Disputation with Pyrrhus*, PG 91: 352AB. See also Sherwood, *The Ascetic Life*, p. 39: "The motion is ontological, by which creatures are seen in
their respective inalienable identities, whence we understand Him who preserves each of them inviolate according to its proper logos." See also Meyendorff, *Christ in Eastern Christian Thought*, p. 135.

4. *Ambigua*, PG 91: 1217AB.

5. *Ambigua*, PG 91: 1073B; see also 1217A. See Sherwood, *op. cit.*, p. 58:
"Hence this mutability (tropi) is not to be referred to the 'everlasting motion
toward the fair or divine'. This latter is a 'natural operation' and therefore
never ceases. Mutability consequently is 'weakness', a 'falling away', a 'motion contrary to nature'."

6. *Ambigua*, PG 91: 1084D.

7. The expression is Florovsky's (*Creation and Redemption*, chap. 3).

8. See Sherwood, *The Ascetic Life*, p. 39: "The motion meant is that of the power and operation essentially consequent on the logos of each creature."

9. *Ambigua*, PG 91: 1080C.

10. *Ambigua*, PG 91: 1089A.

11. Ibid., 1072B.

12. Detailed treatment of the relations between motion and time and space falls outside the scope of this work. On this subject see Balthasar, *Liturgie Cosmique*, pp. 89–95; cf. *Cosmic Liturgy*, pp. 137–144.

13. *Ambigua*, PG 91: 1072B and 1073B. See also Sherwood, *The Ascetic Life*, pp. 55–56.

14. PG 91: 1217C.

15. PG 91: 1072A.

16. See Sherwood, *The Ascetic Life*, pp. 47ff.; Staniloae, *Philosophika kai Theologika Erotemata*, p. 132 n. 21.

17. Cf. Staniloae, *op. cit.*, p. 22. Sherwood (*The Ascetic Life*, p. 47) gives Origen's triad as *becoming, fixity, motion*. What is implied in this case is the creation of souls, their repose in God and their motion as a result of *koros*, satiety. We regard Staniloae's formulation as more correct and according follow that, even though the difference is not substantial.

18. See Meyendorff, *Christ in Eastern Christian Thought*, p. 134; Balthasar, *Cosmic Liturgy*, pp. 137ff.

19. Meyendorff, *op. cit.*, p. 133; Sherwood, *op. cit.*, p. 49.

20. See Staniloae, *op. cit.*, p. 132. The right motion of things takes place when they move in accordance with their norm and measure. See *Various Texts* 5.3, PG 90: 1349B: "The norm for entities should be knowledge of their cause through desire, and the measure should be to honour their cause in action, as far as that is attainable for them. But when desire carries things movable beyond their norm and measure, this makes their path fruitless because they do not attain to God."

21. See Sherwood, *The Ascetic Life*, p. 48; also Staniloae, *loc. cit.* Florovsky considers that the idea of creation moving toward God comes from the Areopagite, as does Meyendorff (*op. cit.*, p. 134). As Florovsky writes: "[the world] is moving toward God, toward God the logos. The whole world is in motion, is striving. God is above movement. It is not He who is moving, but the created and roused world which He created, which moves toward Him. Here the thought is similar to that found in the *Corpus Areopagiticum*" (*The Byzantine Fathers*, p. 221).

22. See Meyendorff, *op. cit.*, p. 137: "But [God] also assigns to the creatures a goal to reach, and in the case of man this goal implies a free movement toward God."

23. *Ambigua*, PG 91: 1217C.

24. Ibid., 1217CD.

25. Ibid., 1217D.

26. Cf. G. Florovsky, *Creation and Redemption*, p. 46; "created becoming."

27. Balthasar, *Liturgie Cosmique*, p. 95; *Cosmic Liturgy*, p. 143.

28. Sherwood, *The Ascetic Life*, p. 48.

29. *Ambigua*, PG 91: 1217D: "Movement is naturally preceded by becoming, and movement is naturally prior to fixity; hence it is clear that becoming and fixity cannot possibly exist at the same time, because between them there is the middle term of motion which naturally keeps them apart."

30. ". . . the ascent and restoration to the *logos* according to which they were created." See *Ambigua*, PG 91: 1080C.

31. *Opuscula*, PG 91: 301AC. See also Sherwood, *op. cit.*, p. 55.

32. *Opuscula*, PG 91: 17CD.

33. PG 91: 16B.

34. PG 91: 16D.

35. PG 91:, 17C.

36. PG 91:, 17D.

37. PG 91:, 12C.

38. PG 91:, 12CD. Cf. *To the Monk Theodore*, PG 91: 280A: "Natural will is the simple and consistent impetus and desire for whatever is by nature constitutive" [of the subject that wills]. Also *Various definitions*, PG 91: 153A: "Natural will is essentially the desire for whatever is by nature constitutive" [of the subject that wills]. The inspiration for this doctrine of Maximus's concerning the will is to be found in Aristotle and the Stoics, principally as adopted by Nemesius; see R.A. Gautier, "Saint Maxime le Confesseur et la psychologie de l'acte humaine," *Recherches de théologie ancienne et médiévale* 21 (Louvain, 1954), pp. 53–77. See also J.D. Madden, "The Authenticity of Early Definitions of Will," *Actes*, p. 61.

39. *Opuscula*, PG 91: 17C.

40. PG 91:, PG 91: 13A, 16C, 17C.

41. PG 91:, 17D–20A. According to J.D. Madden ("The Authenticity," pp. 65–66), introducing free will and self-determination into the concept of will "implies a radical re-shaping of any known secular Greek psychology, and had never to our knowledge been proposed before."

42. *On the Two Wills*, PG 91: 192AB.

43. *Disputation with Pyrrhus*, PG 91: 293A: "Having will by nature is not the same thing as willing; just as having speech by nature and speaking are not the same thing. . . . So it belongs to nature always to have the natural ability to speak, but how one speaks is a property of the hypostasis. So it is with having will by nature, and willing." Cf. Meyendorff, *Christ in Eastern Christian Thought*, p. 149: "*gnomê* is intrinsically linked with hypostasis, or human person." Also Staniloae, *Eisagogi*, p. 61.

44. As we know, Maximus believes that there is energy and will in human nature, as there is in the divine nature. See *The Life and Struggle of the Venerable Maximus the Confessor*, PG 90: 152D: "It has been entrusted to us to believe and confess that as Christ is two natures, because He is from two

natures, so also He has natural wills and energies as appropriate to One who is by nature at once God and man, the same [person]." Cf. *Opuscula*, PG 91: 157BC.

45. *Opuscula*, PG 91: 196A.

46. PG 91:, 192B.

47. PG 91:, 196B.

48. PG 91: 25A.

49. We see here the immense significance of the distinction between natural and gnomic will in Maximus's "eschatocentric" thought. As we have said above (see especially chap. 2.5), the distinction between natural and gnomic will can be seen as analogous to the distinction between *logos* of nature and *mode of existence*. We will say more about this below, but here we may underline the immense importance of this tenet of the Confessor, which is quite literally fundamental to his thought. The gnomic will is an operation of free choice belonging to the hypostasis or the person: as such, it precisely gives the natural will *hypostasis*, "substance" or mode of existence, a mode capable not of course of freeing, that natural will from the constraints of (created) nature, as, for example Zizioulas claims, but of realizing the eschatological vocation of this natural will to fulfill nature's divinization. This means that it can possibly offer nature an opening into a divine future, i.e. a mode of existence which is no longer bounded by the restrictions of fallen creaturehood but is precisely dialogically reciprocal. This is why in Maximus's Christology, which is a response to the Monothelite controversy, Christ has two natural wills (because He has two natures, a human and a divine), while His gnomic will simply does not exist (*Disputatio Cum Pyrrho*, PG 91, 292D–293A) as it is always bound with decision and personal disposition usually linked with hesitancy, uncertainty or ignorance. Here we have the *logos* of the natural human will absolutely open to the mode of the natural will of God the Word, because of the Hypostatic union. This is the eschatological fullness and actualization of the truly natural existence of created nature in Christ. In consequence, the distinction between natural and gnomic will in Maximus has to do with the very foundations of his eschatological ontology. Furthermore, this is one of the greatest spiritual discoveries in the history of human thought, unknown prior to the Confessor. It would take an extensive special study to demonstrate the value of this discovery, e.g., for Aristotelian studies or, above all, for philosophical anthropology, psychology, sociology or pedagogy, for all of which this distinction offer new horizons in interpretation and, above all, an opportunity for radical revisions. The impasse facing these disciplines is due precisely to the fact that they deal with man as a closed individual nature within the limits of (this created) world. Through the distinction between natural and gnomic will, Maximus offers the possibility of opening into a new mode of existence, characterized by the fulfillment of the uncreated *logos* of nature in its truly natural mode of existence, which is hypostatic-personal in the image and likeness of God.

50. PG 91: 192A.

51. PG 91: 193A.

52. PG 91: 25AB.

53. PG 91: 25B.

54. Maximus mentions the following Scriptural passages concerning Christ: "Nevertheless, not as I will, but as Thou wilt" (Matt 26:39) and "It is no longer I who live, but Christ who lives in me" (Gal 2:20). And he goes on: "Do not let this saying trouble you. For I am not saying that free will is destroyed, but rather that it finds its natural state, fixed and unchangeable— there occurs a cession of the *gnomê* in order that we may long to receive our movement from the same that is the source of our being." *Ambigua* 9, PG 91: 1076BC.

55. *Opuscula*, PG 91: 25C: "the human [will], moved through imitation toward the [divine] will which is good by nature . . ." Cf. Meyendorff, *Christ in Eastern Christian Thought*, pp. 143–144.

56. *On the Lord's Prayer*, PG 90: 896AB.

57. Ibid., 896BC.

58. *Mystagogy* 23, PG 91: 701BC.

59. *On the Lord's Prayer*, PG 90: 905D.

60. See his *Communion and Otherness,* chap. 8, esp. pp. 306–307, in the footnote text.

61. See my *Orthodoxy and Modernization; Byzantine Individualization, State and History in the Perspective of the European Future* (Athens, Armos, 2006) pp. 61–103.

62. Chapter 2.6.

63. *Ambigua*, PG 91: 1260B.

64. As we know, energy derives from essence. Thus relationship of energy relates us with essence itself, in the only way this can happen, without confusing the essences: through nature's (always en-hypostatic) energies.

65. Dionysius the Apeopagite, *On the Divine Names* IV.13, PG 3: 712AB: "To tell the truth, we should be so bold as to say even this: that He who is the cause of all, in His beautiful and good intense longing (*eros*) for all, is carried outside Himself in His providential wills for all creatures through the superabundance of His loving goodness, and is as it were beguiled by goodness and love and intense longing. And from being above all things and removed from all, He comes to be in all, according to an ek-static superessential power inseparable from Himself."

66. *On the Divine Names* IV.14, PG 3: 712C.

67. *Ambigua*, PG 91: 1206C.

68. *Ambigua*, PG 91: 1385B.

69. Sherwood (*The Ascetic Life,* pp. 42ff.) examines the text quoted above, and contends by concluding that "the reply is wholly and consciously based on Denis." In fact, however, it is clear that Maximus interprets and supplements the Areopagite's teaching, explaining how it is that God is in ek-static motion: within created things, and through their *logoi.*

70. Commentary on *On the Divine Names*, PG 4: 265D. We thus see
that there is a certain reciprocity of love between man and God, regardless
who initiates it. The relationship thus created is not *asymmetrical* as Levinas and Zizioulas claim (see *Communion and Otherness*, chap. 3) but truly
symmetrical: God loves to be loved, longs to be longed for, and thirsts to be
thirsted, according to Maximus and the Areopagitic texts. Zizioulas seems
to ignore the concept of reciprocity in Patristic Trinitarian theology. (See
on this my "Person instead of Grace, and Dictated Otherness: John Zizioulas's Final Theological Position"). However, the Levinasian God seems to
be rather the God of the Old Testement: He is a non-incarnating God, i.e.,
a God without reciprocity indeed, a God who only creates *asymmetrical*
relationships.

71. Unfortunately Sherwood is unable to understand the notion of ek-
stasis in this way, and regards the Areopagite primarily as the greatest Christian neoplatonist (*The Earlier Ambigua*, p. 126). He then devotes several
pages to exploring how Maximus combines the inwardness of Evagrius with
the Areopagite's ek-stasis as a process whereby the being goes outside itself
(pp. 124–154, esp. 124–128 and 153–154). He finally comes to the conclusion
that Maximus is not an entirely faithful disciple of either Evagrius or Dionysius, but corrects them both (pp. 153–154). Similarly in his *Maximus the
Confessor: The Ascetic Life* (p. 96) Sherwood, in agreement with Balthasar
and Hausherr, regards the difference between Evagrius and the Areopagite
as simply "a difference of mystical technique" (!). He considers that Maximus transcends the problem of inwardness *versus* outwardness when he
affirms that, "God is above every relation of subject and object, of thinker
and thought. Immanence and transcendence fall easily into such a dyadic
polarization. God is Himself therefore above them." We think that Sherwood's problem (as with Hausherr, "L'ignorance infinie," *Orientalia Christiana Periodica* 2 [1936], pp. 351–362; Viller, "Aux sources de la spiritualité de
St. Maxime," p. 248, n. 141; Balthasar, *Liturgie Cosmique*, p. 33) is a failure to
detect that for Maximus, inwardness in contemplation and the ek-static impetus of love are inseparable in spiritual life, precisely because the personal
relationship of love is what saves and gives meaning to inwardness. In the
following pages, we shall see that the fulfillment of the ek-static impetus of
love in communion with God is the one thing that ensures true knowledge
of all things.

72. See Aristotle's *Metaphysics* IV.viii, 1012b: "For there is something
that ever moves things that are in motion, and the prime mover is itself
unmoved." Ibid. XII.vii, 1072a: "There is something that is not in motion but
moves [things], something eternal which is both essence and energy." Ibid.
XII.vii, 1072ab: " The object of desire and of thought causes motion: it causes
motion without being in motion . . . it causes motion because it is an object
of love." Cf. Florovsky, *The Byzantine Fathers*, p. 219.

73. *Centuries on Theology* 1.39, PG 90: 1097C. We can nowhere find any
kind of position between nature and person because of ecstasis, in Maxi-

mus. Rather it is nature itself that is eschatologically fulfilled through the ecstatic gnomic movement of the natural will toward God's loving will.

74. *To Thalassius*, PG 90: 548CD.

75. *To Thalassius*, PG 90: 548D–549A.

76. *Ambigua* 9, PG 91: 1073CD.

77. As we read in the continuation of this passage, 1076A ff.

78. PG 91: 1076C.

79. Ibid., 1077AB.

80. Ibid., 1077B.

81. *To Thalassius*, PG 90: 449A: "Therefore love is the offspring of the coming together and union of the faculties of the soul around things divine—those faculties being the reason, the incensive faculty and the faculty of desire."

82. *Ambigua*, PG 91: 1248D–1249B.

83. PG 91: 1249B.

84. Ibid.

85. *To Thalassius*, PG 90: 401A: "He calls 'good wine' the *logos* of nature which is ek-static, going outside itself so as to be deified."

86. See chap. 1.2, and *Ambigua*, PG 91: 1193C–1196C. It is of great interest at this point to recall the texts referred to in notes 58 and 59 (*Mystagogy* 23; *On the Lord's Prayer*, PG 90: 905D). When our adoption is fully accomplished, we shall be children of God, "all of us carrying within us in all purity Him who is the author of this grace and the Son of the Father by nature, in His entirety yet without His being circumscribed," in the Spirit. The essence of this "Christification" lies in being gathered "to the Father . . . to the oneness of His hidden presence, ek-statically separated from all things" (*Mystagogy* 23, 701B). Thus the believer enters empirically into the very ontology of the internal relations of the Trinity, by participation, i.e., by grace, and in proportion to his receptivity.

87. *Ambigua*, PG 91: 1077A.

88. See PG 91: 1077B: "knowledge . . . singular and subject to participation."

89. Ibid., 1084BC.

90. A treatment of this ek-stasis in connection with the Holy Spirit is lacking in Christos Yannaras' *Person and Eros* (Holy Cross Orthodox Press, 2007). The question is a crucial one: it is through the Holy Spirit alone that communion can be constituted, so any treatment of ek-stasis without reference to its pneumatological precondition contains equally the danger of being imprisoned in the traditional Western "monism of the subject" (Y. Belaval), and ultimately that of being trapped in a concealed individualism, narcissistic in character (to use the traditional terminology of psychoanalysis). It should also be stressed again and again that ek-stasis in Maximus's theology is not connected with transcending nature, (as Yannaras and Zizioulas claim—see, for example, the latter's *Communion and Otherness*, pp. 162–168, where the ecstatic "personal" escape from nature seems to be

the only way to "freedom"/salvation) but with opening creaturehood to the uncreated. On the contrary, to transcend nature, is for Maximus, a sheer absurdity, as we have already seen, because the nature's uncreated principles/logoi, when they become spiritual ways, guide us to God. Here there is a serious mistake common for many Orthodox personalists, thinking that person is exactly this kind of ekstasis, in the sense of an *escape out of nature*, this latter identified with necessity and practically with the Fall. There is a strong neo-Platonic tendency here. For Maximus, to speak of an ekstasis out of nature, is a serious ontological and existential error and a practical abolishment of the Logos' incarnation. Ekstasis, for the Confessor, is an ekstasis of *nature itself* through the gnomic movement of natural will toward the eschatological vocation made for it by God's uncreated logoi, a vocation that is fulfilled in Christ's Incarnation and Resurrection (see my Closed Spirituality . . . , p. 283–300). But that is totally impossible to accomplish through the powers of the creature in itself: it is a work of the Holy Spirit. So ek-static love, as we shall see below, is a result of victory in the Holy Spirit over the demonic powers of division and self-love. In Zizioulas's aforementioned work one can nowhere find even the slightest allusion to Grace, as the author of nature's fulfillment. Here the concept of person substitutes for Grace! This approach is similarly lacking in N. Matsoukas's work mentioned earlier, *World, Man, Communion according to Maximos the Confessor* (cf. especially pp. 128–135). By contrast, Meyendorff has grasped the fact that "this going beyond or ecstasy, is produced because of the presence of the Spirit, who co-operates with the free choice and effort of man" (*Christ in Eastern Christian Thought*, p. 151).

91. *Centuries of Various Texts* 1.71, PG 90: 1208C.

92. Ibid. 72, 73, PG 90: 1208C–1209A

93. Ibid. 73, 1209A: "and in all Christians He is also present in an additional way, in that He makes them sons by adoption."

94. *Ambigua* 9, PG 91: 1076C. Ek-stasis can never be given only a «volitional» definition such as that ultimately given by Sherwood (*The Ascetic Life*, p. 96): "The over all sense is that of an outgoing of the volitive power, which effects the final gnomic harmony and unity in love." Rather, ekstasis is communion, as we have seen.

95. PG 91: 1076C.

96. The term is borrowed from Fr. Justin Popović.

97. The idea of "constituting" and the way this notion is used have been taken from Zizioulas's chapter "Christ, the Spirit and the Church" in *Being as Communion* (p. 140): "In a Christological perspective alone we can speak of the Church as *in-stituted* (by Christ), but in a pneumatological perspective we have to speak of it as *con-stituted* (by the Spirit). Christ *in-stitutes* and the Spirit *con-stitutes*. The difference between these two prepositions: *in-* and *con-* can be enormous ecclesiologically. The 'institution' is something presented to us as a fact. . . . As such, it is more or less a provocation to our freedom. The 'con-stitution' is something that involves

us in its very being, something we accept freely, because we have part in its very emergence" [italics orig.]. This position is not significantly different from that expressed in Lossky's *Mystical Theology of the Eastern Church*, although Zizioulas tends to refuse this fact as he himself never speaks of the "Economy of the Spirit" separated from the "Economy of Christ." However, this separation remains because, in Zizioulas, we are first presented with Christ *as a fact* and then with the Spirit *as the freedom* from this fact, and that happens because Zizioulas retains (and wants to further support) this "institutional" aspect in ecclesiology, so common in some Orthodox and Roman Catholic Orthodox circles today. For Maximus, there is no such separation (and so he never says that the Christ "institutes"—alone?—and then the Spirit "constitutes"), because he never conceived of something other than a purely existential ecclesiology such as that which is described in *Mystagogy*. What I mean is that *Ecclesia* is for Maximus an "image" (*eikon*) of the kingdom to come, insofar as She is moving toward it through an "imitation" (*mimesis*)—a term which, for Maximus, means participation—of God's uncreated logoi/acts. Exactly because of this fact, the Church, as an image of the *eschata*, cannot be said to be a given structure "presented to us as a fact," a structure from which we try to escape (or try to be assimilated into) by the Spirit, but an existential event of becoming-in-communion with Christ, as we shall see. Thus, the Church is never something that is just *given*, but it is always something that is *achieved*. Or, we could say that the Church is given on the part of God, but the Church we know is a contingent event of a certain degree of participation. Thus, if we insist to speak of structures, then the only structure is this existential imitation/participation by and in the Spirit, Who always possibly constitutes Christ, Who in His turn, was never previously instituted by Himself alone, i.e., as a rigid structure (see my *Apophatic Ecclesiology of Consubstantiality* pp. 68–93, 105–109, 150–176 and, for readers of English, pp. 359–384). This lack of balance between Christ and Spirit produces a tension between the institutional and the charismatic aspect of the Church in Zizioulas's work. See on this my *Christian Life and Institutional Church*, in *The Theology of John Zizioulas. Personhood and the Church*, (Douglas H. Knight ed., Ashgate 2007, pp. 125–132).In the same volume D. Bathrellos in his *Church, Eucharist, Bishop : The Early Church in the Ecclesiology of Zizioulas*, repeats some of the above claims of mine, that can be found in my aforementioned book, albeit without any reference to it.

98. See Meyendorff, *Christ in Eastern Christian Thought*, p. 138.

99. *Ambigua* 15, PG 91: 1116C.

100. *Ambigua*, PG 91: 1093A.

101. *Mystagogy* 1, PG 91: 668B.

102. *Ambigua*, PG 91: 1076A–D. See also the two previous sections.

103. See chap. 4.2, above.

104. *Mystagogy*, Epilogue, PG 91: 708C.

105. *Mystagogy* 1, PG 91: 667D.

106. We use the term "becoming" in its simplest philosophical sense, to mean a movement involving a series of changes. This is the first definition of becoming in dictionaries of philosophy, usually connected with the notion of time as does the *Cambridge Dictionary of Philosophy*, second edition, R. Audi, ed., 1999, p. 920.

107. *Mystagogy* 1, PG 91: 668AB.

108. See J. Meyendorff, *Christ in Eastern Christian Thought*, p. 139: "Man's natural movement toward God thus possesses a cosmic impact. Man finds God in the world and the world needs man in order to find its Creator again. Through the image the world recovers the Prototype."

109. See chap. 3.6.

110. We will examine the passage in *Mystagogy* 1, PG 91: 664D–665B. A section of this passage was discussed in chap. 2.2, from a different angle.

111. Ibid.

112. Ibid.

113. *To Thalassius*, PG 90: 760A.

114. PG 90: 757D.

115. PG 90: 757D–760A. Cf. also 781BC.

116. PG 90: 760A.

117. See chap. 2.

118. See chap. 3.2.

119. *To Thalassius*, PG 90: 781BC.

120. See also chap. 2.2 and chap. 2.1.

121. Cf. 1 Cor. 13:12.

122. So the two main ontological characteristics of the person are becoming and communion, as described here, while its essential texture is eschatological.

123. *Centuries of Various Texts* 3.31, PG 90: 1273A.

124. *To Thalassius*, PG 90: 616A.

125. *Centuries on Theology* 2.32, PG 90: 1140B.

126. Ibid.

127. *Mystagogy* 5, PG 91: 680D–681A. This text has been studied before from a different angle.

128. PG 91: 681D.

129. PG 91: 684A.

130. *Mystagogy* 24, PG 91: 704D. Let us recall once more what was said in note 84. By "holy partaking" (i.e., Communion), the Christian communes and is identified, as Maximus says, with God. In other words, the Eucharist is precisely the way he enters into experience of, and participation in, the ontology of the internal relationships within the Trinity, as an experience of personal "communion" with God who is personal and communal. The Eucharist "transmits" this ontology to the created being.

131. It is equally clear, however, that this becoming also ontologically justifies and saves history itself, this concrete and unrepeatable moment in history. To the extent that it is not a free choice of self-annihilation, contrary

to nature, the concrete historical consciousness, the historical act, can freely open itself to this eschatological liturgical becoming, making the transient historical material into something revelatory—a testimony to the Christocentric and Christonostalgic impetus which preserves the truth of historical becoming amidst the chaos of contradictions.

132. As we have shown already in chap. 1.

133. Balthasar, who has different presuppositions and a different perspective, is rather unable to appreciate the questions posed in this chapter or contribute to discussion of them. Mainly on the basis of the *Mystagogy*, he distinguishes three sorts of worship: that of the Church, the "cosmic liturgy" and the spiritual unification of the two in a "worship of love" (*Liturgie Cosmique*, pp. 242–253; *Cosmic Liturgy*, pp. 314–330). He believes that "the basic idea of the Mystagogy is that the sacramental ritual of the Church is the effective symbol of the transcendent, universal and cosmic liturgy" (*Liturgie Cosmique*, p. 246; cf. *Cosmic Liturgy*, p. 322). Our view is of course totally different. It is not a matter of the cosmic liturgy being symbolised in the sacramental: that is a defective understanding of the spirit of the Confessor. The sacramental liturgy is the ideal content of the cosmic, and its sole ontological justification. Woefully inadequate, likewise, is Balthasar's understanding of the place of the Eucharist in the *Mystagogy*. Understanding Maximus in Origenist terms, he regards the Eucharist as symbol rather than reality, as a representation of what is true (*Cosmic Liturgy*, p. 324): "The sacraments—of which Maximus treats only baptism and the Eucharist thematically—stand completely within the dynamic of the movement from sign to reality. The Eucharist is essentially 'symbol, not reality', 'an image of true things' [*On the Ecclesiastical hierarchy* 3, PG 4: 137A, 145B; *Queastiones et Dubia* 41, PG 90: 820A].") The basic thesis of this study is precisely the opposite. The Eucharist is the heart of truth and reality, for Maximus in general and the *Mystagogy* in particular. Indeed, one may say that precisely on the basis on Maximus's eucharistic theology, we are able to transcend the antithesis between truth and symbol (whether of Platonic or of Origenist origin). In Maximus, this whole neo-Platonic impasse has been left behind. Here an image (icon) means precisely ontological participation in the truth, and the mysteries are ways and paths whereby we can approach the truth even now. So not only is there no antithesis, but the Eucharist is the royal ontological road (precisely the icon) to ultimate truth. A non-ontological understanding of the Eucharist also prevents Riou, in his important book, from correctly perceiving the "iconic" character of the Church (see *Le Monde et L'Eglise*, esp. pp. 135–146). So despite the fact that "the Church is the hypostatic, iconic presence of God in the world" through Christ, the ontological manner in which creation is brought into the mystery of Christ remains obscure (Riou does of course speak of "faith" and "grace" in reference to Baptism or the Eucharist [p. 144], but we find neither ontology, nor incorporation, nor hypostasis). So ultimately, "the Church is an icon. It is nothing more than

the 'symbolic' passage, the paschal and eschatological 'incoding' of the Mystery in the world and of the world in the Mystery" (p. 145). Not being ontological, the "iconic" becomes once again "symbolic."

Chapter 5

The Eucharistic Ontology of Becoming in Communion as an Ontology of Dialogical Reciprocity

1. The Original Traditional Philosophical Contrast between Being and Becoming

THE DISTINCTION AND EVEN CONTRADISTINCTION between being and becoming is very ancient, as old as philosophy itself; it is also one of the classical contrasts in the history of philosophy, characteristic and definitive for the cultural history of the West. That which becomes is not yet in being. That which is, has ceased to become. Being "resists every onsurge of becoming."[1]

It is of course beyond the intent and scope of this theological study systematically to trace the formation and development of this classic duality of contrasting concepts, or to describe the tireless philosophical efforts to reconcile them which continue even to our own day. We must say, however, that the roots of this contrast are to be found already in pre-Socratic thought, manifesting themselves in the polarity between the Eleatic view of being (mainly as it appears in Parmenides) which holds that being is qualitatively stable (immovable), and the view of Heraclitus who holds that the reality of becoming is primary.[2] All the "inquirers into natural causes" of the fifth century BC work to reconcile this accepted antithesis, which nevertheless expresses, in the words of Windelband, two equally valid "necessities of thought."[3]

According to Parmenides, then, the properties of the One or of Being are eternity, being ingenerate and indestructible, and in particular (as Xenophanes had earlier maintained) complete unity, i.e., overall homogeneity and absolute changelessness.[4] For Heraclitus, by contrast, the order of becoming which is the only reality has two definitions: the harmony of opposites and the cyclical succession of matter in the universe. From his observation of the continuous flux and change of all things, Heraclitus will be led to the conviction that all things are continuously being changed into their opposite. This continuous change is ultimately an unceasing battle (war is father of all things, according to the sage of Ephesus). So everything that appears at a given moment to be, comprises the coincidence of opposing motions and forces which balance each other out ("*enantiotropia*"). Thus the universe is at every moment a unity that is broken apart and continuously reconstituted ("one thing differing from itself"), a constant war that tends toward reconciliation; the essence of the universe is the "invisible harmony" which unifies the tensions pulling in opposite directions.[5] We must emphatically stress that in the dialectical thinking of Heraclitus, this harmony does not at all mean that the opposites are amalgamated or reconciled: on the contrary, each entity is the unity of itself and its opposite within the dramatic process of becoming which is warlike and not at all peaceful, animated by conflict, negativity, war as the supreme Justice, the inexorable fate of the world.[6] Even God is for Heraclitus bound up in this cosmic becoming.[7] The One, Being, forms a unity, but in this sense of warlike harmony, dramatic tension and contrasts tearing each other apart: being is "the being of becoming."[8]

Windelband in his *Handbook* gives a fine (indeed classic) exposition of the whole of pre-Socratic thought in the light of precisely this quest to reconcile these primal polarities of ancient thought, Elea and Heraclitus, and comes to the following conclusion: "Heraclitean becoming does not bear any kind of being—as well as from Parmenides' being no becoming is born. Indeed, the Heleatus's doctrine of being, along with the exception of change and manifoldness, also considers becoming as impossible. According to their metaphysics, becoming is unthinkable, it is impossible."[9] This opposition, which even its contemporaries worked to resolve, is present even to our own day. The philosophies of Hegel and Marx, of Nietzsche and of Bergson, of Kant, and of the existentialists have their contributions to make to the long-running effort to reconcile this primal contradiction. We shall focus our attention on the most authoritative analysis of the subject, that of Heidegger; here we have the preeminent modern attempt to understand the contradistinction between being and becoming, and at the same time the most radical modern effort to transcend it, always within the framework of Western thought.

Heidegger tries to bridge the gap: Heraclitus and Parmenides want to say the same thing, he is forced to affirm.[10] And to explain this, he goes on to analyze the second primal dualistic opposition, that of Being and appearance. Heidegger connects the two pairs:

> What is situated in becoming is no longer nothing and is not yet that which it is destined to become. In view of this "no longer and not yet," becoming is shot through with non-being. Yet it is not pure nothing, but no longer this and not yet that and as such perpetually other. Consequently it looks now this way and now that. It presents an intrinsically unstable aspect. Thus seen, becoming is an appearance of being.[11]

So for Heidegger, becoming is the appearance of Being; and to make this better understood, he proceeds to the third fundamental dualistic pair of opposites, a modern one this time, that of being and thought: "Accordingly, becoming and appearance are defined in the perspective of thought."[12] This means that "critical thought" is ultimately what identifies becoming with movement, change of place, transposition. On the other hand, it is thought that ultimately sees appearance as a logical error, a falsehood, an oversight. Thus Being ultimately shows itself to be permanance, in contrast to becoming—and correspondingly, in contrast to appearance it is the enduring prototype (the paradigm), the always identical. In contrast to thought, finally, it is the subject, the given.[13] It is clear, however, that becoming, appearance, and thought all have entity: they are not nothing but exist and determine the ontological state of essences. So they are beings themselves, Heidegger says. How are they then set in opposition to Being? The philosopher's answer attempts a radical criticism of Western metaphysics: "Then the sense of being that has been accepted up until now does not suffice to name everything that 'is.'"[14] So Heidegger proposes a further broadening of the concept of Being to encompass all beings, everything that is seemingly in opposition to the notion of Being. Despite all this, their relationship with being will be that of Being and beings ("the essent");[15] Being is clearly given preeminence in Heidegger as the sole and supreme "power which still sustains and dominates all our relations to the essent as a whole, to becoming, to appearance, to thinking and to the ought."[16]

So Being is always "other," something different from "what is," something different from becoming. Even though Heidegger tries to transcend the antithesis between being and becoming, and does manage to place them in a relationship of dependence (becoming is a being which depends on Being) even he is not able ultimately to avoid differentiating them: Being is "greater" than becoming, different from becoming, which is simply a particular being. This attempt on Heidegger's part, the probably supreme and boldest attempt of its kind in modern Western philosophy, in its own way preserves the dichotomy between being and becoming. This dichotomy, insurmountable as it is, really seems to be written into the "fate" of European philosophy.

Certainly, the question of the solution to this problem is not simply an exercise in academic philosophy. The consequences of this dichotomy are enormous for Western education (as they were for that of ancient Greece). The separation of becoming from being (or the establishment of becoming as the primary reality) raises profound questions, such as: What is the meaning and ontological value of becoming as a factor in nature, society, and history? What is the ultimate goal of becoming, or, conversely, what is the ontological meaning of continuous becoming? What is the beginning of becoming, and why should becoming exist? How to ensure that becoming has a positive, constructive direction, and how to avoid it taking a negative and destructive force? Which is ontologically prior, being or becoming, and why? What sort of moral, social and historical behavior flows from each interpretation of becoming? Who is ultimately the lord of becoming: how far is man able to control natural, social, or historical becoming? Is man or is he not subject to a cosmological and historical becoming which transcends and crushes him? What is the meaning of freedom, and what are the possibilities for true freedom within an inexorable natural and historical becoming? What is the value of the specific and unrepeatable human person amidst the rapidly changing movement of all things which crushes the particular? On the other side, the separation of being from becoming (or the establishment of being as the primary reality) also raises enormous intellectual problems, such as: If this is what Being is like—eternal, unchanging, incorruptible, and unapproachable—does it not run the risk of being objectified? (Berdyaev has given us remarkable insights on this subject, criticizing the Western philosophical view of that which is and showing the necessity of going beyond the idea of Being as a set, objectivized entity.[17]) How can being be perfect if it cannot move? On the other hand, how can it avoid falling into nothingness if it does move? How can being exist if it does not move?[18] How can being commune and be communed in if it does not move? (a question that literally demolished Western theology). How can being be alive if it does not move? On the other hand, how can being be absolute, if it does move? If being

is thus immobile, how can it move? How is freedom ontologically preserved if movement is nothingness? What are the consequences of this
absolute lordship of being over ethics and aesthetics, sociability and history? How are the freedom and otherness of the person preserved when
they are absolutely subject to its essence?

Some of these question were given answers in the course of this
book. Let us summarize our reflections.

2. The Identification of Being with Communion, and Its
Basis in the Divine Eucharist

THE NATURAL "RELATIONALITY" OF THE INNER PRINCIPLES of entities,
their "principle of union," and the "loving affinity" between them impel
them to become part of the universal realization of being as a dialogical
reciprocity, through a "unifying relationship," which operates through
human nature, in Christ.[19] This "pressing things together" into communion as gift-giving belongs to God's Providence, and is intended to
bring them into the "changelessness" of the Kingdom: ultimately, the
many inner principles of entities becomes "one and the same *logos*"
through unifying communion, as all things are conjoined "to God and
to each other through the Spirit." What we have here is an eschatological event, imaged in Pentecost[20] and activated in Christ. Christ closes up
the five ontological divides, fulfilling "in obedience" God's loving and
providential will[21] and showing creation to be "one" given and shared
gift, crowning the work of creation out of nothing with this absolute
communion. Without this communion, the being of things will fall back
into nothingness. Nothingness is non-being precisely because it is absolute non-connection, non-communion. According to Maximus, being
is constituted as a dialogical communion of gifts: being cannot be conceived without communion as gift-giving and gift-sharing.[22]

The actualization of being as communion is eschatological and
comes into history through the Eucharist; or rather, history itself is
elevated through the Eucharist, which is the supreme real manifestation of the communion of entities in Christ. The Eucharist is the heart
of the Church, communion as love and reciprocal distribution of gifts,
i.e., communion in the Person of Christ: communion in Christ through
love is what brings entities into the truth of the Kingdom of God's love.
Christ's love is a kenotic and sacrificial "divine solicitude" which produces a peaceable communion of all things, put into operation "by His

Blood." This love is incarnate, according to Maximus, in the Eucharist, as
the eucharistic love of Christ, a conjoining and incorporation of rational
beings in Christ which leads them to partake even now in divine life, in
Trinitarian unity-in-communion, as a foretaste of the perfect participation which is to come. The Lord's love is revealed to us in its fullness in
His eucharistic Body and Blood, through which He constitutes and preserves the ultimately one inner principle of creation in communion with
the Father.[23] The personal life of the faithful in the Church is put into
action as participation in the eucharistic love of Christ, a participation
which is a consequence of personal ascetic obedience to God's life-giving
call to communion in Christ, as opposed to the division wrought by self-
love. It is the believer's response to God's will that the world should be
given life in the eucharistic universality of the ecclesial body.[24] The being
of entities, joined as they are in communion in the Church, is fulfilled
and accomplished in the Eucharist: the Eucharist causes beings to be as
gifts, because it is the living and active communal expression of being
as life, as a loving-adoptive gathering of entities by God in Christ and a
unique expression of the reality of the Church, because the Eucharist is
God's love itself as the eucharistic Body and Blood of Christ.[25]

Through the Eucharist, therefore, the concept and the reality of
communion in being are definitively authenticated. Real being, the true
life of existent creatures, is communion in Christ. Following Christ, the
human being is fulfilled as a person as he is introduced through baptism,
by grace, into the personal mode of existence of Christ; and through the
Eucharist, which is the culmination and "essence" of all the mysteries,[26]
he participates (also by his voluntary ascetic obedience to the Lord) in
the sacrificial eucharistic love of Christ, which is the fulfillment and con-
solidation of man's personal mode of existence, in the likeness of God.
Man exists as person, the more completely he participates in the eucharistic love of the Lord. Following Christ in everything, man becomes by
grace a person similar to His unique Person—he becomes the unique
locus and mode of existence for the entire cosmos. Within himself he
identifies being with communion, revealing life to be an eternal experience of personal communion, that communion of which Christ is the
author and mystagogue.

Through the Eucharist, then, we know being, and experience it
within the Church, as a free communion of a dialogical reciprocity of
gift-giving, a communion of creation and God in Christ, in the image of
the personal communion and unity of the Trinity. Being owes its stability and unity to the fact of this active continuous circulation of gifts that

constitutes being and holds it together in its essence: this is precisely what the eschatological foundation of ontology means in the work of the Confessor. The profound post-Kantian crisis in ontology and its "exhaustion" in our day[27] objectified in the polarity of subjectivism and objectivism which permeates the whole of Western thought, philosophical and theological alike, marks the inability of Western philosophical thought to conceive of the fact of communion ontologically and in absolute relationship to the very essence of being.[28] And this inability on the part of Western philosophy leads directly to its inability to conceive of becoming as ontologically inherent to being, as we shall see immediately below.

3. The Introduction of Becoming into Being through Eucharistic Communion: The Eucharistic Ontology of Becoming-in-Communion as an Ontology of Dialogical Reciprocity

As we have seen, the divine Eucharist brings being as dialogical reciprocity, into ontology, and indeed makes it the ontological foundation, the ontological ground on which the being of things is founded. Yet love, that "internal inter-subjectivity,"[29] has also another precondition according to Maximus. This is the precondition that follows from the mobile quality of creaturehood which, as a component of its uncreated principle of existence, is an absolutely positive "passion" of creaturehood and at the same time one of its "active operations," a means whereby entities are able to evolve and have evolved toward their coinherence in unity, as a becoming which provides the basis for their eschatological communion.[30]

In a rational creature, the gnomic will makes use of the operation of the natural will, but now as a personal movement of its nature toward the fullness of that nature's life. Thus, no separation between nature and personhood can be possible in the Confessor's thought, as some modern Orthodox personalists claim. Redemption for Maximus is a redemption of—what else but—the nature itself, as it is created by God the Word and assumed by Him; but, of course, this a redemption of nature as a restoration of its very being as personal dialogue. The personal activation and direction of this natural movement through the gnomê leads thus to the dialogical "agreement of wills" between God and man as a "yielding of the gnomê," a process of a step-by-step opening of man's will to God out of love. The mode of this gnomic step-by-step movement of the will is prayer, the quintessence of which lies in offering to God's will the totality of becoming (not only the personal human movement, but also through it the movement of all inanimate entities as through a "cosmic liturgy," in Balthasar's phrase); and God's will is His desire to be given and simultaneously adored, according to our author.[31]

Just as God, who is by nature immovable, goes outside Himself in creating a personal relationship of love with His creature, so man's movement is in its ultimate essence a response of *eros* to the ek-stasis of God in His goodness and love, as a "sober madness" of personal ek-stasis of nature in favor of this dialogue between man and God mentioned above. When through the virtues the gnomic will attains to love, it is sanctified and the human movement becomes an ek-stasis, with prayer as its vehicle, which is thus "the love which opens man's free will to God."[32] The author of human ek-stasis is the Holy Spirit, who overcomes the comprehensive evil of narcissistic self-love and assists man in his ascetic effort to acquire selfless love, whereby he joins in the sacrificial eucharistic love of Christ.

This ek-static love ultimately sustains the becoming-in-communion of man's personal movement.[33] Becoming is inseparable from communion, just as communion is inseparable from being. Becoming in Maximus is not simply an instrument or an underpinning for communion: it is an ontological datum on a par with it. We are talking about a profound communion interlinked with becoming, incomprehensible and non-existent without becoming. Static communion and becoming without communion both destroy the creature. Becoming in Christ has to do not simply with deeper communion, but with true communion. Communion is the aim and truth of the entity in process of becoming; becoming is the mode of existence of the entity that is in communion. What causes beings to be is becoming-in-communion, in the senses given to these terms in this book, and in the sense that the Confessor himself gives to this teaching of his with the terms "ever-moving fixity" and "fixed motion-in-sameness."[34] Here we have another possible correction of "being as communion," so strongly supported by Zizioulas. It has not been noticed how strong is Maximus's emphasis on the ontological importance of becoming. Without it, any possibility of being as communion to be real and not institutionally or even existentially imposed upon creatures, simply vanishes. The Church and the Eucharist themselves become merely some "monophysite" reflections of divine logos, without a step-by-step existential dialogical becoming, consisting in divine proposals and human responses. *Micro-eschatology*, which is the voice of the little beings of the world, is thus destroyed and God becomes again an onto-theological giant, arrogantly closed in His solipsisitic castle of self-sufficiency. Becoming is not a becoming of God Himself, as we have already said, but it is His becoming through His uncreated loving wills/ *logoi* within creatures; a becoming by which He also becomes, through the Human response, *a God for the creatures*. Thus by introducing becoming in ontology, Maximus introduces the real history in theological cosmology and anthropology, an act which prevents ecclesiastical communion from being *transcendental*, i.e., a heavenly structure imposed by God on things. Maximus's only "structure" *is an event of a historical becoming in communion*, step-by-step, by imitation of (or participation in), the divine Logos, through His uncreated *logoi*, through our gnomic will. The event of the Church is thus an absolutely existential one, one of a freely-stepping historical dialogue between man and God. Thus historical happennedness acquires spiritual meaning and this uncreated meaning makes God present in it.

The natural space within which beings *are*, as they experience this becoming-in-communion, is for Maximus the Church, and above all its heart which is the divine Eucharist. Of course the Church is not a product of the Eucharist, as she also exists before it; but the sacraments culminating in the Eucharist *express* what the Church is, in the same way that the divine energies express what God is. Thus in the Eucharist, as an expression of ecclesial being, we find encrypted the truly natural mode of existence of entities as gifts, i.e., as an ontological event of dialogical reciprocity and loving unity, an event involving Providence, the divine economy and love. Here we find the culmination of the Spirit's activity in bringing about our adoption,[35] which leads to the absolute, immortal, and incorruptible life of eternal well-being. Indeed, the ontological dimensions of the Eucharist are dimensions of this incorruptible and irrepressible eternal life, which is identical with eternal knowledge of the deifying truth of adoption in Christ—of the recapitulation of the created order in Christ, which is operative *par excellence* within the framework of eucharistic ecclesial communion.[36] Hence also becoming has a liturgical quality, according to the *Mystagogy*, and leads the believer to the eschatological place of Christ's "sitting at the right hand," to deification. This personal, liturgical becoming succeeds and achieves its goal, according to Maximus, when, and to the degree that, it is incorporated in the Holy Spirit into the one and only ecclesial-eucharistic becoming.[37] The Spirit assists and supports the gathering together of beings in the Risen Christ, just as He supports their ek-static movement toward Christ.

This eucharistic ontology takes as its starting point Maximus's idea that being is not only fulfilled in well-being, but even exists "eschato-logically," i.e., for the sake of well-being, for the boundless divine vitality which as "fixed motion-in-sameness" is offered to personal beings and through them to the entire created order; and it reveals to us that every movement of things and every action of persons is ontologically justified inasmuch as it is directed toward the *eschaton*, the eternal well-being which is perfect incorporation into the risen Body of Christ.[38]

Here we have a revealed ontology outside-the-created, the only true ontology of the personal mode of being as it is uniquely under-stood "in the divine Trinity," which shatters the closed, intra-mundane or rather intra-creational ontology of the ancient Greeks; and it equally shatters the modern Western ontology, creation-centred in all its mani-festations, to the extent that the latter proceeds from a theology inca-pable of comprehending the irruption of the last things into the present which lies at the heart of Orthodox ecclesiology—an irruption that is charged with vitality, actual in a realistic and not a metaphysical sense, and continuous. This is a Christocentric ontology founded on Trinitar-ian theology, and is in consequence eucharistic, in the sense that it is in the Eucharist (as the culmination of all the mysteries) that the authentic life of all entities, their very possibility of being, is revealed and activated even now. None of the traditional philosophies are able to grasp this. What we have here is a new ontology (new in the sense that philosophy has not yet discovered it, and indeed is never going to), an ontology that is purely theological, eschatological, and eucharistic.[39] Is this ontology a new step beyond ancient Greek ontology, i.e., beyond Plato and Aris-totle? I would reply, yes. Indeed E. von Ivanka in his *Plato Christianus*, a work regarded as a classic, is unable to get beyond an understanding of the doctrine of the *logoi* in Platonic and Aristotelian terms. And quite naturally so, because he is unable to understand the eschatological basis of Maxi-mus's ontology except in the light of ancient teleology. So the Confessor's originality lies, according to Ivanka, in that he unites into a single ontologi-cal understanding the natural, earthly, actual being of entities with a su-pranatural openness to the ideal beyond, which is to say that he unites the Aristotelian "nature" with the Platonic "idea." In that case, of course, the "real being" of entities is nothing more that a form of "decadence" (*déché-ance*) which must be transcended. This dialectic is however foreign to the spirit of the Confessor . . . And so, despite recognizing the ontological value

of movement in Maximus, Ivanka cannot but regard it as merely a component part of the perfectly fulfilled nature of creaturehood in the last times,
certainly not part of the essence of created being even now. These views
betray an inadequate understanding of the eschatological texture of Maximus's theology. For from the perspective of that theology, it is a moot point
whether we can even speak of a just given "essence" of creaturehood, and
especially of a distinction between "essence" and "fulfilled nature," when
the ontological foundation of being is eternal well-being. This means that
the Confessor is neither an Aristotelian, interested in the ontological mini-
mum of the nature or form, nor a Platonist concerned with the ontological
maximum of the full development of the nature's potentialities. We are
dealing—and this too must be particularly emphasized—with a truly new
ontological understanding with a theological basis, which transcends both
(and does not simply create a synthesis of the two). So this is not a synthesis of nature and the perfecting of nature, but rather being in the very
process of becoming, being as a dialogical event of becoming-in-communion. The notion of *logos* in philosophy is of course originally protological,
having to do with the beginning of being; but here, in the Confessor, this
"beginning" is revealed in the end, by the "nonconditional" Incarnation
of the Word, who takes creation as His body. The end is the ontological
beginning; it is a new ontology which is personal and eschatological. Being
in its original form is not a fall, but an eschatological gift offered as part of
a cooperative dialogical co-creation, a gift that can freely enter upon the
path of ecclesial-eucharistic becoming and ultimately true being as a fruit
of divine-human dialogue; through dialogue being realizes its true nature,
which is grounded in eternal well-being. What has this got to do with Plato
and Aristotle—despite the fact that it justifies or rather transcends their
wildest philosophical dreams? As to the eschatological unity of all things in
Christ, here too Ivanka misses the point, regarding it as neo-Platonic, and
criticizes the Confessor's "false" conclusion which supposedly dictates that
"the specific is swallowed up in the general."[40] He comes to the conclusion
that this whole progress toward the unity of entities in the Word is quite
secondary for the interpretation of Maximus's thought—which, according
to him, is "theological, not ontological." The whole of the present book is
an argument against these views. Ivanka fails to understand fundamental
themes in Maximus's theology, such as his dialogical ontology and above
all his Christology in its hypostatic-personal context and the theology of
the two wills, which is connected with his Trinitarian theology, equally hypostatic and personal, and thus with ontology. And this hypostatic, onto-

logical Christology has nothing in common with ancient philosophy, even when it seems to justify some of its most brilliant premonitions.

But is this ontology essentially different also from modern Western philosophy and theology? We shall try in the next chapter to search for a Western future for this eschatological ontology of being as dialogical reciprocity, in discussion with some very essential Western theological and philosophical issues.

Notes

1. Cf. M. Heidegger, *An Introduction to Metaphysics*, tr. Ralph Manheim (New York: Anchor Books, 1961), p. 81.

2. See W. Windelband, H. Heimsoeth, *Handbook of the History of Philosophy*, chap. 1. In this volume, the formation and contrasting of the concepts of being and becoming are systematically examined. See also K. Axelos, *Heraclitus and Philosophy*, p. 253, and Heidegger, *Introduction*, pp. 105–106.

3. W. Windelband, H. Heimsoeth, pp. 51, 60 etc.

4. Ibid., *p. 50.*

5. Ibid., p. 62

6. See also Axelos, p. 274.

7. Axelos, p. 250.

8. Axelos, p. 277.

9. Windelbrand, p. 63.

10. Heidegger, *Introduction*, p. 83.

11. Ibid., p. 97. Heidegger uses Being with capital B and being with a small b to indicate the distinction between Being and beings ("the essent"). In this chapter we use the lower case for the most part, because we have no further interest in this distinction of Heidegger's.

12. Ibid., p. 163.

13. Ibid., p. 169. Heidegger has already attempted to analyze the fourth and final dualistic pair of opposites, that of being and the ought, which we will not go into.

14. Ibid., p. 170.

15. Ibid., p. 170.

16. Ibid., p. 169.

17. See N. Berdyaev, *Essay in Ontological Metaphysics*, esp. (gk) pp. 171–189.

18. For the distinction between *being* and *existing*, see Berdyaev, ibid., pp. 176ff.

19. See chap. 1.1.

20. See chap. 3.2.

21. On the connection between Providence and God's will (*inter alia*), see *Ambigua*, PG 91:1189B: "Providence is God's will through which all entities receive the direction appropriate to them."

22. See chap. 3.3.

23. See chap. 3.4.

24. See chap. 3.5.

25. See chap. 3.4.

26. It should be recalled once again that this is the traditional Orthodox theological position: Baptism, like the other Mysteries, is "fulfilled" in the Eucharist (see also p. 157.) See also A. Schmemann, *Of Water and the Spirit*, chap. 4. On pp. 117–118, he writes: "But if the Church's ultimate being and essence are revealed in and through the Eucharist, if Eucharist is truly *the sacrament of the Church* and not only one of the Church's sacraments, then of necessity to enter the Church is to enter into the Eucharist, then Eucharist is indeed the fulfilment of Baptism." See also St. Symeon of Thessaloniki: "This constitutes the fulfilment of all sacraments that, being free from sinful uncleanness, and having become pure and sealed to Christ in the Holy Spirit (*sc.* through Baptism and Chrismation), we would partake of the Body and Blood of Christ Himself and would be bodily united to Him" (quoted in Schmemann, *op. cit.* p. [168], n. 5). Cf. Boris Bobrinskoy, *The Mystery of the Trinity: Trinitarian Experience and Vision in the Biblical and Patristic Tradition* (Crestwood: St. Vladimir's Seminary Press, 1991), pp. 161–162. In chap. 2.2 of the present work, we saw how Maximus makes the connection between, *inter alia*, the triads *being, well-being, eternal being* and *birth, baptism, resurrection*. This Father distinguishes between the natural birth "through which we receive being," the birth "by baptism, in which we receive well-being in abundance, and the birth by resurrection, in which we are reshaped by grace so as to come into eternal being" (see p. 163). As we strive to fulfill our existence, which is given as an uncreated but "natural" proposal to us, we cross over through baptism (again, see the eleven triads in chap. 2.2) to the purely ecclesial mode of existence, which is well-being, a mode of existence culminating in resurrection, in deification (which is imaged and brought about by the Eucharist).

27. As Heidegger would have it.

28. See my *Apophatic Ecclesiology of Consubstantiality*, chap. 2.

29. The phrase belongs to D. Staniloae, "The Holy Trinity, Structure of Supreme Love" in *idem*, *Theology and the Church* (Crestwood: St. Vladimir's Seminary Press, 1980), p. 77. Certainly for Maximus love is not only internal but also external intersubjectivity.

30. See chap. 4.1.

31. See chap. 4.2. It is quite clear that personal otherness is always retained in the course of this dialogue. This "step-by-step" movement truly safeguards the "personal" character of this dialogue, which may, at times, comprise also hesitation, delay, anxiety, aggressiveness, doubt, complaint,

on the part of man—all this "wrestling with God," known to us from Scripture (Jacob, Jonah, Peter, Paul, etc).

32. See chap. 4.3.

33. See chap. 4.4A.

34. Ibid.

35. See chap. 1.4A. Cf. *Centuries of Various Texts* 1.73, PG 90: 1209A: "and in all those who are Christ-like, [the Holy Spirit is present] in addition to the ways already mentioned as [the spirit] of adoption."

36. See chap. 1.5.

37. As we have shown in chap. 4.4B.

38. Thus an eschatological eucharistic ontology of being as gift, as presented in this book, is diametrically opposed to the Hegelian model which, from Joachim de Floris to Marx, turns Christian eschatology into something merely historical, imprisoning it in historicity. In Hegel (where this understanding finds its fullest expression), the Spirit, or God, or the Word has to abandon the abstract indefinability of pure thought in which, as Absolute, he identifies being with nothingness, and turn into a material universe in order to pursue self-awareness (see Hegel, "Precis de l'Encyclopedie des Sciences Philosophiques," *La Logique*, Paris, Vrin, p. 77). This "transformation" of the Word is precisely an obligatory fall, a passage through the inorganic, the organic and the animal, to the culmination in the subjective, the objective, and ultimately the absolute spirit; and this passage and its culmination are the only possible opportunity for the Spirit to realize itself, because this self-realization must take place purely within history. Here history, as a deterministic and rationalistic reality, is the very essence of truth, the necessary locus and mode of the Word's real existence, which means his existence as a specific historical whole. Thus the Hegelian eschaton has as its essence precisely historicity as the self-awareness of the Spirit-Word, who, in order to have true being, ultimately has to be totally contained within the world. In consequence, history is the sole locus of ultimate truth; historicity is eschatology as a plaything of the dialectical wiles of the Word. Cunning which identifies freedom with the acceptance of the ultimate coercion as its very essence: the necessity that earthly rational wholeness will come about in history through a deterministic process. As an ultimately historical state with a fate of its own, a historical collective subject including both nature and spirit, this wholeness is the only, exclusively earthly, opportunity for God to realize Himself. So in Hegelian philosophy, it is necessary for God to create, just as it is altogether necessary for Him to subsume all beings into one whole, a tragic process that perforce takes place in history. This is not, of course, a communion of beings as reciprocal or dialogical gifts; that requires the freedom of personal loving dedication. There is no such thing as the "dialogical" person in Hegel (although he has so many things to say about relationship), and his "word" bears no relation to the loving personal Christ-the-Word of St. Maximus. Hence the Confessor's thought is, as we have seen, quite literally poles apart from Hegelianism: if Hegel historicizes

eschatology, thus becoming the precursor of all modern forms of totalitarianism, Maximus by contrast opens history up to its eschatological center. Eucharistic ontology means that the world and history are brought into the mystery of enhypostatic human nature in Christ, into the true dialogical being of the personal mode of divine Existence. So eschatology is not to be found (as Western theology would have it) simply at the end of history. History and eschatology are not mutually exclusive. For us, as Cabasilas puts it so well, "that life which is to come is as it were contained in this present life and intermingled with it." This does not, however, mean "ahistoricism," nor is it a form of deliverance from a "secular" history. (The Augustinian distinction between sacred and secular history, a distinction non-existent and unacceptable to the Confessor, was a source of profound confusion for later Western philosophy [and theology] of history.) What we have here is rather an ontology of history and historicity, founded on the pre-eternal loving Counsel of God, who in Christ becomes the eschatological locus of history, the dénoument of the historical drama and the justification of history, even now present as in an image. Here eschatological meaning embraces historical "happenedness," understanding historical process as a step-by-step progress toward a final opening to God who thus becomes, through this dialogue a God-for-His-creatures. The history of the world will end at some point; but in Christ, in the Church, it is already justified even though not already completed. It is already open, ontologically open—through the Eucharist especially—to the Kingdom of God which will come in the future (without of course being identified with it). This has consequences for becoming: in Hegel, becoming is presented as necessary, a necessary unity of being and non-being (*La Logique*, p. 78), arising in some way out of the inability of being, as pure abstraction, to avoid flowing into non-being; whereas in Maximus there is a deifying becoming-in-commmunion, communion as a historical dialogue between God and creaturehood, which alone comes out of nothing and as a result has an innate risk of "fading into non-being." This becoming renders the being of creaturehood ever more open to its communal actualization in Christ—it is the very movement of the free and personal divine *eros* which yearns for a ever-deepening enrichment of the living communion of love as dialogical reciprocity of gifts between God and the world, and among human beings themselves. As ever-moving fixity, becoming-in-communion has an eschatological character (as an icon of ultimate truth) and constitutes even now the surety and leaven of true being, of the Kingdom of God. For if in Hegel the only justification for God is for Him to be fixed within history and thereby altered, in Maximus the only justification for history and the universe is for them to be brought, through the Church and its Mysteries, into the eternal communion of love between the Father and the Son. They must be incorporated into the mystery of the living Christ, in the Holy Spirit; through the mystery of the free personal *ascesis* which wrestles with ego-centric self-love in all its forms, existentially experiencing the mystery of the Cross and so participating in the Lord's resurrectional eucharistic love, where being as dialogical reciprocity of gifts is portrayed.

39. It is perhaps possible here to attempt a preliminary explanation of the difficulty which Western students of the Confessor characteristically experience in connecting eschatology with ontology in his work, and connecting both with the Eucharist. This difficulty is related to the fact that, in Western theology in general, eschatology is sometimes not clearly connected with the event of Christ's Resurrection. Thus Riou (*Le Monde et L'Eglise*, p. 175), true to his Roman Catholic presuppositions, writes: "This eschatology of creation is rooted in the eschatology of God Himself, which is accomplished only through the Cross and descent into the Tomb, through the extremity of the Word delivered into the hands of His enemies." Eschatology is fulfilled in the Cross: this is an eschatology of suffering, of martyrdom, of the Cross, not the Patristic eschatology of the Resurrection (where the Cross and Passion already bear the character of Resurrection, and the Lord's sacrificial, kenotic love is already the gateway to the Resurrection). Further on in Riou's book (p. 193), there is a special chapter entitled "L'eschatologie de la Passion," in which the eschatology of the Cross, the suffering of the ascetics and martyrs is quite explicitly linked with "the fulfilment of the divine Plan for the world, absolute in its fullness," and becomes a reference to the Confessor's own martyrdom. And of course, this whole effort to attach eschatology to the Cross is connected with a liturgical and eucharistic understanding centred exclusively on the Cross. For this reason, Riou cannot see that eschatology in Maximus is linked with "eternal well-being," or that his ontology, his teaching on the *logoi* of entities, is founded on that same "eternal well -being," only revealed in its fullness in the Resurrection of Christ.

40. E. von Ivanka, *Plato Christianus*, PUF, pp. 280–288.

Chapter 6

Theopoiia, the Other Side of Theo-Humanity
Some Remarks on the Western Future of Eucharistic Ontology

1. *Introduction*

THE MOST IMPORTANT THING TO EMPHASIZE insofar as St. Maximus the Confessor's contribution is concerned, is that he does not merely represent one personal theological view among those of other Greek patristic theologians (although he has a strong personal style), but is also an excellent key to the understanding of a considerable portion of the theology of other Fathers. Having assimilated almost every kind of theology before him, Maximus also opened the ways of its future: there is not one important theological figure after him who does not bear his influence in same way or other. Thus when we speak of Maximus, we do not speak of another patristic figure, not even an eminently important one, but rather of one of the centers around which the Greek patristic tradition constantly gravitates. However, it is not in the context of this "gravitation" that I call my understanding of Maximian work in this book a "Eucharistic Ontology." Rather, it is, because I believe his theological achievement provides an impetus to discover again today the core of the author's inspiration in the light of our own need to be inspired again today. In this way we are also capable of reworking some of the most delicate contemporary theological-philosophical issues: tradition always means reinterpretation, a new perception and evolution, without losing its center. As such, the most ground breaking spiritual "discoveries" are, in this sense, nothing different than a reworking of some of the "cores" of tradition.

2. The Khora of Another Intentionality

THIS KIND OF "SYSTEMATIC" EFFORT FORCES US to leave the historical field intact and look beyond Maximian work, in order to catch a glimpse of its author's aforementioned inspiration and assimilate it in our own terms by putting it in the perspectives of our own contemporary quests. Let us thus attempt a free understanding of Maximus's theological macrocosm faithful to his spirit, but also as if he were to be read according to our own conditions, in a constructive and poetic manner, like his own.

The doctrine of *logoi*, to start with, refers to the divine *intentionality* outside God, i.e., how God becomes a *God for the world* or, in other words, a *God in the world*. What is crucially important here is that this becoming is not a becoming of God's very essence, but of His will. This fact is probably difficult to understand in a Thomistic theological context in which God *is* His own will,[1] while divine essence is the principle object of this divine will.[2] According to this perspective which reformulates a theological claim descending from Augustine,[3] such an intentionality could then even transmute God's essence by making it penetrable by created beings. However, for Maximus, to create means for God to establish a real and full otherness outside Himself. By otherness, we do not mean a fixed and immoveable being *in se*, built upon the ineffable, irreducible, and atheological no-place of absolute alterity which Derrida and Caputo name the Khora, but exactly this Khora in the form of another radically different intentionality indeed. God creates the unthinkable and impossible: an *intention* incredibly and absolutely independent of His own. That means that he does not create a senseless cosmos, but an absolutely God-like image of His own freedom, as an equal partner for an eternal, adventurous discussion. God the Logos creates His Dialogos, i.e., the human world, full of intentions-*logoi* culminating and assumed in many ways in human *logos*. This anthropological cosmology, according to which createdness is a whole universe of ontological tendencies assumed in the human priestly intentions is thus expressed as a constant dialogue of two equal freedoms. Creation is an unexpected, contingent and "useless" intention of God's will, not to fulfill His own super-abundant essence, but to annihilate its absoluteness out of love, in the created intentionality of a God-like creature. That means Khora is created by God as an incredibly free other intentionality, i.e., the essence of beings is an abyssal and bottomless God-like freedom. What I want to say here is that, in light of the doctrine of *logoi*, createdness is somehow *against* being. It is exactly the possibility of an ineffably irreducible and atheological no-place of absolute alterity (that also explains the mystery of evil, in case that this alterity remains self-centered and self-sufficient) that can also turn to be *for being*: this is exactly what is meant by the famous Maximian distinction between a κατά φύσιν (according to nature) and a παρά φύσιν (against nature) gnomic movement of beings. If we say that Khora or nothingness is something "existing" somehow (even in a way irreducible to any notion of being) outside of God as a kind of His own non-ego (for example in a Fichtean manner) then by "creation-out-of-nothing" we would mean a kind of co-creation, similar to the one we notice in the works of Plato, where God is a co-creator along with this nothingness or Khora. When Maximus speaks thus of "creation-out-of-nothing" he means it in an absolute and philosophically inconceivable way, that is he means that the world was an act of God completely unexpected, radically contingent and useless to God, as we have already said—that the world was a possibility of *getting out of God* completely and ineffably. Thus Khora (or Levinas's *il y a* or Caputo's "abyss") is rather a created possibility and not creation's independent presupposition as an ineffable irreducible non-being *per se*. That means that what is given by the divine *logoi* to beings is not a concrete and immutable essence but, fundamentally, the possibility of an abysally free response; what is thus established is not a hierarchy of beings but a free discussion on what each essence *could finally be: Biblical eschatology is thus introduced in ontology as a new dimension of it*. Created being can be fallen or restored, distorted or resurrected, annihilated or fulfilled, in dependence on this eschatological dialogue where God is given or not the possibility to become a God for His creation.

Thus the *logoi* are a proposal for real Otherness outside the Sameness; it is the will of God as Logos to put Himself in an eschatological dialogue with a really God-like partner. Not to fulfill His eternally fulfilled (in an intra-Trinitarian communion) essence, but eternally overcome His own transcendentality in a *double transcendence* which makes Him possibly nothing in the Other's freedom: this is what we call divine love. But if this kind of kenotic ecstasy, not out of God's nature but out of its exclusiveness, takes the form of an ontological proposal, then the mode of existence proposed by God can only be described as a possible, as we saw, *exchange of gifts* in a context of dialogical reciprocity. The uncreated *logos* of created being causes a created gift of otherness which is so absolute that it is totally ontologically different from its origin—that is, it is exactly created. This created gift of otherness needs, as its logical core, a totally free, created agent, whose absolutely free, other intention-

ality accepts the offering and thus makes this gift of otherness exist in reality by assuming its principles in his possible intentional reference back
to his Creator, while there is also a possibility to refer it back to himself.
In the first of these two instances, created being is returned back to its
Creator as a free and unconditional gift to Him, according to Maximus,
i.e., as a *eucharistia*, a thanksgiving to God as He is the first Who gives
creation to itself out of love. In this way only, creation is really a gift back
to God because it comes out of free intentional and unconditional love
emerging from a real and free created otherness. Thus what is offered to
God, as we have already said, is the possibility of His becoming a God
for the created world, fulfilling eschatologically created beings' natures,
i.e., transforming them in His Body; created beings themselves really
exist in this dialogical process which makes them co-creators of their
own unknown and mysterious final being. Thus the reality of evil can
also be partially overcome, and the resurrection of the dead, i.e., the
final victory over death, is anticipated. As this ontology of being shared
and returned is a *Eucharistic Ontology*, then the very initiator must in-
evitably be the only completely eucharistic being we know: *Jesus Christ*.
Christ is God completely and kenotically offered to man out of love and
man freely and eucharistically offered out of love to God, and thus we
have man as the intention of God and God as the intention of man, the
logoi of God and the *logoi* of man in an absolutely kenotic, dialogical
reciprocity, by the mystery of the Cross; this is why Maximus so strongly
insists that Incarnation was an unconditional purpose of God before the
ages and not a decision following humanity's fall.[4] That was His initial
purpose to "save" (in ontological, not moral terms) creation from stay-
ing "against" being, hence the doctrine of *logoi* can only describe exactly
the suspending ambiguity of well-being and ill-being as the two eternal
options of creatures.

   Paradoxically, the uncreated *logoi* are thus deeply connected but,
at the same time, also independent from creatures; they are not meant
to express God in His own essence, but only in His essential movement
within creation. In this way, the *logoi* are, according to the Confessor's
expression, "the fire existing in the essences of creatures," but curiously
enough for any Platonizing mentality the essences themselves, which
are the created results of the *logoi*, although full of divine glory, are also
independent, by the freedom of their agents, from their burning, divine source. For a typically western mind nourished by Augustinian and
Thomistic doctrines that means, as we shall see below, a real danger of
losing participation because of this self-positing freedom. On the other

hand, the typically western theological mind will probably search for seeds of semi-Pelagianism in any expression of this kind of freedom. But for Maximus, created freedom is not self-sufficient but it must *imitate* divine freedom in order to become *positive* and not self-destructive. Divine freedom is ontologically linked with love as the latter is the very expression of the profound communion that the supreme Trinitarian relationship has achieved. In the same manner, created freedom's *becoming* has to be verified by *communion*. That means that a being can only fulfill his essence in a dialogue which discloses step-by-step, as its proper eschatological vocation, its mode of existence as *becoming-in-communion*, as a likeness of his creator. That also means that the divine mode of existence, which is finally expressed as the eternally achieved "homoousion" (consubstantiality), is finally conveyed into creation by man in the form of a step-by-step imitation and a possible achievement in human history (and here the Cross is again not only a symbol but an existential reality).

Here we have a very delicate point for a possible correction of what was expressed by Orthodox theologians during the last decades as a theology of communion (based usually on the Eucharist). As we have said in a previous chapter, and as we shall see better below, if we abolish this very crucial element of free becoming in our theological understanding of communion, then we risk understanding communion, the Eucharist, and accordingly the Church, as a direct reflection of divine things, as a structural mirroring of the Kingdom to come, as an immediate achievement of divinization *hic et nunc*. Becoming introduces a decisive historical and existential dimension in communion and, thus, a possibility for its verification. It is because of the lack of this dimension that we see the so-called "eucharistic ecclesiology" of today to be unable to avoid a rigidly structural understanding of the Church as a kind of supposedly eschatological elevation or ecstasy out of history instead of a step-by-step, humble effort to transform it.[5] What corresponds to this "ecstatic" ecclesiology, as a supposed reflection of the Kingdom, is of course an "ecstatic" anthropology, where human nature is supposedly bound with necessity, while human person is (like the Plotinian mind) supposed to be, by nature, free, as an outlet or ecstasy out of this forever fallen nature.[6] In that case the need of the Incarnation remains, after all, obscure. And the possible meaning of ascetical struggles for a step-by-step crucial transformation of human nature and thus also the further achievement of "contemplation of the divine *logoi*" as Maximus calls it, is dangerously concealed. Thus we

can only speak of being as becoming-in-communion and never of being as communion as this risks over-emphasizing an easy and effortless
ecstasy out of suffering nature and history, as a happy gazing at *eschata*
without the self-less and kenotical struggle for the restoration of what is
fallen, by the long and painful *assimilation* of grace.

I understand of course that, after my above claims, many theologians who are accustomed to think in more classical ways would have
some points to make. And the most classical question is surely the question concerning the difference between divine and created freedom. In
the context of the contemporary Orthodox theology, things seem to be
very simple: divine freedom is unlimited, while created freedom is absolutely limited. But if we ask those modern Orthodox theologians why
they proclaim such a view, their response will be that God is the only one
who is absolutely free because His essence is not given to Him, while
the freedom of the creatures is limited exactly because their essence is
presented to them as a given fact. Such theologians identify, as we have
said, consciously or unconsciously, essence with necessity, so that freedom is always meant to be a kind of "personal" escape of it. This neo-
Platonic (or, we dare to say, monophysite) sort of freedom is, in its initial
stage at least, a *negative* one. In this sense createdness cannot be said to
be *ontologically* free; its possible freedom consists in the submission of
this limited freedom to God's really ontological freedom, as a splendid
reflection of His own glory. Those Orthodox theologians (as well as so
many of their Western colleagues) usually think of freedom negatively,
i.e., as a freedom *from* something and not of freedom as freedom *for*
something. I think that, in light of Maximian thought, freedom cannot
be conceived as a freedom from nature or essence (because as I have
argued throughout this book, Maximus completely refuses to identify
nature or essence with necessity and person with freedom) but can only
be conceived *positively*. It is a freedom *for* relationship. According to this
perspective, the "scandal" of also having a God-like *created* freedom, i.e.,
the scandal of this strange "equality" between divine and human freedom can be explained. The only difference between divine and human
freedom, is that in God freedom is, before all ages, deeply linked with
love, while human freedom can accept or reject this deep existential link.

But divine freedom "educates" human freedom. God's loving freedom becomes a divine Providence that is "co-extensive" with human
freedom. That means that God's freedom, in the form of His unlimited
loving Providence, "follows" the abyssal human freedom, teaching man
love, in some incredibly manifold ways, throughout history. This can

probably be the ultimate *common* definition of freedom: God *is* wherever human being is, out of His love, and human being *can possibly be* wherever God is, out of a possible human loving response.

3. Analogy with or without Dialogue?

AND THUS WE COME TO DISCUSS THE CRUCIAL POINT of participation, comparing Maximus with an equal theological giant of the West, that is to say Thomas Aquinas.

How can we relate *analogia entis* with the *ontological dialogue*, the latter of which seems to be the Maximian foundation of participation?

As we have seen, that which is derived from the Maximian doctrine of *logoi*, is first, that each being is unique and unrepeatable as it consists of a unique uncreated call to existence out of nothing, thus being a created effect of God's divine will. In God's providence, all these unique beings are put in a process of possible unification as an image of divine eternal unity, without separation or confusion–a process or a becoming that can be promoted by human agency only. This is because only logical creatures can also respond to God's uncreated call and proceed to a conversation with Him, concerning the *mode of existence* of the given essences. No created being or part of any created being can be left out of this dialogue, which can be finally conceived as a reciprocal/ dialogical exchange of gifts out of love. This exchange forms a full eschatological ontology of participation, by grace, in the Trinitarian mode of existence, conveying step by step, *homoousion* to creation. Two remarks are necessary here: first, in this perspective participation is not something that takes place only *by mind* (as this is usually conceived in the context of western theology). If participation is achieved by mind only, then as St. Gregory Palamas forcefully insisted, expressing Maximos's way of thinking, that means that participation is not real but imaginary. In order for participation to be real, it has to happen "μετὰ παντός εἴδους κτίσεως . . . ἵνα τὸ τῆς εἰκόνος ἀπηκριβωμένον?" (with every kind of creature . . . for the image of God to be insured).[7] Palamas likes to sometimes use the word ἀνάκρασις instead of participation, a word which is not easily translated into English, though we could probably say "mutual indwelling and blending without confusion," of divine and human. This means that every kind of being is, in its true mode of existence, by grace, an object of dialogue: there is not the slightest possibility of any kind of "pure nature" that could be left out of this "conversation." As every being consists of a response to a divine eschatological call, nothing can be just "given" as "essence" or "origin," because this would mean (and this is my second remark, related to the first one) that an original passivity—in the form of a pure nature—relies on the essence of created beings, i.e., something we need to get out of (instead of offering it), by a kind of Platonic ek-stasis, an outlet in order to supposedly receive grace as a *superadditum*. This also would mean that we would need a created means as a vehicle for this outlet, which is of course, for Augustine and Aquinas, human mind conceived as an image of God on man. Even if we then admit that all this pure nature is destined and dedicated to the "supernatural," as De Lubac pointed out in the series of his remarkable works on the *Supernatural*, this is still a passive mirroring of God's glory as this pure nature remains speechless and falsely "independent," i.e., it does not take an active part in this "destination." And what is more, the reception of grace here cannot help also being at least partially passive; R. Jenson is probably right when he sees here the seeds of another semi-Pelagianism.[8] Does all this have something to do with a western understanding of *analogia entis*? But we shall return in detail to these issues very soon.

What is the Greek patristic conception of analogy? We have to keep in mind that the Areopagitic texts are here the common source of both eastern and western theological traditions. We thus approach these texts in order to find out what the sense of analogy is there. It seems obvious that analogy is very closely linked to participation in the Areopagitic work[9]: participation takes place analogously, i.e., by an analogous free response to God's freely proposed analogy, which here is identified with His divine will, predestination, and finally, *logos* of each being.[10] This is an exchange of love, as Roques describes it, where God proposes a harmonious order to creatures and they respond by tending existentially toward it. What is important here is first, that analogy can be only be identified with God's uncreated *logoi* and not with His internal Trinitarian existence and second, that analogy ultimately functions as a *dialogue* between man and God and not as a kind of passive reflection of divine harmony upon creation. This identification of analogy, not with any passive (or semi-passive) mirroring but with dialogue, is very clear when Denis insists that the elevation of beings happens only according to their own analogy, i.e., capacity of elevation or participation (καί ἀεί ἀνατείνειν αὐτάς ἐπί τά πρόσω κατά τήν σφῶν εἰς ἀνάνευσιν ἀναλογίαν). Participation, thus, is a personal expression of a dialogical devotion to divine order and harmony.[11]

Secondly, this is why analogy is finally linked with synergy in the Areopagitic work: ἑκάστη τῆς ἱεραρχικῆς διακοσμήσεως τάξις κατά τήν οἰκείαν ἀναλογίαν ἀνάγεται πρός τήν θείαν συνέργειαν[12] (every kind of hierarchical order is elevated toward divine synergy according to its own analogy). Of course this last concept is not an Areopagitic invention as it also belongs to Proclus.[13] But what Denis has in mind here is 1 Cor 3:9; his own understanding of synergy is completely different, as this is not a kind of ontological necessity as happens in Proclean hierarchies but a free dialogical response to God. This "dialogical" character of Dionysian analogy also distinguishes this kind of analogy from the derivational and returnable, by necessity, Proclean one.[14] Analogy is here not a necessary derivation but a possible free dialogue and, consequently, a possible synergy between God and His creation. That simply means that analogy reveals us a God Who acts dialogically, i.e., analogously, proportionately to His creatures' needs and capacities and does not impose Himself upon them as a distanced supreme Being. God behaves analogously with His creatures' abilities of understanding and feeling Him—as we do with our children. Thus the fact that analogy refers to the synergy between God's acts/energies and human acts/energies ultimately means that God puts Himself in our position when He acts; He teaches, takes care of, elevates, fulfills creation in this becoming-in-communion through His loving will/energy, by way of a constant dialogue.

Thus analogy is for Pseudo-Dionysios the very expression of a dialogical phenomenology of synergetic participation, which is radicalized in St. Maximus the Confessor's work. Similarly, Maximus refuses any kind of an ontological analogy between God and creation except for the analogy between the divine logos of a being and the possibility of a participational response to it. In *Mystagogy*, Maximus decisively substitutes the notion of analogy for that of "eikon." "Eikon" is not exactly an image according to the usual English translation of the term. "Eikon" means exactly a dynamic analogy of activity and not a static reflection of the divine super-being. An image can be static, but an "eikon" is rather a tendency, an existential response, and an act of motion toward its archetype. Maximus identifies "eikon" with the final *truth* of beings,[15] a truth that is already given by divine will, but it is also accepted, explored, and assimilated by beings as their own *telos*, the double meaning of this Greek word being "end" and "goal" at the same time. What is thus constituted is an eschatological-dialogical and synergetical-ontology, where analogy as an "eikon" is not only made by God, but also returns to Him as a likeness. Likeness is the eschatological/ontological core of "eikon," which is the most dynamic ontological term we have in Maximus. In this way, the last remnants of neo-Platonic passivity (which Denis also obviously tried to get rid of) are definitely overcome. Man and cosmos are fulfilled in God by becoming His own body, but also, God becomes by man a God-for-the-world; if there is a kind of human passivity due to human createdness, this is not something that is *ontologically* passive, as von Balthasar thinks,[16] but it has to do with the need of an analogical synergy in order to fulfill human capacities. So there is no need for a "personal" overcoming or outlet or ek-stasis out of a nature ontologically passive, but a synergetical ek-stasis or outlet of this personal nature itself. Analogy, here as a dialogical "eikon," is a process of divinization out of divine love, which makes a man into God, having previously made God into man, a *theopoieisis* of man out of the *anthropopoieisis* of God; as we shall later claim, we could daringly say that we have a *theopoiia* within creation. Man's analogical "givenness" to God is not a prolongation of a created passivity but an active return of an image to its archetype: and "eikon." Eschatological synergy is thus not a rupture but an active and conscious eucharistic self-deliverance; even if vision of divine glory surpasses human capacity, as it does, human nature is not left behind, but transformed in this light. For passivity ultimately means a lack of transformation—or a passive, dictated transformation that finally violates man's nature, instead of changing its mode of existence.

4. *The Supernatural Nature of Natural*

LET US NOW TURN TO THE THOMISTIC CONCEPT of analogy that also "presupposes not just a metaphysics of participation but also a phenomenology of participation," as Milbank says.[17] Let us start from the beginning.

The first thing that someone learns as he starts his research by reading some classical contemporary works such as Gilson's *Le Thomisme*, is that Thomistic analogy, contrary to the Areopogitic or Maximian approaches, refers not to the divine *logoi* or energies but *to God's very essence.*[18] What is also obvious is that "the objective foundations of analogical predication in natural theology is the dependence of creatures on God as their efficient and exemplary cause."[19] Thus, analogy is a way of speaking of God, not equivocally, i.e., a way to avoid theological sophistry.[20] However "we necessarily think and speak of God in terms which, from the linguistic point of view, refer primarily to creatures, and we can only approximate two words, while never reaching an adequate understanding of what is meant by saying God is "wise" or "good" or "intelligent" or "living." Aquinas therefore distinguishes between what he calls the perfection signified by a term and the mode of significa-tion.[21] All of the above mean that Thomas claims a certain knowledge of God's essence when we speak analogically of Him, albeit this restriction is valid only for this life and not for eternity.[22] That is, in this life we speak of God, as Copleston writes "by a negation as when we say that God is eternal or infinite, or by a relation as when we say that God is first cause of supreme good."[23] It seems that for Aquinas in the life to come, con-trary to the Greek fathers of the first millennium,[24] direct contemplation of God's essence is not only possible but also something bestowed upon the righteous, and this is because, in an Aristotelian fashion, actuality for Thomas means pure intelligibility. That means that the *telos* of any rational subject has to be an act of understanding, especially of what is the most perfect intelligible object, i.e., God Himself.

However "the objective ontological foundation for predicating terms analogically of God is the creature's *participation in* or *reflection of* (italics mine) the divine perfections" as Copleston insists.[25] And thus we come to the crux of our discussion. Can we equate *participation* to *reflection* when we speak of the ways of an analogical divine knowledge and its ontological presuppositions? Of course it is of the highest im-portance that Thomas's theological intention was to describe a way of sharing in God's very being, a form of union with God, an anticipation of beatific vision as Anna Williams claims.[26] I am not quite sure, however, whether Williams—while describing Thomist beatitude as an operation of the mind—when she thinks that contemplation for Thomas is not identified with any particular method of prayer but is rather an activity of the mind, because mind is the very essence of human being com-mitted to the knowledge of the highest intelligible object (God Him-self!), takes into account how decisively different is the Palamite psycho-somatic and prayerful "existential" way of participation. Nevertheless, what matters here—although we admit that the theological intentions are similar—is to search also for the differences of the two ways of par-ticipation proposed and of course for a possible complementarity.

However, Thomist participation seems at first sight to be a kind of *double passivity*. The first passivity comes from the fact that created nature (which for much of the Thomist tradition is in fact a *pure* nature) is just given as a replication of God's *esse*, i.e., as a created similitude, as Bradshaw has admirably argued. Analogy here refers directly to God's *esse* as we have already said, because divine simplicity entails that the divine activity *is* the divine essence. Thus if we say that creatures *are* in a dialogical and synergetical analogy with God, then that would mean, for Aquinas, that creatures participate in the divine essence itself. So, as Bradshaw claims, "in effect Aquinas ignores (within this context) the active dimension of *esse,* treating *esse* instead as a kind of quality that is possessed by God and replicated in creatures." [27] While strictly the active dimension of essence is not a quality of God, but his very essence, I personally prefer the word *reflection* or even *mirroring* in order to describe this passive replication without or before dialogue, which seems to characterize Thomas's *analogia entis.* What makes us speak of a *second passivity* is the way that grace is imparted to these pure natures. As it is commonly known, Thomas also insists that, because of the divine simplicity again, which entails the full identity of the divine will to the divine essence, it is impossible to admit an external cause of God's willing.[28] Thus grace seems to be imparted without any real dialogical presupposition; it is rather an extrinsic *superadditum* because of God's efficient causality. Thus we have a kind of *double passivity* as we have said—nature as a mirroring of divine essence and grace as a reflection of divine efficient causality. Human response is something that possibly matters only after the predestined offering. Here God does not seem to put Himself in His creatures' position. When analogy refers to essence and not to act/energy, then God undoubtedly becomes a kind of supreme Being, Who simply orders and acts alone upon created beings. But shall we stop here? As everything in this delicate quest is a matter of interpretation, can we re-read the Thomist claims in the light of any modern reconsideration of them?

I think that the author that made the most significant modern contribution in order to carry this discussion a few steps further is undoubtedly Henri de Lubac. De Lubac's immense theological work[29] can help Christian theology today toward a deeper self-knowledge. His contribution to the solution of the question of the supernatural specifically is of paramount significance for all of us today. It is not, of course, the appropriate place to give an account of this remarkable work as a whole; suffice to say that de Lubac is the first who realized so seriously what Aquinas has in common with the unbroken patristic tradition of the first millennium: the deeply decisive connection of natural to the supernatural. Furthermore, he stressed the fact that every being is sacred by destination, that the only possible destination for what is natural is the supernatural, which can only be reached by participation. I think that de Lubac represents probably one of the most serious steps taken by western theology during the last century.

De Lubac realized Cajetan's tremendous error of ascribing to Aquinas the claim that we cannot find any natural desire for God in human being, unless this is given special grace as a *superadditum*. Natural human desire is thus not for God but for the natural things of this biological life. De Lubac has brilliantly shown that the truth is just the opposite: human being has in itself a natural desire for God that is constitutive of man's very essence. The French theologian attributes exactly this point to Aquinas. Four centuries of a toxic theological separation between nature and grace, falsely ascribed to Aquinas, are now to be corrected by de Lubac. Thus, according to him:

> Paradox of the human spirit : created, finite, it is not only a double nature ; it is nature itself. Before being a thinking spirit, it is a spiritual nature. Irresoluble duality, and at the same time an indissoluble union. Image of God, but pulled from nothingness. Therefore, before it loves God, the spirit is attracted by him. God alone is not something different from love without desire, because God does not have any nature imposed upon him : pure being, pure Act, he is also pure Love. The spirit is therefore desire for God. Every problem of the spiritual life will be to free this desire, and then to transform it : radical conversion, μετάνοια without which it is impossible to enter the Kingdom . . .[30]

De Lubac's definition of human spirit as a desire for God according to Aquinas and the western Scholastic tradition, changes profoundly the conditions of Western theology. Something that, in a sense, belongs only to God lies,[31] at the same time, in the unfathomable depths of human existence. But have we yet overcome the non-synergistic analogical passivity that we described when discussing Thomas's claims? This is still not clear enough. De Lubac writes, "Natural desire for the supernatural: this is in us the permanent action of God which has been created by God who created our nature, as grace is in us the permanent action of God who created the moral order."[32]

I have two points here. The first concerns the human quality of this desire: if it belongs to God, where is human agency, i.e., where is human free *logos* or initiative? I am personally sure that when de Lubac says that my natural desire for God is His own permanent action in me, he wants to say that there is a kind of *synergy*: if my natural desire is really mine, then *I make this desire active* simultaneously with God. It is in this way only that we can overcome passivity, and this is why I think that de Lubac made something really new when he took this step. But was he ready to accept this final consequence of his own thought?

My second point is also crucial: if grace has to do only with the moral order, that means only with the resemblance of creatures to God and not with His image on them, as de Lubac writes elsewhere,[33] then how can we avoid a separation between nature and grace again?

It is useless to avoid these questions. We see that, although de Lubac's interpretation seems revolutionary, some deep Thomistic structures remain uninterrogated. Almost all of the Thomistic passages he provides in the pages of his book[34] make us think that we still speak of a separately given human nature with some natural capacities and an additional grace that elevates it from earth. Of course, the difference here is that we cannot separate the two orders any more: on the contrary, natural order is made for the supernatural one. We cannot conceive of the former without the latter; the first is to be dedicated to the second and this is exactly de Lubac's revolution in the midst of Western theology. But it seems that he could not surpass some of its fundamental structures! In the context of the Greek patristic theology, nature is *already* grace and analogy means dialogue. Maximus, for example (as I have argued throughout) never separates nature from its constitutive divine grace and a dialogue that forms its mode of existence "according to nature," that means according to God's will. Furthermore, in the concept of *logos*, both ontology and ethics are so deeply connected, as we have seen above (chap. 2.3) where *logos* means not only being but also acting out our human essence.

Thus we *are* according to our divine *logos*, but we can also *act* according to it in order to fulfill it in freedom, and in dialogue with our Creator. Consequently, no nature (whether pure or otherwise) can be left out of this dialogue, as nothing is just given as a passive reflection of divine glory upon nothingness. In our times, to connect analogy with dialogue again is the most urgent task of both Orthodox and Western theology alike. Because Orthodox theology also has its own temptation to neglect dialogue in favor of a fleshless spiritualism, which disregards nature's graceful otherness in order to "overcome" it, for some reason. Of course this transcendental spiritualism comes from the West, but centuries of bitter historical troubles, with the subsequent tragic loss of many of its written sources, pushed a part of Orthodox theology toward this kind of spiritualistic transcendentalism, which is the opposite of Hesychasm's sacred materialism. The subsequent danger for modern Orthodox theology is a kind of "monophysitic" tendency in the midst of the recent "philokalic" and "neptical" renovation. I have written a book in which I try to show how this danger threatens modern Orthodox theology.[35] In its most recent editions, this monophysitism is in danger of becoming a kind of disguised pantheism, and this phenomenon usually derives, unfortunately, from a complete misunderstanding of Greek patristic tradition. It is not without a kind of embarrassment that I shall refer to D. B. Hart's book *The Beauty of the Infinite: The Aesthetics of Christian Truth*,[36] a book that could normally give a high and genuine spiritual joy to its reader, in spite of its linguistic pretensions. Hart thinks that if we are to understand God, not as the world's highest principle, but as its transcendent source and end, we must use (in order to overcome any current metaphysics) the notion of analogy.[37] I completely agree that we must have this analogical relation, but we must ask, how does he understand it? I shall quote some characteristic passages from his book:

> By the analogy, each thing comes to be as pure event, *owning no substance* (my italics), made free from nothingness by the unmerited grace of being other than God, participating in the mystery of God's power to receive all in giving all away– the mystery, that is, of the truth that God is love.[38]

> (Creation) attends God, *possessing no essence* (my italics) apart from its character as a free and open utterance within the infinity of His self-utterance [because] in the strictest sense theology can use a term like ousia of God alone.[39]

It seems that for Hart, to derive from God and to stay in relation with Him means to not possess an essential otherness as this is diluted in the divine ocean of being. This certainly saves us from the horror of the Prime Mover but, at the same time, Hart surrenders us to the other horror represented by Archimandrite Eutyches: only one essence or substance is real; what is touched by God exists only without a real essential otherness. Monophysitism returns each time we seek the divine fountain of being without having a created pot in which to put the Divine water—and thus we have a flood instead of quenching our thirst. However, in Orthodox theology, during the last two centuries, monophysitism has never been alone as an idea. Indeed, monophysitism has usually been coupled with some form of pantheism. Hart again: "(Things) in themselves *have no essences* apart from the divine delight that crafts them: they are an array of proportions, an ordering a felicitous parataxis of semeia, and so have *nothing in themselves* by which they might divert attention from the God, no specific gravity, no weight apart from the weight of glory."[40] It is obvious that this glory is absolutely void of real, willing, suffering, understanding, and struggling creatures! Hart insists: "The transcendence of Being over beings—of God over creatures—is such that the very otherness of the transcendent is the intimate actuality of every being in its particularity."[41] By this implicit rejection of any kind of created freedom, we have here the mono-energetic aspect of mono-physitism. Pantheistically, then, "creation is . . . an aesthetic moment to the divine," while, "the Christian God never goes out into His opposites, because the active motion of condescension—creation, covenant, incarnation—is already contained in the perichoretic motion of the Trinity: in the eternal going forth of the Son, the everlasting spiration of the Spirit, the eternal restoration of all things to the Father."[42] Thus theology, in a characteristically Western fashion, is melded with economy, and creation becomes, by necessity, a part of the Trinity because, according to Hart, "moreover it is *only* within these intervals of beauty that the sublime—as delay, intensity, dissonance, immensity—*occurs at all.*" Finally, "the here below, is like a *mirror* without a taint, a depth that is pure surface, and a surface *composed entirely of the light it reflects.*"[43]

It is not so easy to be a logical creature in Hart's totalitarian world, which consists of God alone without any kind of real acting and responding otherness, but full of a dictated harmonious glory. Despite his rare references to Gregory of Nyssa, Hart constantly misunderstands patristic texts.[44] The fact that created essences are in becoming because they *are* as part of a continuing dialogue between God and creation does not mean that they do not essentially exist in themselves or that they are mere reflections of God's mirroring upon nothingness. In that case God's creative logos or act would be completely ontologically void, without any ontological result, that is, without any real and concrete *essential* proposal necessary for initiating a dialogue. We do not make any conversation in response to an empty call, we only accept something in order to give it back—this "something" is the given essences of things in their perspective of an analogical, eschatological, and dialogical becoming. The fact that we cannot define (or confine) createdness as a static essence, does not mean that it consists of an undifferentiated reflection of God's grace. Creation delightfully reflects God's glory indeed. But this is magnificent only because it is so deeply connected with created freedom!

Apart from my above critique on the point of analogy without dia-logue or synergy, I have many good words for Hart's book as a whole. Hart has, along with a convincing awareness of contemporary philoso-phy, a genuine sense of theology as *life in God*, which is embodiment and participation, glorious wisdom and kenotic transformation, death and resurrection in Christ, beauty, light, splendor, and Eros. But what we need indeed is an agent wounded by divine love, but yet active, who not only reflects, but also undertakes the mystery of divinization as a synergetic response, in the most personal, free, and intimate manner. Even when we speak of the deepest submission of our own will to God's loving will, human act/will still remains intact; otherwise we have an assimilation of human hypostasis by God, rather than a divinization of it. Of course human freedom cannot *oblige* God to collaborate with it, but it can only show human agent's *loving intention* (that the Fathers called *proairesis*) something that makes God's response possible. In this way the human person becomes someone who, moreover, can discern God's traces in the dramatic course of History—not only someone who criticizes modernity but also someone who can liberate the secrets of its deep and painful wanting, of its unconsciously Christo-nostalgic ter-rible wandering. If the seeds of post-modern destructive nihilism can be easily found today almost everywhere, the divine seeds of God's logical call, Who "claims what is His own," according to the Confessor's wise suggestion, must also be searched for, by everyone that is really inspired by the mystery of Incarnation.

We thus come to realize that although the Thomist or the Ortho-dox, pure or graced nature, reflects God, we crucially need to complete this kind of analogy with Maximian eschatological dialogical reciprocity, if we understand the abyssal horrors of passivity, whether it is double, in a western fashion, or single, in an Orthodox fashion. Maximus has to be read today word by word by some Augustinian and Thomistic scholars in both the East and West—except our confessional regressions do not allow us to do so. Fortunately, he still belongs to our common Christian tradition.[45]

Of course it is not easy to understand Maximus. Today we have books on related topics, which although brilliant, completely misunder-stand the Confessor's work, such as D. Farrow's *Ascension and Ecclesia*.[46] This is an outstanding modern theological work with which I exten-sively agree,[47] while completely disagreeing on the way in which he treats Maximus. Farrow understands the Confessor in a rather superficial way: "In other words, the Maximian vision remains very much a monastic one; ascensus and ascesis are virtually synonymous. This translates once again into a serious loss of continuity between the old creation and the new [. . .] To enter the kingdom man must attain to a more angelic mode of being, exchanging the active life for the contemplative life."[48] Farrow seems radically unable to follow Maximus, when he claims that creation and fall are simultaneous in Maximus and this "suggests that his correction of Origen is incomplete, that a confusion between ktisiology and hamartiology is still operative and that behind this maxim lies a lingering doubt about the goodness of the temporal and material world. If we hope to be God-like we must wash away our fondness for matter 'like dust from our spiritual eyes.'"[49] This "simultaneity" does not mean that creation *had* to fall for some internal reason, as Farrow thinks. There are a great deal of Maximian texts which claim that this fall happened because of the personal choice of creatures. What Maximus wants to imply here, as it is obvious from some other of his texts, is that the first man did not sufficiently behold God's face and turned immediately to this narcissistic account of createdness that culminates in what we call a fall. Farrow becomes totally confused when he asks "can such teaching do other than cultivate a process of interiorization[. . .]? Can it sustain [. . .] an ontology which takes seriously the many as well as the one, or support an ecclesiology which elevates koinonia over contemplation?"[50]

Alas, Farrow ignores the Maximian doctrine of the *logoi*, which explains all of the above issues. It explains, to wit, how ascension is, for Maximus, a *eucharistic one* while contemplation derives from a realistic *change* (in the eucharistic and relational manner of the change of the *mode of existence* of human being and not from a neo-Platonic outlet or ek-stasis out of it by "contemplation"). It also explains that matter and its movement is really an absolutely good and positive one. Matter is a divine call of spiritualization, it is an uncreated *logos* fulfilled in Incarnation. It is only bad to think of matter not as a divine call for the spirit to be incarnate but as an antithesis to this process.

Farrow also destructively ignores the many passages, (quoted in this book), where Maximus astutely disconnects ktisiology from hamartiology, condemning any abolition of the "good and Godly logical" material world.[51] The Confessor insists in many passages, on the contrary, that "the power of the Holy Spirit never abolishes the natural power of beings, but, as this is already abolished by being practiced in manners which are against nature, He makes it active again by restoring its function in a way that is according to nature and by introducing it to the knowledge of the divine things."[52] Only this passage (between so many similar to it) would suffice to show how Farrow incredibly misconstrues Maximus. We must move beyond the inadequate dichotomies that so plagued patristic discussions in earlier times!

5. *The God Who May Be or the God Who May Act?*

LET US NOW SWITCH TO CONTEMPORARY PHILOSOPHY, and particularly to that kind of modern phenomenology that seems to turn to theology, suggesting as Richard Kearney says, a "hermeneutics of religion." In his masterpiece, entitled *The God Who May Be*, Kearney to start with, takes again Cusanus's step (against Aquinas, as he claims), to conceive God, not as *esse*, but as *possest*—a word he creates by fusing *posse* and *est*.[53] Thus "God who is traditionally thought of as an act or actuality, might better be thought as possibility."[54] What is extremely important for us is that, as we already see, what is overcome here is exactly the metaphysical divine *esse* of Thomist origin, identified with act or actuality. Kearney brilliantly understands that such an *esse*, as *Unum*, *Verum*, and *Bonum* challenges the truth of the everyday embodied life and abolishes the possibility of what he (and we, as we have seen in this book) calls a *micro-eschatology*, instead of metaphysics, i.e., a dialogical co-creation of God-with-us.[55] For Kearney this can be called a "fourth reduction." Thus, as Kearney's disciple Manoussakis explains,[56] in Husserl we have the first reduction that he calls the "transcendental," as intentionality, which is the intentional movement of consciousness that seeks and constitutes phenomena as objects. Here the "I" is an "I" which elevates upon phenomena by constituting them. The second reduction occurs in Heidegger's *Being and Time* when he attributes to his *Dasein*, which is thrown-into-the-world, the existential experience of Being. The third takes place in Marion's *Reduction and Givenness*, in which he replaces the Kantian/Cartesian notion of subjectivity hidden in the first reductions by his own *interloqué*, namely the one to whom whatever givenness gives is given. Finally, we enter the fourth reduction where *mutual exchange* prevails decisively.[57] Thus, as Kearney defines it, "Platonism might to be said to mark the first reduction; Aristotelianism the second; neo-Platonism the third; and a certain return to the ordinary world (Augustine's questing heart, Duns Scotus's 'thisness,' Teresa of Avila's 'pots and pans') the fourth."

Thus Kearney opens a philosophical chapter for relatedness. As he clearly expresses himself "this is a contribution to the phenomenology of the gift. I usually call the gift by other names: (1) the "transfiguring" God; (2) the "desiring" God; (3) the "possibilizing" God; (4) the "poeticizing" God, that is the creating God (*qua poiesis*). They would be my four categories of gifting. Poiesis or the poeticizing God engages in a co-creation with us. God can't create the Kingdom unless we create the space for the Kingdom to come."[58] The question is: how God is the Lord of History after all this possibilization? In what sense is He finally the One who is going to judge the world? If "God cannot stop evil [. . .] because evil is the absence of God,"[59] then how can He *judge* evil? All these questions made by the common Western theological mind cannot be answered, as we shall see, only in the context of Western theology today. I deeply agree with Kearney when he says that God is not responsible for evil, for "He knows things only as He wants them to be," as Maximus claims, but can we say that, by consequence, History finally has two or many Lords, or that, human negation refuses not only God's desire for a *perichoresis* with creation, but also His very being as such? A deep western theological problem seems to lie somewhere here: the fusion of theology and economy of God, due to the inability to make a proper distinction between essence and will or *logoi* or energies in Him. But not this only!

By insisting that God neither is nor is not, but may be, Kearney thus makes human agency a decisive element of the realization of God's very being. However, he has been criticized as Hegelian when he asserts that "God can be God only if we enable this to happen." Desmond continues: "Kearney does not overtly say, as Hegel does, that God is not God without the world, though he does imply that God could not be God without us enabling Him to be God[. . .] but a God who needs us to be God would be pitiable[. . .] Maybe the God who may be is another idol . . ." He concludes: "Just ask: could you love absolutely, love unconditionally, a beloved who may be? With your whole heart, and your whole mind, and your whole soul? A beloved who, in some sense seems not yet to be?"[60]

I think that both Desmond and Kearney have been caught in the same spider's web. We owe our theological gratitude to philosophers like Kearney and Jean Luc Marion[61] for bringing forth the most essential and difficult Western theological problem—something that Western theology could only partially do. These phenomenologists manage to show how the Augustinian/Thomist God, or at least a certain long-living understanding of Him, was, in a way, absent from creation; which creation in its turn was pure passivity or a vain reflection of Him, whether or not it is dedicated to Him. Kearney represents a decisive moment in the history of western thought: he realized and he so strongly emphasized that without *dialogue* (or *trialogue*, as he intelligently insists) God is *not*, as no one knows Him as God, no presence of Him can be experienced—although our mind constantly makes us sure of His supreme analogical existence. But at the same time, he identifies God's undeclared *esse* with His *logoi*, to wit, with His *historical* partnership in this dialogue. And thus while he successfully distinguishes God's being from His logical activity, he tends to abolish the former in favor of the latter—or better, he tends to put the essence of the former in the place of the essence of the latter. This is the opposite of what Desmond (and many who are of the same mind) does. But the problem, for both sides, lies in the fact that they cannot keep both ontological sides of God intact, to wit, His unchangeable essence and His many essential realizable potencies *ad extra*, which derive from the essence without being identified with it (in the same manner as the external activity of any one of us does not *exhaustively* express the whole of his personal being, although it *really* expresses it). Thus we have either an almighty divine *esse*, that eliminates the world's essential existence in a double passivity of essence and grace, or an activation of the created being, which probably eliminates God *per se*, transforming Him into a historical God-for-the-world. I do not want to say here that Kearney is another representative of process theology. It is true that, for Whitehead or Hartshorne, God is completely reduced to an immanent, historical process, while Kearney puts the question of an original call beyond history. But he seems to think that this historical Godly process is really a part of God's being.[62]

The temptation to consider history as part of God's being is common in a significant part of modern theology. Two of the most eminent examples are probably Pannenberg and Jüngel. For the former, the divine essence is not immutable but it will be constituted also by God's historical acts of love or wrath that He exercised in time as the Lord of History.[63] For the latter "what was already worked out in the doctrine of the Trinity is now confirmed from working out a concept of being appropriate to God: God's being is constituted through historicality"[64]—not of course in the Hegelian sense but in the sense in which this affirmation can be used in order to express the Old Testament's experience.[65] However, Kearney takes a further step in that he asserts that it is only because of His acts in History that God is said to be. And thus as I believe, he puts, whether he realizes it or not, the question of dialogue in the midst of any analogical approach to God. Moreover, he overtly puts the question of *synergy* in the midst of western theological/philosophical thought.

The outcome is a dialogue or synergy that may risk the abolition of God's *esse per se*, as we have said, but, nevertheless, this is at the same time a demand for a possible *realization* (which is to say Incarnation) of God beyond His metaphysical idols. Thus Kearney is "Orthodox" in that he tends to correct analogy with dialogue, as we want to do, although he endangers the divine essence's immutability in order to accomplish this.

As we have already said, Maximus's doctrine of *logoi* offers exactly the possibility for God to become a God-for-the-world, not by losing or risking His own unchangeable essence, but by realizing its uncreated personal potencies/energies *ad extra*. This analogical dialogue does not exhaust God's essence, nor does it constitute an essential part of it—in the same way my own human essence remains intact whether I decide to communicate with you by writing this essay or not. The potential/energetic expression of a hypostatic essence always constitutes a dialogue (or tria-logue, or poly-logue) out of it, but neither as an ontological substitute for it, nor as an ontologically necessary part of it. That means that energies/potencies are a kind of free realization of essence *in communion ad extra*, but this communion should not take the place of an essence, because although it is this essence that is expressed by these potencies *ad extra*, this essence is not exhausted in them. But we must be very careful insofar as this point is concerned, for other reasons as well. When Kearney, or any other western philosopher or theologian, says that God's historical acts or dialogues constitute a part of His very essence, he is not, of course, necessarily a pantheist; he probably tries to stress that what God does in history, *really belongs to Him*, it is *Himself acting and working in space and time.* Sometimes I think that we are closer than we think we are! That is, every Orthodox theologian, ancient or modern, could immediately accept the above position. This is exactly what the Orthodox mean when they say that the potencies/energies are *essential* and not only simply hypostatic: that God *Himself is acting and working in space and time.* Then what do we mean when we assert that, although uncreated energies are God Himself acting, they are not His very essence? In think that an answer is possible after all we have said so far. We mean that although God's essence is expressed in a free communion with creation, this expression is not a substitute for His essence. In the Trinity, relationship is constitutive of the Persons, without any person being identified with His relationship to the Others; Persons are *in relation*, without being relations themselves. *Ad extra*, God *is* in relation again, without these relations substituting His own unchangeable, essential Otherness: God *is* always Himself when He acts in various ways outside Himself. I believe that Greek patristic theology is a little more accurate or delicate than the Western thought concerning that point. While affirming God's real ("essential," we could say, by its essential energies) presence in creation and History, it refuses to completely identify this real and essential presence with the transcendent divine essential otherness, in the sense that the essential energies carry the wholeness of divine essence, although it is exactly this divine essence that they express. The God Who may be is indeed a God Who may act.

This is why this potential divine expression is called exactly *logos* (speech, word) by Maximus. *Logos* implies active engagements in real dialogues in which created essence/substance is realized as *consubstantial*, i.e. it is united while retaining the essential othernesses of beings, step by step, in the course of history and in the Spirit, while God as the divine *Logos*-Son of the Father, where the Spirit rests, is Himself consubstantial with the two other Persons, in His eternal dialogical Being, before ages. Thus the world, along with human nature, is an already graceful analogical gift of God to man, while the latter's possible dialogical gift to God is this world as Eucharist; that means that man offers to God the gift of a possibility to be also a God-for-the-world, while He is always a God in Himself. But this last claim does not imply that if humanity once refuses synergy with God, He is automatically chased away from His creation! He is still creation's uncreated foundation, but without being able to fully embrace it, i.e., without being able, because of human denial, to *fully explain Himself as He really is* to His creatures. All the monstrous or metaphysical idols of God were given birth in this way, throughout history. Thus we can finally say that by dialogue or synergy, God becomes analogically a God-for-creation-as-He-really-is and not another metaphysical monster or idol. Furthermore, this mutual possible exchange of gifts (divine *logos* offered to humanity and human *logos* offered to God) makes us understand that created nature exists only in the Holy Grace of this mutual giveness, in which God is the very source of any giving, the first and the last Who gives, the Alpha and the Omega.

6. Beyond Immanence, Before Transcendence

AND NOW THE TIME HAS COME TO SAY A FEW WORDS on the notorious and persistent western distinction between immanence and transcendence, a distinction so challenged in the context of Post-modern theology. Secular theology brings to the fore, through some of its distinguished representatives, such as G. Vahanian, what Deleuze calls "a plane of immanence."[66] Let us recall that Deleuze's persistent idea, as expressed, for example, in his work *What is Philosophy?* is that we must search for transcendence in the interior of immanence, and it is from the latter that we expect the emergence of the meaning of the former. The notion of " l'évenement"[67] is exactly this mystical potentiality, absolutely real and not abstract, which brings things out of chaos, without being transcendent itself, as it is pure "reservation." I believe that Deleuze's challenge is not to lose immanence because of the need of an ontological foundation for it. We shall return to this question later on.

As Clayton Crockett puts it "one of the trajectories of modern theology has been toward an elimination of other worldliness in favor of an attention to the concrete, immediate reality in which human beings live, think, suffer, and die."[68] Let us not forget that for Vahanian, secular does not mean the opposite of sacred, but rather it is a theological notion that implies that we live in a world of immanence, which functions as the location of human and divine meaning and value. If this immanence becomes identified with a naïve belief in human progress, etc., then the whole of this scheme will finally become nihilistic, not only in the view of such a great defender of divine transcendentality, such as Karl Barth, but also within those of the most recent theological trend, which is called *Radical Orthodoxy*.

The Radical Orthodox theologians seek to overcome the modern rejection of the medieval synthesis of faith and knowledge that ends up in nihilism, because of its secular presuppositions. What is needed is a restoration of a deep theology of participation along with the restoration of an autonomous theological reason illuminated by a revitalized Christian experience of faith as an erotic assumption in divine harmony and transcendence. This is not the place for a critical evaluation of *Radical Orthodoxy*[69] but what I am sure of is that whether or not they speak of transcendence, both Radical Orthodox as well as the secular theologians want primarily not to escape from but to illuminate immanence again. To save the name of God means to see again the world as a place of singularities, empiricities, and heterologies. And then, as Charles Winquist puts it "we can say yes to the ordinary things because the ordinary is now extraordinary."[70]

This is very important in the eyes of an Orthodox. We should not forget that modern Western secular theology began with the "death of God" theologies (J. J. Altizer, G. Vahanian, W. Hamilton, R. Rubenstein, Paul van Buren) where history and society were understood as thoroughly secular, and theology as a simple textual reality. This has been accomplished with the introduction of Derrida's deconstructive philosophy and Ricoeur's "hermeneutics of suspicion" in theological discourse (i.e., *The Alchemy of the Word,* C. A. Raschke; *Deconstruction and Theology,* Altizer, et. al.; *Erring: A Postmodern A/Theology,* Mark C. Taylor). Here we have some special points to make.

Although this turn is seen by the Radical Orthodox theologians as nihilistic—and this is fair when we see things from the angle of the *analogy of being* as they do—there is still a possibility for a positive evaluation of it. For example, the notorious "undecidability" (of Derrida and Caputo) is not only a negation of metaphysics or revelation, but it can also be seen as an appeal to (textual) experience, and, indirectly, to theological empiricism. An empiricism that calls theologians to save God's name from metaphysics by defending its radical otherness toward the world. Of course, this radical negativity, which the *differance* makes possible, (in a place of non-conceptual negativity that is called, as we saw, in a Platonic fashion, *Khora*) risks to also separate us completely from God; this Hebraic-like radical transcendentality has to be re-thought if we are to truly stay in the field of a *theological experience* of the world. In a theological perspective, any kind of radical transcendentality has to be complemented with a way of participation. On the other hand, as I insisted earlier in this essay, we cannot ontologize "*Khora*" or "*differance,*" or "*me-on*" (nihil), along with God, because in this way we still lose His absolute transcendentality. In a way, all of the above consist in a context in which the divine freedom is made manifest—and this context is also *created.* Furthermore, the "*differance,*" which can be called apophatic, does not necessarily mean that God is unparticipated in, but, as we said, that he is Other than any participation is able to comprise, although it is Him we participate in. Apophaticism, for Orthodox theology, is a spiritual situation, a position we are in, a state of dialogical participation in divine actuality and not a sterile gnosiological abstinence.

However, it seems to me that, what both immanentists and transcendentalists want to ultimately defend, is the existential priority of experiencing the ultimate divine meaning from the inside of beings, to feel God in the depths of creation, to see divine light transfiguring eschatologically the *mode of being* of the essences of things, without losing body and history or anything of the inner-worldly sphere. I believe that we have a kind of convergence on that point, between Western and Eastern Christian theology, for the first time in history: *divine*

reality within creation seems to be the deepest common demand of the
ecumenical Christian theology today. After so many ek-stases and out-
lets and monophysitisms and inner-worldly nihilisms or sterile moral-
isms, the most essential project for theology today is to overcome any
dualism of immanentism and transcendentalism in order to vouchsafe
both in the unique spiritual dimension of the world-in-God, or of God-
in-the-world. But how can we make either of these two claims, without
implying a kind of pantheism, in which the world enters the very essence of God? How can we say that our minds are able to "see" God,
without implying that they are parts of divine essence?

I believe that the doctrine of divine uncreated *logoi* of things
allows us to say, along with Deleuze, that transcendentality is found
within immanent things, or to say, with Vahanian, that supreme divine
and human meaning are located within this world of immanence, and
then, as Winquist says, ordinary things become absolutely extraordinary. So, there is not a sacred and a profane world, no tension between
matter and spirit, or body and mind, or history and *eschata*, because
everything has its own unique divine logos and thus can be thought of
as expressing divine uncreatedness in the conditions of the worldly createdness. Otherworldliness is the very condition of innerworldliness,
while the latter can be a location of the former, for us. The distinction
between enhypostatic essence and enhypostatic will/*logoi*/energies/
potencies allows God to be really and absolutely immanent without
violating either the freedom of creatures or His own transcendentality.
And so He exists in the midst of createdness as a vocation and invita-
tion for dialogue, while He maintains His divine essence intact from
any sort of pantheistic trespass or confusion. Thus we have God and
His world in an undivided union without separation and without confusion. Divinization is the only purpose for everything that is created,
as it consists exactly of a divine call, whether it is material or spiritual,
bodily or psychic, individual or communal or even political. Divinization can happen only within the real conditions of History, without any
outlet out of nature or time. Transcendence can only be immanent, as
a possible dialogical transformation of the *mode of existence* of these
given created things, in the perspective of their micro-eschatological
vocations, which are realized as little "eucharistic incarnations" of divine Logos in the world. Nature is not only made for grace, but it is
made, from the beginning, *out of grace.* We are beyond "immanence"
and before "transcendence," as we have both simultaneously.

But this also means, as we have strongly insisted in the course of this book, that God is not present within His creatures like a cause in its effects, as philosophical metaphysics claims.[71] Rather, He is present, allowing for the danger of a totally other intentionality to exist; an intentionality, which He permits to emerge, out of love, risking a real possibility of a radical denial of His presence, an intentionality which is a gift of freedom and of a possible ontological reciprocity. And this also means that He exists as a pure loving givenness, although He exceeds, by His surplus of essence, any immanent pure phenomenology of gift.[72] Paradoxically, while God *shows* Himself in His gifts, He is not simply His gifts. However, He is truly inside His creatures, but also ready to deny–out of love–the *exclusiveness* of His own intentionality in favor of the radically other intentionality of His creatures: that is, the theological way of a pure, non-metaphysical givenness,[73] which can be described, by the Orthodox theological term *synergy*. I appreciate Marion's substitution of subject with the "gifted,"[74] "he whose function consists in receiving what is immeasurably given to him, and whose privilege is confined to the fact the he is himself received from what he receives." This *intergivenness* (in the place of classical phenomenological inter-subjectivity) as "the exceptional phenomenological situation in which a gifted shows himself, therefore gives himself, to another gifted according to several levels of the one and only giveness,"[75] can be accepted in the context of the Greek patristic synthesis only under two conditions. First, in God, His absolute and unutterable transcendence is so absolute that He, as a hypostatic essence, transcends Himself out of love, in also locating divinity within the created depths of worldly things, by the divine personal activity, without this absolute immanence destroying Godly absolute transcendence. Second, whenever we speak of the gifted (instead of subject), then this gifted is completely *active* and *present* in His own personal will and activity. This means that we cannot substitute the personal reality of the gifted with any a-personal *relatedness*, as many Orthodox and non-Orthodox personalists tend to do nowadays. Relatedness, as a given structure, (ecclesial, eschatological, or anything like this) annihilates what we call *a personal givenness out of love* and makes it, probably, a passive dictation imposed upon living and desiring individuals as a pre-existing ontological structure. We have strongly denied such a relatedness that ultimately makes givenness void of real otherness, i.e., void of *desire* in its manifold, conscious or unconscious, adventures.

7. Desire Creator

LET US NOW SAY A FEW WORDS ON DESIRE. I have published an essay on Lacan and Maximus the Confessor[76] in order to show how subjectivity is always constituted by desire, thus establishing a strange affinity between two radically different authors and two radically different epochs. There is no place in this essay for a detailed discussion, but I must stress something that I think is essential: desire is the only means we human beings have to consubstantiality. Desire is the only vehicle of the Whole, whether I speak of the unconscious "desire for the desire of the Other," or the conscious ascetical struggle through prayer, which makes possible the existential realization of the eucharistic-ontology-of-becoming-in-communion in which divine grace cooperates with human free intention.

It is impossible to build a Christian anthropology without an ontology of desire. Desire makes human being a relational image of the Trinity—it is this *koinonetic* or *perichoretic* nature of desire that so abundantly flows from Greek patristic spiritual literature, and makes it so decisively anti-idealistic. Because desire refers, as we said before, to "every kind of creature," thus making any valid attempt at participating in God, not only mental or imaginary, but also historical and material. We could also claim[77] that this desire, divine and human alike, abolishes any pyramidal cosmological model, thus making it possible for us to create a new theological/epistemological context for modern physics; there, Cusanus's brilliant presentiments can be fulfilled in the Maximian doctrine of *logoi* of natural things. Modern physics is too "strange" to be thought of in terms of the classical, Aristotelian or Thomist, ontological hierarchy; that is without this personal divine presence within the universe that is God Himself, a God-for-the-world, a God making the world full of His own unworldly and hyper-logical harmony, a God becoming in communion in the loving economy of His own eschatological activity. Physics could become the most "existential" science today, as it no more describes "logical," but "personal," i.e., dia-logical natural structures that bear the image of their relational archetype upon them. But we shall need another essay for this.

8. Theopoiia, the Other Side of Theo-humanity

BY CONSIDERING HUMAN ESSENCE AS A HYPOSTATIC "aspect of the Whole"[78] (and not as the a-personal sum of human body and soul) Maximus lays the foundations of another kind of anthropology, which is bib-

lical and not philosophical. The human person as a hypostatic essence, is
not just given, but it is also an existential achievement of *perichoresis* of
beings; that is, an ecclesial achievement of *consubstantiality*,[79] through
the assimilation the grace of the sacraments in the kenotic overcoming
of *philautia* in the light of the Cross. Thus human hypostasis, as Christ's
divine hypostasis, becomes synergetically the place and the mode of
communion of beings, the place where the world becomes a "macran-
thropos," while man becomes a "microcosmos." The ultimate content of
the divine-human analogical dialogue is this type of transference of divine *consubstantial* mode of hypostatic existence in creation, by grace.

That means that man not only becomes God out of a theopoiesis
through grace (which is given by the sacraments and assimilated by the
ascetical outlet of gnomic will out of philautia, as we said), but it also
indicates a previous *theopoiia* of God Himself, as He becomes a God-
for-the-world, not by essence (as Hegel and a whole swarm of western
philosophers claim) but by His acts/*logoi*. This doctrine of divine *Logos*,
Who "becomes thick" (παχύνεται),[80] in creation by the *logoi* (according
to the good will of the Father and with the cooperation of the Spirit, as
Maximus insists), is accomplished in the doctrine of His many incarnations in the words and meanings of Scripture and then in His incarnations in the virtues[81] and ultimately, after His Incarnation in Christ, in
His many "eucharistic incarnations," as we may call them.[82] All these "incarnations" that frame or follow Christ's Incarnation, constitute not only
a *theopoiesis* of creation, but also a *theopoiia* inside creation, through the
Logos's acts that culminate in theo-humanity. God is made by His acts of
grace, which culminate in the Incarnation, a *God-in-creation* in order to
ultimately become a God-for-creation. Christian theology usually thinks
of the Incarnation in the sense that creation is assumed by the divine *Logos* and forgets that the divine *Logos* is, at the same time, offered to His
creation, thus inaugurating a real dialogue where He first offers Himself
as a gift to creation, and then assumes it, as a gift given to him through
the Theotokos. We thus speak of this divine givenness as a *theopoiia* that
represents the other side of Theo-humanity, in the sense that the former
reveals the *telos* of the latter: Theo-humanity starts with *theopoiia*, and
paradoxically ends with it again, in the sense that God's absolute self-
givenness forms the ultimate meaning of the Incarnational assumption
of creation. God assumes creation in order to completely give himself to
it. It is exactly because of this manifold theopoiia that each one of the
believers can participate, through the Eucharist, not in Christ *in general*,
but in a certain part of His body. Thus each part of Christ's body (breast,

eyes, ears, hands, legs, fingers, belly, etc.) represents a participated charisma for the believer, a *charisma* that is already communicated to him
by Baptism and Chrismation, and fulfilled in the Eucharistic embodiment. So, *theopoiesis* or divinization, is an ontological consequence of
the incarnational *theopoiia*; here we have the accomplishment of that
simultaneously immanent and transcendental mode of existence that
characterizes the fate of the world-in-God, through Christ and in the
Spirit. Thus, in Christ, we find our *personal* way of divinization, because
this way has already been prepared by Him for us, as His own *theopoiia*,
in many unique fashions. I receive my personal existential way as a gift
from Him, i.e., as a personal *charisma* of participational embodiment
in Him, which means also a dialogical synergy with Him. His *theopoiia*,
that reflects His Incarnation in many *charismata* is the perfect sign of
His personal love for each human being and for the entire spiritual and
material world. A new *theo-humanism*, along with a new *theo-cosmism*
emerge because of this *theopoiia* out of love–beyond any philosophical
ambition of honoring nihilistically any inner-worldly singularity, em-
piricity, or wisdom. *Theopoiia*, as the source of theo-humanity, is the
only Godly wisdom concerning creation.

 Theopoiia and *Theopoiesis* form the two sides of this eschatological ontology of dialogical reciprocity which is in this book expressed
as a Eucharistic ontology. From what we have said above, it seems that
Western and Eastern Orthodox theology have today reached a mean-
ingful point of convergence. It is the problem of God-in-the-world and
God-for-the-world. It is the attainment of the greatest anti-Platonic
maturity of the postmodern theological quest—although it was exactly
this demand that even Plato wanted with his broken words to express in
his latest period. What Orthodox theology has to offer to this perspective is its concept of *dialogical reciprocity*, as an ontology based on Eucharist and expressed as a personal synergy/analogy between man and
God. This concept, insofar as the notions that uphold it (the *logoi* of beings, the enhypostatic energies, the synergy) constitute the way beyond
every kind of passivity that undermines every really analogical ontology. Perhaps modern secularization, atheism and its related nihilism
were born exactly from the melancholy of the passivity of a relationship
with God without synergy and without dialogue? Perhaps the secularized *theopoiia* of God as a merely intra-mundane sense is linked exactly
to the oblivion of this dialogical *theopoiia*, in which God primarily and
primordially *is offered* to the world, inaugurating a kenotic dialogue full
of humble love?

A dialogue in which the depth of the godlike freedom of the creature is made evident as well as the miracle of his transfiguration by love. The world is not a dictated text, but a poem continuously written and certainly by at least *two* poets. And the end of this poem remains unknown. We know only that what expects us is the inexhaustible erotic surprise, the discovery of an infinite and wise erotic Otherness and her infinite exploration in communion, that begins "in a glass darkly," from this time forth.

The eschatological ontology of dialogical reciprocity is exactly the course of this inexhaustible erotic surprise . . .

Notes

1. *Summa Contra Gentiles*, I, 73.

2. *Summa Contra Gentiles*, I, 74.

3. See the first part of my *Closed Spirituality and the Meaning of the Self: Mysticism of Power and the Truth of Nature and Personhood* [in Greek] (Ellenika Grammata, Athens: 1999).

4. In his famous text, *Quest. ad Thalassium* (60) it is extremely important that many Western Church Fathers agree on that point, starting from Augustine (*De Trinitate*, XIII, 17). Thus, Rupert of Deutz (*De Gloria et honore Filii hominis super Matthaeu*, Lib. 13, PL 148, 1628), Honorious of Autun (*Libellus octo questionun de angelis et homine*, PL 172, 72), Alexander Halensis (*Summa Theologica*, dist. 3, qu. 3, m. 3), Albertus Magnus (in. 3,1 *Sententiarum*, dist. 20, art. 4) and Duns Scotus (*Opus Oxoniense*, 3, dist. 7, qu. 4, schol. 2), completely agree that Christ's Incarnation has not been caused by sin. The only great Western theologian who essentially disagrees is Thomas Aquinas, arguing that he had not been able to discover any biblical witness for this claim (*Summa Theologica*, 3, qu. 1, art. 3 in 3 sent. dist. 1, qu. 1, art. 3).

5. This happened with Metropolitan John Zizioulas's work. For a different understanding of his thought, see Paul McPartlan's *The Eucharist Makes the Church: Henri DeLubac and John Zizioulas in Dialogue* (T&T Clark: Edinburgh, 1993). In pp. 265–274, where McPartlan tries to defend Zizioulas from his critics' accusation of over-identifying Christ with Church, he ultimately claims that, "For Zizioulas, it is by the rhythmic acquiring and losing of our eschatological identity in the Eucharist that the stability expressed as 'our deification in space and time' is imparted" (p. 270). Thus the Christian identity is "a rhythmic identity that Zizioulas conveys by his description of the *homo eucharisticus*" (p. 273). What Zizioulas and McPartlan fail to take into account here is the fact that innumerable pages were written by hundreds of spiritual authors, not only in the East but also in the West, on the existential dimensions of this sort of identity—and Maximus is a prominent

figure among them. This is why he not only speaks of the Church as an *icon* (image) of the Kingdom, but also as a striving toward an *imitation of* (in the sense of *participation in*) the many divine energies, which are the *charismata* of God to His Church. (Regarding this, see the English summary in my *Apophatic Ecclesiology of Consubstantiality* [in Greek], Armos: Athens, 2002, pp. 359–384.) Without such an *imitation*, always in the Greek patristic sense of *participation*, we risk losing also the *Image*, because the *event* of the Church is both. Furthermore, the problem according to the spiritual tradition is not only, as it is according to Zizioulas, to repent more or less after our eucharistic communion, but the question is chiefly about the possibility of a human *assimilation* of the grace imparted by the sacraments. We are only able to transform history or our—despised by Zizioulas—biological hypostases, while being in the process of this sort of *assimilation* of grace, step by step, by our own personal movement of prayer and ascesis; this movement is of course not an individual one but ontologically based on the communal becoming-in-communion by and in the Eucharist. Without this "existential" dimension, our "rhythmic identity" becomes, practically speaking, rather a rhythmic outlet out of real history, as a sort of eschatological consolation for its shortcomings. Note that by "assimilation of grace" the spiritual authors usually mean something much more than a recognition of the necessity of repentance because of grace—they rather mean a synergy, a collaboration and a further dialogue with it in order for man to ultimately contemplate (which also means participate in) the uncreated works of God in creation. Of course, the question is too big to be dealt with in a footnote. For another critique of this lack in Zizioulas's work see Aristotle Papanikolaou's *Being with God: Trinity, Apophaticism, and Divine-Human Communion* (Notre Dame: Indiana, 2006, pp. 142–161).

6. Concerning this, see my *Closed Spirituality and the Meaning of the Self*, pp. 283–300.

7. *Antirretikos*, Z, 1136. See also my *Closed Spirituality. . .* , pp. 240–242.

8. Robert Jenson, *Systematic Theology*, vol 2 (Oxford UP: 1999), p. 68.

9. See R. Roques, *L' Universe Dionysien: Structure Hiérachique du Monde selon le Pseudo-Denys* (Cerf: 1983).

10. See C.H. 292D–293A; Div. Nom. 824C; C.H. 165A; Div. Nom. 700D–701A.

11. Ecclesiastical Hierarchies, 373A.

12. C.H. 168A.

13. El. of Theol., prop. 70, p. 66, 25–27.

14. El. of Theol., prop. 100, p. 90, 9.

15. Ad Mar. Presb. PG91, 9A–11A.

16. *Cosmic Liturgy: The Universe According to Maximus the Confessor* (Communio Ignatius: San Francisco: 2003), p. 87: "Rather, the very passivity of creatures comes from God, is inseparably tied to their createdness, it is not pure imperfection, because even being different from God is a way of imitating Him. So to the degree that the creature comes closer to its own

perfection, its passivity is also made perfect; and its perfection is the pure state 'undergoing God,' a state in which, as we will see, its 'activity' is also perfected."

17. J. Millbank and C. Pickstock, *Truth in Aquinas* (Routledge: 2001), p. 48.

18. E. Gilson, *Le Thomisme. Introduction à la Philosophie de Saint Thomas d'Aquin* (6th rev. ed., Vrin: 1989), p. 125: "Signes et effets de Dieu, les perfections des choses ne sont pas se qu'est Dieu lui-même, est, sous un monde infiniment plus haut, ce que choses sont. Parler de Dieu par analogie, c'est donc dire, dans chaque cas, que Dieu est éminemment une certaine perfection." See also Reg. Garrigou-Lagrange, *Le Synthèse Thomiste* (Desclée de Brouwer, Paris: 1946), p. 147.

19. Copleston, *Aquinas* (Penguin Books, 1982), p. 137.

20. Gilson, p. 124: "Ce que saint Thomas demande à la notion d'analogie, c'est de permettre au métaphysicien, ou au théologien qui use de la métaphysique de parler de Dieu sans tomber à chaque instant dans l'équivoque pure, et par conséquent dans le sophisme. [...] Pour éviter l'équivoque pure, il faut donc s'appuyer sur le rapport qui relie tout effet à sa cause, le seul lien qui permette de remonter, sans erreur possible, de la créature au créateur. »

21. Copleston, p. 135

22. Aquinas, *In epist. ad Rom.*, cap. I, lect. 6.

23. Copleston, p. 136. See also Garrigou-Lagrange, p. 150.

24. Concerning Aquinas's misunderstanding of Greek patristic tradition on this point, see David Bradshaw, *Aristotle East and West: Metaphysics and the Division of Christendom* (Cambridge UP: 2004), p. 256.

25. Copleston, pp. 137–138.

26. Anna Williams, *The Ground of Union: Deification in Aquinas and Palamas* (Oxford University Press, 1999), pp. 34–101.

27. Bradshaw, p. 252.

28. S. Th. 1.19.5

29. I refer to his works *Le Surnaturel* (1946), *Le Mystère de Surnaturel* (1961), *Augstinisme et Théologie Moderne* (1965), and *Petite Catéchèse sur nature et grâce* (1980).

30. De Lubac, *Le Surnaturel* (Desclée de Brouwer, 1991), p. 483.

31. De Lubac, *Le Surnaturel*, p. 485.

32. De Lubac, *Le Surnaturel*, p. 487.

33. De Lubac, *Le Surnaturel*, p. 390.

34. De Lubac, *Le Surnaturel*, pp. 431–471. See in particular S.T. Ia, q. 23, a. 2; Ia, 2ae, q. 5, a. 5; Ia, 2ae, q. 62, a. 1; Ia, 2ae, q. 109, a. 5 ad 3m. In all these passages, two different "ends" are affirmed, in various ways, for human beings: one attained only by natural human forces and the other "supernatural" and transcendental, attained only by grace.

35. This is my *Closed Spirituality . . .* , mentioned above.

36. David Bentley Hart, *The Beauty of the Infinite: The Aesthetics of Christian Truth* (Grand Rapids, MI/Cambridge, UK: Eerdmans, 2004).

37. Hart, p. 243.

38. Hart, p. 249. My italics.

39. Hart, p. 252.

40. Hart, p. 255. My italics.

41. Hart, p. 273.

42. Hart, p. 257.

43. Hart, p. 259. My italics.

44. And thus he thinks that Gregory and Basil, when they say in various texts that material creation consists of non-material attributes, these attributes are the uncreated acts of God themselves (while, on the contrary, they are *spiritual but created results* of the latter); or he thinks that the Cappadocians claim, in a pantheistic fashion, that divine will itself is the very matter and substance of the creatures. Maximus himself, after having written so many pages on the doctrine of logoi, asserts that, "If God thinks of entities in the process of thinking of Himself, then *He is those entities*" (PG 4, 320B ff), but he explains a few lines below that he claims so because "God's intellections are existent things." That means that he distinguishes God's essence from God's creative act, although He Himself is the one Who is active in creation. Only a poor knowledge of Greek patristic literature could cause one to claim differently.

45. A theologian whose thought is very close to the assertions made above is probably Robert Jenson. On p. 65 of his aforementioned work, he writes, "We have seen: it is not only our salvation that is accomplished by God's address, but our being as such. 'Let there be' and 'Christ is risen' are but two utterances of God within one dramatically coherent discourse. We are indeed prepared in our very nature for the divine address of God, because we have a nature only in that we have already been caught up by the dialogue in which this concluding address occurs." What Jenson and other Western theologians are likely still unable to imagine is that nature is dialogue itself, by and in grace, that is, nature is by grace uncreated, that nature is already dialogically "supernatural" in its very essence, in the initial divine call that constitutes its existence.

46. Douglas Farrow, *Ascension and Ecclesia: On the Significance of the Doctrine of Ascension for Ecclesiology and Christian Cosmology* (T&T Clark: 1999), pp. 141–147.

47. See my *Orthodoxy and Modernization: Byzantine Individualization, State, and History, in the Perspective of the European Future* [in Greek] (Armos, Athens, 2006), where in the chapter entitled "An ecclesiology of the lost subject," (pp. 211–218), I endeavor to show, between many other things, that Farrow's claims regarding Augustine, Origen, Iraneus, and some other Christian authors are basically correct.

48. Farrow, p. 143.

49. Farrow, pp. 142–143.

50. Farrow, p. 145.

51. What Maximus writes against "the ascetical mutilation [κολόβωσις] of human and worldly nature" (PG 90, 756B) would suffice for witness.

52. Thal. PG 90, 608A

53. Richard Kearney, *The God Who May Be* (Bloomington, Indiana University Press, 2001). See also his *On Stories: Thinking in Action* (Routledge, New York: 2001), and his *Strangers, Gods, and Monsters: Ideas of Otherness* (Routledge, New York: 2003). The best collection of essays and discussions regarding Kearney's thought is *After God: Richard Kearney and the Religious Turn in Continental Philosophy* (John P. Manoussakis, ed., Fordham UP, New York: 2006)

54. Kearney, *The God Who May Be*, p. 1.

55. I refer here to Kearney's "Epiphanies of the Everyday: Toward a Micro-Eschatology," in *After God*, pp. 3–20.

56. "Toward a Fourth Reduction?" in *After God*, p. 23.

57. Kearney, "Enabling God," in *After God*, pp. 50–51.

58. Kearney, "In place of a response," in *After God*, p. 367.

59. Kearney, "In place of a response," in After God, p. 372.

60. See William Desmond, "Maybe, Maybe Not: R. Kearney and God," in *After God*, pp. 74ff.

61. With his remarkable *God without Being*, (Trans. Thomas A. Carlson, Chicago: University of Chicago Press,1991).

62. *After God*, p. 332.

63. See Pannenberg's *Basic Questions in Theology*, vol.1, (Philadelphia: Fortress Press, 1971) pp. 27–30.

64. Eb. Jüngel, *God's Being is in Becoming. The Trinitarian Being of God in the Theology of Karl Barth*. (Ediburgh: T. and T. Clark, 2001) p. 81.

65. Jüngel, *God's Being*, pp. 126ff

66. Gilles Deleuze, Felix Guatarri, *Qu'est-ce que la Philosophie?* (Ed. de Minuit, 1991) chap. 2.

67. Deleuze, *Qu'est que la Philosophie?*, chap.6

68. See his *Secular Theology. American Radical Theological Thought* (C. Crockett ed., London and New York: Routledge, 2001) p. 1.

69. See my, "Ontology Celebrated: Remarks of an Orthodox on Radical Orthodoxy," in *Encounter of Radical Orthodoxy with Eastern Orthodox Theology*, (Grand Rapids: Eerdmans, 2009).

70. C. E. Winquist, *Postmodern Secular Theology*, in *Secular Theology* p. 36.

71. See Spinoza, *Ethica* I,18: *Deo est omnium verum causa immanens, non vero transiens*.

72. See J. L.Marion's brilliant remark, "The Trinitarian gifts are given in such a way that, for us at least, they never show themselves without remainder–by which they transgress the phenomenological field. The triple reduction of the gift and its reconduction to givenness exclude on principle the possibility that even the least bit of transcendence could subsist–especially transcendence in a theological (or supposedly theological) sense" in *Being*

Given: Toward a Phenomenology of Giveness, J.L.Kosky transl., (Palo Alto, California: Stanford University Press, 2002) p. 115.

73. This can be taken as a first little comment on Derrida's and Marion's philosophies of gift. But the discussion should carry on.

74. Marion, *Being Given,* p. 322.

75. Marion, *Being Given,* p. 323.

76. See the first two chapters of my *Psychoanalysis and Orthodox Theology: On Desire, Catholicity and Eschatology* (Athens: Armos, 2003, in Greek).

77. See my "Ontological and Cosmological Encounters between Theology and Natural Sciences," in *Analogion* (5) 2003.

78. See my *Closed Spirituality,* pp. 303–306.

79. See my *Orthodoxy and Modernization,* chap. 2.

80. P.G. 90,1141CD.

81. For example, P.G. 91,401AB.

82. See chap. 1,4. See also PG91,1364A–1365C.

INDEX

About the Author

Rev. NIKOLAOS LOUDOVIKOS is Professor of Systematic Theology at the University Ecclesiastical Academy of Thessaloniki, Greece, Visiting Professor at the Institute for Orthodox Christian Studies, Cambridge, UK, and Adjunct Professor at the University of Wales (Centre for Orthodox Studies). His books include: *The Terrors of the Person and the Ordeals of Love: Critical Thoughts for a Postmodern Theological Ontology* (Armos, Athens 2009); *Theopoiia: Postmodern Theological Aporia* (Armos, Athens 2007); *Orthodoxy and Modernization: Byzantine Individualization, State and History in the Perspective of the European Future* (Armos, Athens 2006); *Psychoanalysis and Orthodox Theology: On Desire, Catholicity and Eschatology* (Armos, Athens 2003); *An Apophatic Ecclesiology of Consubstantiality* (Armos, Athens 2002); *Closed Spirituality and the Meaning of the Self* (Ellinika Grammata, Athens 1999).